THE DEVELOPMENT OF THE RULE OF LAW IN ASEAN

An interdisciplinary work that comparatively studies rule of law practices and the relationship between the rule of law and regional integration, a topic largely explored in European integration. By looking at the function of the rule of law in ASEAN rather than what it 'means' measured on normative conception, this book situates the rule of law in broader institutional and political processes in the member states and in regional relations to show the motivations of member states in adopting a peculiar type of regional architecture. It asks whether forging the rule of law in the region can help build it internally for member states. The book revisits discourses on the 'spill-over' of economic integration, the impact of globalization in reshaping the state, and generating new tools of the rule of law. It makes a comprehensive comparison – the European Union, Africa Union and MERCOSUR – showing the uneven pathways to rule of law in various contexts.

IMELDA DEINLA is a Research Fellow at the School of Regulation and Global Governance (RegNet) at the College of Asia and the Pacific, Australian National University (ANU). She is the inaugural Project Director of the Philippines Project at the ANU, which focuses on research and policy engagement on Philippine politics, economics and trade. Her research interests are law and society, legal pluralism, conflict and peacebuilding.

THE DEVELOPMENT OF THE RULE OF LAW IN ASEAN

The State and Regional Integration

IMELDA DEINLA
Australian National University, Canberra

CAMBRIDGE
UNIVERSITY PRESS

CAMBRIDGE
UNIVERSITY PRESS

University Printing House, Cambridge CB2 8BS, United Kingdom

One Liberty Plaza, 20th Floor, New York, NY 10006, USA

477 Williamstown Road, Port Melbourne, VIC 3207, Australia

4843/24, 2nd Floor, Ansari Road, Daryaganj, Delhi – 110002, India

79 Anson Road, #06-04/06, Singapore 079906

Cambridge University Press is part of the University of Cambridge.

It furthers the University's mission by disseminating knowledge in the pursuit of education, learning and research at the highest international levels of excellence.

www.cambridge.org
Information on this title: www.cambridge.org/9781107193604
DOI: 10.1017/9781108147934

First published 2017

Printed in the United Kingdom by Clays, St Ives plc

A catalogue record for this publication is available from the British Library.

Library of Congress Cataloging-in-Publication Data

Names: Deinla, Imelda, author.
Title: The development of the rule of law in ASEAN : the state and regional integration / Imelda Deinla.
Description: Cambridge [UK] ; New York : Cambridge University Press, 2017. | Includes bibliographical references and index.
Identifiers: LCCN 2017006683 | ISBN 9781107193604 (hardback)
Subjects: LCSH: Rule of law—Southeast Asia. | ASEAN. | Southeast Asia—Economic integration. | Southeast Asis—Politics and government.
Classification: LCC KNC514 .D45 2017 | DDC 340/.11—dc23 LC record available at https://lccn.loc.gov/2017006683

ISBN 978-1-107-19360-4 Hardback

CONTENTS

FIGURES

ACKNOWLEDGEMENTS

I have always been intrigued by the paradox of the rule of law, first as a legal practitioner and later as a development worker and academic. Over the years I was writing this book, there has been little consensus on the 'meaning' of the rule of law. It has grown however into a huge international enterprise deploying professionals, academics and the many innovations on the technologies of law all over the world. I hope that this work focused on ASEAN can contribute in better understanding of the many misunderstandings – or confusion – about the rule of law.

This book was written over the course of more than five years, first as a doctoral dissertation at the University of New South Wales (UNSW) and later during my work as an early career academic at the Australian National University (ANU). I would not have had the stamina and the inspiration to carry through this work to completion without the kind help, advice and criticisms from colleagues in the academe and people I have met in the course of my professional journey. My deepest gratitude to my mentors and colleagues at ANU, UNSW and UP for reading countless drafts and for providing thoughtful suggestions and encouragement: Professor Veronica Taylor, Professor Adam Czarnota, Professor John Braithwaite, Professor Andrew Tan, Professor Paul Redmond, Dr Girlie Abbu, Dr Emma Larking, Dr Bjoern Dressel, Dr Dao Pornsakol Coorey, Professor Hilary Charlesworth, Professor Martin Krygier, Professor Hal Hill, Kristina Simion and Professor Merlin Magallona.

This book is dedicated to my departed parents, Edita and Regalado Sr, who gave me wings to continue my passion for knowledge and service to the less fortunate; to my family – brothers, sister, in-laws, nephews, nieces, cousins, uncles, aunts as well as my neighbours – in Ticao Island, my beautiful birthplace, for their love and support. My heartfelt thanks to my friends and colleagues in the Philippines and Sydney – Inlay Amora, Tess and Peter Jennings, Marcia and Mer Teki, Gie and Eman Candor, Beth Gebilaguin-Ahmadi, Honorato Aquino, Emil and Nenita Suntay, Dr Karen

Valencia, DTP colleagues, Sarah Gembarowski-Torcasio, Suraina Pasha and Dr Sarah Pritchard.

I am grateful for the support of the School of Regulation and Global Governance, College of Asia and the Pacific ANU where I finished the book manuscript. I owe a lot to Amy Hamilton for giving me such dedication and resourcefulness in seeing through the publication of the manuscript. I thank the Cambridge University Press for giving me their trust and confidence in publishing my modest contribution to the rule of law literature in ASEAN.

TABLE OF CASES

European Court of Justice

Germany

African Court of Human and Peoples' Rights

African Commission on Human and Peoples' Rights

Southern African Development Community Tribunal

Economic Community of West African States Court of Justice

International Court of Justice

World Trade Organisation

United Nations Materials

International Centre for Settlement of Investment Disputes

ASEAN Arbitral Tribunal

TABLE OF LEGISLATION

Constitutions

Philippines

Singapore

TABLE OF TREATIES

ABBREVIATIONS

ACA	ASEAN Cosmetics Association
ACC	ASEAN Coordinating Council
ACC	ASEAN Cosmetics Committee
ACCSQ	ASEAN Consultative Committee on Standards and Quality
ACD	ASEAN Cosmetics Directive
ACHPR	African Court on Human and Peoples Rights
ACIA	ASEAN Comprehensive Investment Agreement
ACJHR	African Court of Justice and Human Rights
ACMF	ASEAN Capital Markets Forum
ACTIP	ASEAN Convention Against Trafficking of Persons, Especially Women and Children
AEC	ASEAN Economic Community
AEC	African Economic Community
AEM	ASEAN Economic Ministers Meeting
AICHR	ASEAN Intergovernmental Commission on Human Rights
AIA Council	ASEAN Investment Area Council
AFAS	ASEAN Framework Agreement on Services
AFTA	ASEAN Free Trade Area
AFC	Asian Financial Crisis
AFMM	ASEAN Foreign Ministers Meeting
AGS	ASEAN Governance Scorecard
AMM	ASEAN Ministerial Meeting

APEC	Asia-Pacific Economic Cooperation
APSA	African Peace and Security Architecture
APSC	ASEAN Political and Security Community
APRIS II	ASEAN-EU Program for Regional Integration and Support – Phase II
APT	ASEAN Plus Three
ASA	Association of South-East Asia
ASCC	ASEAN Socio-Cultural Community
ASEAN	Association of Southeast Asian Nations
ASEAN PTA	ASEAN Preferential Trading Area
ASW	ASEAN Single Window
AU	African Union
BOC	Bureau of Customs
BPP	Brunei People's Party
CCA	Community & Corporate Affairs
CCRR	Center for Cosmetics Regulation and Research
CEE	Central and Eastern European
CFSP	Common foreign and security policy
CLMV	Cambodia, Laos, Myanmar, Vietnam
Charter	ASEAN Charter
COMESA	Common Market for Eastern and Southern Africa
CoR	Committee of Regions
CORPER	Committee of permanent representatives
CMTA	Customs Modernization and Tariff Act
CPP	Cambodian People's Party
CPV	Communist Party of Vietnam
DOH	Department of Health
DRBs	Domestic ranking bodies
DSP	WTO Dispute Settlement Body

EAC	East African Development Community
EAFTA	East Asia Free Trade Area
EC	European Community
ECB	European Central Bank
ECCJ	ECOWAS Community Court of Justice
ECJ	European Court of Justice
ECOWAS	Economic Community of West African States
EC Treaty	European Community Treaty
ESC	Economic and Social Committee
ECSC	European Coal and Steel Community
EEC	European Economic Community
EIPR	Egyptian Initiative for Personal Rights
EMU	Economic and Monetary Union
EPG	Eminent Persons Group
EU	European Union
FDA	Food and Drug Administration
FDI	Foreign Direct Investment
FSJ	Freedom, Security and Justice
GIZ	German Cooperation Agency
GMA	Greater Mekong Area
HAS	Health Sciences Authority
HLTF	High Level Task Force
ICJ	International Court of Justice
IIAs	Inter-Institutional Agreements
ICSID	International Centre for Settlement of Investment Disputes
IGCs	Intergovernmental Conferences
LSAD	Legal Services and Agreements Division
MERCOSUR	Mercado Común del Sur

MRAs	Mutual Recognition Arrangements
NAFTA	North American Free Trade Area
NEP	New Economic Policy
NGO	Non-Governmental Organisation
NTB	Non-Trade Barrier
OAU	Organization of African Unity
OMC	Open Method of Coordination
UNESCO	United Nations Educational, Scientific and Cultural Organization
PACER	Pacific Islands Agreement on Closer Economic Relations
PICTA	Pacific Island Countries Trade Agreement
PLCs	Publicly Listed Companies
PSC	Peace and Security Council
PTR	Permanent Tribunal of Review
REC	Regional Economic Community
RECs	Regional Economic Communities
RoO	Rules of Origin
SAARC	South Asian Association of Regional Cooperation
SADC	Southern African Development Community
SADCC	Southern African Development Co-ordination Conference
SEOM	Senior Economic Officers Meeting
SSA	Special Service Agreement
TAC	ASEAN Treaty of Amity and Cooperation
TAC	Treaty of Amity and Cooperation
TEC	Treaty Establishing the European Community
TEU	Consolidated Version of the Treaty on the Functioning of the EU
ToR	Terms of Reference
UMNO	United Malays National Organization

VAP	Vientiane Action Program
WG	Working Groups
WTO	World Trade Organization
ZOPFAN	Zone of Peace, Freedom and Neutrality

1

From ASEAN Way to the ASEAN Charter: Towards the Rule of Law?

1.1 A General Background

Writing a book on the rule of law is bound to generate debates, especially where it concerns countries and regions where the rule of law is not generally highly regarded or its very existence is challenged. The Association of Southeast Asian Nations (ASEAN), a highly plural organization with diverse rule of law practices among member states, invites those questions and debates even for those who hope that the rule of law can provide the foundation for intra-regional relations. Finding the rule of law in regional integration, a phenomenon that has emerged almost simultaneously with globalization, can be a difficult task where 'the rule of law' itself is an unsettled concept.

By examining the processes of regional integration within ASEAN and extrapolating from the experiences of the European Union (EU) and other projects of regional integration, this book attempts to locate factors and conditions by which the rule of law develops during regional integration. It explores the possibility that regional integration influences the development of rule of law in member states in ASEAN, as it has in European integration.

One of the most significant developments in ASEAN has been the adoption of the ASEAN Charter (Charter) on 20 November 2007 on the occasion of the Thirteenth ASEAN Summit. The Charter was widely regarded as turning a new page in the 40-year history of ASEAN. It came into force on 15 December 2008 after ratification by its 10 member states. The five original member countries were Indonesia, Malaysia, the Philippines, Thailand, and Singapore, whose foreign ministers signed the two-page ASEAN Declaration (Bangkok Declaration) on 8 August 1967 establishing ASEAN. Brunei Darussalam joined ASEAN in 1984 while Vietnam was admitted in 1995.[1] Myanmar (Burma) and Laos PDR joined in 1997 while Cambodia was formally admitted in 1999.

[1] The ASEAN Declaration (Bangkok Declaration), Bangkok, Thailand, 8 August 1967.

The Charter, aimed at giving ASEAN a legal personality and a more rules-based regime, is a groundbreaking achievement for a regional organization better known for its informal and flexible manner of cooperation and a form of decision-making based on *musyawarah* (consultation) and *mufakat* (consensus). This form of consensus decision-making is observed in Indonesian villages and is said to exist to some extent in Malaysia and the Philippines.[2] The ASEAN Way not only describes the conduct of relations of member states but also encapsulates the core principles and values of the association based on strict adherence to the principles of national sovereignty and non-intervention. The Charter, which came as a consequence of ASEAN's initiatives in promoting regional integration, ushers in an evolving framework for regional cooperation in Southeast Asia.

The establishment of an ASEAN Community by 2015 is intended to be the culmination of efforts to deepen cooperation in economic, political, security and sociocultural areas among member states. The ASEAN Community is envisaged as 'a concert of Southeast Asian nations, bonded together in partnership in dynamic development and in a community of caring societies, committed to upholding cultural diversity and social harmony'.[3] Economic integration is the flagship programme of ASEAN integration, representing a departure from the almost exclusively political basis of regional cooperation in the past. This shift in thrust from political to more substantive economic cooperation has opened a range of possibilities and opportunities for change in the region. The adoption of the ASEAN Charter has been hailed by ASEAN state leaders as facilitating the realization of ASEAN Community objectives by investing the organization with legal personality and efficient structures.[4] The ASEAN Charter states adherence to the rule of law, good governance, the principles of democracy and constitutional government as among the key principles to be observed by member states.[5] Thus we see prospects for the development and the promotion of the rule of law at a regional level for the first time.

The impetus for ASEAN cooperation has changed dramatically with the onslaught of combined political and economic events in the 1990s.

[2] Mely Caballero-Anthony, *Regional Security in Southeast Asia: Beyond the ASEAN Way* (Singapore: Institute of South East Asian Studies, 2005), 72–3; See also Koentjaraningrat, R.M. (ed.), *Villages in Indonesia* (Ithaca: Cornell University Press, 1967).

[3] Declaration of ASEAN Concord II (Bali Concord II), Bali, 7 October 2003.

[4] Cebu Declaration on the Blueprint for an ASEAN Charter, Cebu, 13 January 2007; Bali Concord II.

[5] Charter of the Association of Southeast Asian Nations 2007 (ASEAN Charter 2007), Singapore, 20 November 2007, art. 2(h).

These included the end of the Cold War, the dismantling of authoritarian regimes in the Philippines, Indonesia and Thailand, the resolution of the Cambodia conflict and its subsequent democratization, the embrace by socialist states of Vietnam and Laos PDR of the market economy and the Asian financial crisis of 1997. The millennium brought about significant events on the world stage, in particular the terrorist attack on September 11, 2001, and its fallout and the current economic and financial crises in North America and Europe. These events have triggered new challenges in Southeast Asia – in particular, the emergence of Islamist radicalism and transnational crimes – that have prompted state leaders to seek stronger regional cooperative solutions.

In ASEAN, regional and international events since 1997 have prompted profound rethinking on the part of leaders and elites about ASEAN's role in the face of internal and external problems. ASEAN's failure to provide a common front against the impact of the Asian financial crisis, particularly as the crisis severely affected many member states, generated strong criticisms about its continued relevance, and its claim to centrality as a regional organization. At the same time, member states have had to grapple with the challenge of increasing competition from other developing economies as economic globalization intensifies. Globalization has affected the internal political and economic processes in member states and this has prompted state leaders and elites to utilize ASEAN in responding to the challenges and benefits of globalization. The Asian financial crisis also exposed the flaws in the 'Asian values' argument espoused by authoritarian regimes in the region that sought to particularize conceptions of democracy and human rights in a cultural and communitarian context.[6] For civil society in Southeast Asia, the impact of globalization and the idea of a more integrated region have encouraged civil society organizations to reconsider ASEAN as a platform for advocating political, economic and sociocultural reforms.

As with the EU, ASEAN was conceived as a regional grouping to foster peace and stability through greater economic cooperation. Peace-building in most Southeast Asian societies, however, is linked to the wider project of nation-state building. The postcolonial nation-state in the region has struggled to achieve internal cohesion and legitimacy, with the result that most ASEAN members have placed primary emphasis on social unity, cohesion and order. Regionalism, the broader context in which regional

[6] Amitav Acharya, *The Quest for Identity* (Singapore: Oxford University Press, 2000), 155–6.

integration is situated, remains anchored in ASEAN member states' efforts at nation-state building.

In contrast, achieving peace within the EU builds on a history of ending centuries of Pan-European wars and in restraining the re-emergence of German hegemony.[7] This has informed to a large extent the decision among EU member states to surrender some parts of their sovereignty in favour of a supranational authority which is responsible for implementing the member states' obligations under legally binding treaties. The act of delegating or pooling of sovereignty to a supranational body has enabled the EU to transcend a state-centred approach to international relations and international law. This has made it possible for the creation of a model of regional governance that exhibits autonomy from its member states.[8]

1.2 The Early ASEAN, Non-intervention and the ASEAN Way

ASEAN began as a regional mechanism to avert major armed conflict in a turbulent region. Its two precursors, the Greater Malayan Confederation, also known as MAPHILINDO representing Malaysia, Philippines and Indonesia, and the Association of South-East Asia (ASA), failed in the face of interstate conflicts among member states.[9] Ensuing years have seen the stabilization of the region, understood as the absence of any major armed confrontation among member states and was attributed by state leaders and officials to the stabilizing effect of ASEAN's formation. There is wide agreement among academics that ASEAN was established as a security community, though perhaps in a rather implied and limited manner.[10] ASEAN's role in securing peace and security in the region has been partly

[7] See John Gillingham, 'A German Solution to Europe's Problems? The Early History of the European Communities, 1950–1965' in *European Integration, 1950–2003 Superstate or New Market Economy?* (Cambridge: Cambridge University Press, 2003), 3–80, 3–5.

[8] Pierre Pescatore, *The Law of Integration: Emergence of a New Phenomenon in International Relations Based on the Experience of the European Communities* (Leiden: A.W. Sijthoff, 1974), 4–11.

[9] ASA (composed of Thailand, Malaysia and the Philippines) was formed on 31 July 1961 and MAPHILINDO (which stands for Malaysia, Philippines and Indonesia) on 5 August 1963. These two regional organizations failed because of two major inter-state conflicts in the region: the *Konfrontasi* or Confrontation declared by Indonesia in January 1963 against the formation of the Federation of Malaysia and the Philippines' claim over the territory of Sabah which was annexed in the Federation.

[10] See, for example, Donald Emmerson, 'Security, Community, and Democracy in Southeast Asia: Analyzing ASEAN' (2005) 6(2) *Japanese Journal of Political Science* 165–85; Amitav Acharya, *Constructing a Security Community in Southeast Asia: Asean and the Problem of Regional Order* (London: Routledge, 2001), 1–8.

credited to its 'political formula', the preferred method of cooperation in ASEAN particularly during the first 10 years of its existence.[11] This approach, as opposed to legally binding treaties and procedures, gives preference to diplomacy and informal mechanisms of dispute settlement or dispute avoidance.

The primacy of the political agenda in ASEAN was not only driven by the members' desire to achieve freedom from fear of external threats. It was as much dictated by the domestic imperatives of state-building which preoccupied member states in the postcolonial era. Political instability was considered the principal threat to the internal security of member states; ethnic secessionist groups and communist insurgents were deemed to be the 'enemies of the state'. Security threats were expanded to include any opposition to the government such as political parties, activists and the media. By the late 1960s, most states in ASEAN were ruled by authoritarian regimes.

As a regional grouping, ASEAN has vigorously espoused the principle of national sovereignty and non-intervention. This coincided with member states' interests in being left alone to tackle their own political and internal security issues, free from any form of interference from their neighbours. The recognition of security threats as the primary source of insecurity was formally recognized in ASEAN when it adopted the Declaration of ASEAN Concord (or Bali Concord), and the Concord principles of regional and national resilience as key to safeguarding the stability of member states and the whole region.[12] National resilience is understood as 'the security of the nation emerging from the strength of national development' and encompasses all major aspects of nation building.[13] Without having to contend with external interference or pressure, member states could focus on their nation-building objectives, centred on achieving economic growth and development. Regional resilience could therefore be achieved by enabling member states to attain their own national resilience.

The Bali Concord, which came 10 years after the founding of ASEAN, formally elaborated the political framework of ASEAN cooperation. Political cooperation was stated ahead of economic cooperation – a tacit

[11] Estrella D. Solidum, *The Politics of ASEAN: An Introduction to Southeast Asian Regionalism* (Singapore: Eastern University Press, 2003), 79.

[12] Declaration of ASEAN Concord (Bali Concord), Bali, 24 February 1976.

[13] Alan Collins, *Security and Southeast Asia: Domestic, Regional and Global Issues* (Singapore: Institute of Southeast Asian Studies, 2003), 129–30.

acknowledgement of ASEAN's *raison d'etat*. The instrument lays down the components of political cooperation as:

1. Meeting of the Heads of Government of the member states as and when necessary.
2. Signing of the Treaty of Amity and Cooperation (TAC) in Southeast Asia.
3. Settlement of intra-regional disputes by peaceful means as soon as possible.
4. Immediate consideration of initial steps towards recognition of and respect for the Zone of Peace, Freedom and Neutrality wherever possible.
5. Improving ASEAN machinery to strengthen political cooperation.
6. Studying how to develop judicial cooperation including the possibility of an ASEAN Extradition Treaty.
7. Strengthening of political solidarity by promoting the harmonization of views, coordinating position and, where possible and desirable, taking common actions.[14]

Implicit in ASEAN's rationale for regional cooperation is the goal of strengthening the sovereign capacities of member states. Unlike the EU where states agreed to voluntarily surrender certain parts of their sovereignties to a supranational body, ASEAN states had no intention of limiting their sovereign authority, especially in the context of regional relations. This and the political nature of ASEAN inform the processes of ASEAN cooperation. Regional issues that were inherently political in nature called for a political solution or approach. Some territorial conflicts, however, had been referred to the International Court of Justice for legal adjudication. Examples of the latter are the territorial issues between Indonesia and Malaysia involving the *Pulau Ligitan* and *Pulau Sipadan* Islands in the Celebes Sea; between Malaysia and Singapore over *Pedra Branca* and the dispute between Thailand and Cambodia over the Preah Vihear Temple.[15] Most other pressing disputes

[14] Bali Concord, s. A.

[15] The Malaysia–Indonesia dispute was decided in 2002 by the ICJ in favour of Malaysia though it left open issues of maritime demarcation that have remained contentious, and Indonesia is still claiming maritime jurisdiction over Ambalat and East Ambalat. On 23 May 2008, the ICJ ruled in favour of Singapore jurisdiction over the Pedra Branca islet, known as Pulau Batu Puteh in Malaysia. The state parties have so far sufficiently respected and complied with the ruling of the international court. The Preah Vihear was adjudged by the ICJ in favour of Cambodia's sovereignty in 1962 but violent clashes occurred recently. The ASEAN Way which is based on informal and low-key approaches is thought to have managed conflicts but not resolved them as well as lacking clear framework for more

in the region, however, had been dealt with or managed through the traditional method of state diplomacy.

The building of trust and confidence among member states in view of existing intra-state conflicts was a key consideration in developing regional cooperation. ASEAN became a venue for regional diplomacy where issues that were considered too sensitive to tackle are dealt with either through quiet diplomacy or bilateral summitry.[16] Issues that are considered for bilateral negotiations range from secessionism, insurgencies and territorial and border disputes, to foreign policies on non-alignment and neutralization and security problems involving foreign powers such as foreign military bases and military cooperation. ASEAN consciously adopted informal and flexible mechanisms as opposed to formal and institutionalized rules. This is evident from the wording of the 1967 Bangkok Declaration itself where ASEAN is described as an 'Association for Regional Cooperation' consisting of 'the collective will of the nations of Southeast Asia to bind themselves together in friendship and cooperation'.[17]

ASEAN's legal and institutional mechanisms in its early years reflected the political aims of the organization. The ASEAN Declaration only provided for four informal and loose institutions – an Annual Meeting of Foreign Ministers called the ASEAN Ministerial Meeting (AMM), a Standing Committee, under the chairmanship of the Foreign Minister of the host country, Ad-Hoc Committees and Permanent Committees of specialists and officials on specific subjects and a National Secretariat in each member country.[18] It was only in 1976 that the ASEAN Secretariat was established in Jakarta and the first ASEAN Summit, or meeting of the Heads of States, was convened.

ASEAN has developed a mechanism of regional cooperation that state leaders and officials consider to be distinctive of the association, the so-called ASEAN Way.[19] The ASEAN Way has generally defined what the organization is about. It has evolved as the core organizational principles and norms and consists of both behavioural and procedural dimensions. The behavioural aspect comprises what can be collectively called a 'code of conduct' to be observed by member states in relation to one another. The ASEAN TAC

effective security management in the region. For further discussion, see Yukiko Nishikawa, 'The "ASEAN Way" and Asian Regional Security' (2007) 35(1) *Politics and Policy* 42–56.

16 Solidum, *The Politics of ASEAN*, 102–9.

17 Bangkok Declaration.

18 Ibid., para. 3.

19 Acharya, *The Quest for Identity*, 127–8.

states basic principles of international law that have assumed greater (and even peculiar) meaning in ASEAN owing to its colonial history and security perceptions. The core principles embodied in the TAC are as follows:

1. Mutual respect for the independence, sovereignty, equality, territorial integrity and national identity of all nations;
2. The right of every State to lead its national existence free from external interference, subversion or coercion;
3. Non-interference in the internal affairs of one another;
4. Settlement of differences or disputes by peaceful means;
5. Renunciation of the threat or use of force and
6. Effective cooperation among themselves.[20]

ASEAN has invested peculiar meanings in these concepts which are otherwise generally recognized by the international community as norms of international law. For example, the principles of respect for national sovereignty and non-intervention reflect expectations of conduct of member states towards each other that include refraining from criticizing the actions and policies of another member state towards its own people, such as the treatment of human rights. They are also expected to deny recognition, sanctuary or other forms of support to any rebel or secessionist group in a member state, and to provide support or material assistance to member states in their campaign against subversive and destabilizing activities.[21]

The procedural dimension of the ASEAN Way is grounded in the use of informal mechanisms to manage conflicts or to arrive at decisions. Informal means of dispute settlement in ASEAN are underpinned by conflict avoidance or containment. They are usually characterized by observance of particular conduct which is not formally expressed in formal and institutional mechanisms of the association. They place emphasis on self-restraint, respect and tolerance, acceptance of the processes of *mushawarah* and *mufakat*,[22] use of third-party mediation, agreeing to disagree and networking. These norms have been collectively referred to as 'diplomacy of accommodation' or ASEAN's intramural approach to dispute settlement.[23]

[20] TAC in Southeast Asia, Bali, 24 February 1976, in force 21 June 1976, 1025 UNTS 316.

[21] Acharya, *Constructing a Security Community*, 58.

[22] Caballero-Anthony, *Regional Security in Southeast Asia*, 72; Davie Capie and Paul Evans, 'The ASEAN Way' in Sharon Siddique and Sree Kumar (eds.), *The 2nd ASEAN Reader* (Singapore: Institute of Southeast Asian Studies, 2003), 45–51, 48.

[23] Mely Caballero-Anthony, 'Mechanisms of Dispute Settlement: The ASEAN Experience' (1998) 20(1) *Contemporary Southeast Asia* 51–64. See also Michael Antolik, *ASEAN and the Diplomacy of Accommodation* (New York: M.E. Sharpe, 1990).

Formal mechanisms for dispute settlement have been instituted in ASEAN such as the provision for a High Council in the TAC and the Protocol for Enhanced Dispute Settlement Mechanism and the dispute resolution mechanisms of ASEAN's economic agreements. These mechanisms have not been used or even invoked by member states in resolving their conflicts. A prominent example of this vacuum is the continuing dispute between Thailand and Cambodia over the Preah Vihear temple which continues to be a flashpoint to regional security but also an issue that impacts on domestic politics. Since 2008 fresh border clashes started after the recognition by UNESCO of the temple as a world heritage site and ASEAN, through Indonesia, offered to mediate. This was largely unsuccessful. Neither ASEAN's formal dispute resolution mechanisms were invoked by either disputant. Cambodia formally referred it to the ICJ where the latter issued a provisional measure for the cessation of armed hostilities, and authorized the creation of a provisional demilitarized zone pending the resolution of the case.[24] The ruling also urged the parties to continue to cooperate with ASEAN, particularly in deploying observers to the demilitarized zone. Although a ceasefire did materialize, the deployment of the Indonesian or ASEAN observer team was rejected by Thailand, particularly by its military.[25]

The ASEAN Way on decision-making, which emphasizes consensus building through a process of discussion and consultation, has been argued to be Southeast Asian cultural paradigm. It is said to reflect the customary way of arriving at decisions in villages and among the elites in Southeast Asia.[26] The process of consultation entails lengthy negotiations and is incremental. Decisions are made only after several behind-the-scenes or low-key meetings among officials. Leaders may agree to disagree on their positions but disagreements are, more often, not stated publicly. The origins of the ASEAN Way have been traced from member states' nationalist struggle for recognition and security which culminated in ASEAN's establishment as a Zone of Peace Freedom and Neutrality

[24] Temple of Preah Vihear (Cambodia vs. Thailand) (Provisional Measures, Judgment) [2013] ICJ Rep 281.

[25] See Prentice, Jonathan, *Waiting for RI observers at Preah Vihear* (17 March 2012) The Jakarta Post, www.thejakartapost.com/news/2012/03/17/waiting-ri-observers-preah-vihear.html; Bangkok Post, *Preah Vihear Dispute Weighs on Army Brass* (24 May 2012), www.bangkokpost.com/opinion/opinion/294787/preah-vihear-dispute-weighs-on-army-brass

[26] Solidum, *The Politics of ASEAN*, 93–4; See also Pushpa Thambipillai and J. Savaranamuttu, *ASEAN Negotiations: Two Insights* (Singapore: Institute of Southeast Asian Studies, 1985), 3–25.

(ZOPFAN).[27] While there is doubt as to whether the ASEAN Way is distinctively Southeast Asian, there is little question that it has crystallized into ASEAN's diplomatic and security culture, and perhaps mediated to a certain extent 'estrangement and insecurity' in the region.[28]

The ASEAN Way has served the purposes of ASEAN particularly well in its formative years. It has performed a state-building or regime-maintenance function in member countries. Member states were enabled to direct their energies towards domestic problems without fear of intervention or criticisms from neighbouring states. Autonomy, discretion and flexibility have been enhanced in member states through ASEAN's reliance on its core values of sovereignty, non-intervention and informality. It has fostered solidarity among leaders of member states and even the maintenance of dictatorships.

The ASEAN Way has not been inviolable, however. The intermittent armed clashes between Thailand and Cambodia over Preah Vihear show non-observance of the code of conduct on restraint and non-use of force. Various other incidents in the past also show deviation from non-interference, such as the Indonesian protests over Malaysia's expulsion of its Rohingya Muslim inhabitants, the giving of sanctuary to Philippine Muslim rebels in Sabah and Indonesian pressure on the Philippines to ban East Timorese and foreign delegates from attending a conference on East Timor in 1994.[29]

The adoption of the ASEAN Charter in 2007 amounts to an implicit recognition of the limits of the ASEAN Way as the association embarks on an ambitious plan of building a Community. New challenges have emerged that go beyond the traditional conception of security. The 'new' ASEAN now recognizes the principle of comprehensive security that includes both state and human security and extends to all forms of threats such as transnational crimes and trans-boundary challenges that need greater political, security, economic and sociocultural cooperation.[30] To bring about economic integration would require a degree of clarity, stability and

[27] Jürgen Haacke, *ASEAN's Diplomatic and Security Culture: Origins, Development and Prospects* (London: Routledge Curzon, 2005), 16–51.

[28] Ibid.

[29] Jürgen Rüland, 'ASEAN and the Asian Crisis: Theoretical Implications and Practical Consequences for Southeast Asian Regionalism' (2000) 13(2) *The Pacific Review* 421–51, 439–40; See also *East Timor Conference in Manila Tests Southeast Asia's 'Good Neighbor' Policy*, International Herald Tribune (1 June 1994), www.iht.com/articles/1994/06/01/timor.php

[30] ASEAN Charter 2007, ch. 1, art. 1.

predictability of rules as well as functioning institutions to implement, monitor and enforce compliance of agreements. It also demands greater political cooperation of member states requiring a more stable and coherent framework for inter-state cooperation. The EU experience shows the interdependence of economic and political cooperation, which in turn also enhances economic cooperation and other areas of regional cooperation.

1.3 Regional Integration and ASEAN Integration

Regional integration had been synonymous with the process of building the EU but the term has now been applied to more than 400 other regional trade agreements that had been notified to the World Trade Organization (WTO).[31] The proliferation of projects of regional integration in many parts of the world particularly in the 1990s has coincided with increasing globalization and thus with strong economic objectives. Some of these projects evolved as political projects of nation-states due to the necessity for greater commercial cooperation and as instruments for attaining broader political, social and economic objectives.[32] Globalization, understood as an economic project, is regarded as complementary, rather than antagonistic, to regional integration. Regional integration is generally looked upon with favour as a response to globalization through its preferential incentives to prepare industries to be more competitive and to create larger regional markets.[33]

Regional integration is also viewed as an expression of regionalism which in its new wave has been informed by globalization and new dynamics in international relations.[34] Regionalism is understood as a top-down political process imposed and managed by the states for a range of political, security and economic cooperation.[35] Regional integration, in its broadest term, could be regarded as a process by which member states

[31] There are currently more than 400 RTAs notified with the Committee on Regional Trade Agreement of the WTO as of September 2016 that 230 are in force. See World Trade Organization, *Regional Trade Agreements*, www.wto.org/english/tratop_e/region_e/region_e.htm

[32] Robert Devlin and Antoni Estevadeordal, 'Regional Integration, Trade and Development' in *Bridges for Development: Policies and Institutions for Trade and Development* (Washington: Inter-American Development Bank, 2003), 3–17, 4–5.

[33] Ibid.

[34] Jens-Uwe Wunderlich, *Regionalism, Globalisation and International Order: Europe and Southeast Asia* (Hampshire: Ashgate, 2007), 34–6.

[35] Ibid., 3–4.

agree to form regional institutions that promote the attainment of common goals. Integration is the formal expression of regionalism where institutions are formed and different parts are brought together.

ASEAN regional integration has globalization as a catalyst, but member states' state-building objectives continue to underline broader regional cooperation. Some of the key factors that sparked the ASEAN integration initiatives that began with the establishment of the ASEAN Free Trade Area (AFTA) were identified as: '(1) growing interdependence triggered by the rise of production networks; (2) regionalism in Europe and the Americas; (3) the loss of momentum in the APEC and the World Trade Organization (WTO); (4) the Asian financial crisis; and (5) the transformation and resurgence of China'.[36]

However, the enumeration of the first three purposes in the ASEAN Charter 2007 reflects the continuing ascendancy of political and security motivations for ASEAN integration:

1. To maintain and enhance peace, security and stability and to further strengthen peace-oriented values in the region;
2. To enhance regional resilience by promoting greater political, security, economic and sociocultural cooperation;
3. To preserve Southeast Asia as a Nuclear Weapon-Free Zone and free of all other weapons of mass destruction.[37]

Regional integration in ASEAN is aimed at taking advantage of the benefits of globalization while also aiming to protect and enhance the sovereignty of the members. Unlike the EU, ASEAN has adopted an open and non-exclusive integration. It is expressed through the 'ASEAN Plus' concept, which is intended not only to better stimulate trade and investment but also as a strategy to lessen the potential for domination of a single foreign power and thus maintain the member states' sovereign independence.[38] The ASEAN Plus concept has emerged from a series of multilateral meetings in the 1990s that culminated in the formation of the ASEAN Plus Three (APT) in 1997. The APT is the most important regional cooperative framework in East Asia and involves the three powers in Asia – China, Japan and Korea – where ASEAN hopes to enhance its political and economic leverage, with these three countries having competing interests

[36] Ellen L. Frost, *Asia's New Regionalism* (Boulder: Lynne Rienner Publishers, 2008), 110–14.
[37] ASEAN Charter 2007, ch. 1, art. 1(1)–(3).
[38] Frost, *Asia's New Regionalism*, 115–16.

in the organization.[39] The ASEAN Plus Six was subsequently formed in 2004; it has a wider Asia Pacific focus with the inclusion of Australia, New Zealand and India.

With ASEAN's current broader aspirations, observers have asked whether the 'ASEAN Way' remains relevant or whether there is a need to depart from it. There is overwhelming recognition, even from ASEAN officials themselves, of the inherent limitations of the ASEAN Way in dealing with the more dynamic demands of economic cooperation, and the need to evolve into a more rules-based regime.[40] Regional integration in its general sense presupposes more cohesion among member states, not only in the sharing of common ideas of values and ends, but also not least, on the ways and means of achieving them. It has paved the way for public and private non-state actors to be involved or be affected, directly or indirectly, through its activities and its potential impact on domestic institutions, policies and laws. This book therefore looks at whether current legal and institutional developments in ASEAN have signalled a departure from the ASEAN Way as well as a commitment to observe the rule of law in regional cooperation.

1.4 Rule of Law as a Placeholder for Regional Integration

The rule of law has become the banner through which regional integration projects is being promoted. But what does rule of law mean or entail in regional integration, or what it seeks to achieve, is something that has remained ambiguous. At its inception, the discourse on the rule of law assumes that it is inextricably linked to the concept of sovereignty. Sovereignty, like rule of law, is a contested concept, but represents the central idea of statehood as well as that of international relations. There is a minimally acceptable condition for the existence of sovereignty, as the ultimate authority or source of decision.[41] Conceptions of the rule of law have developed from the notion that law has replaced violence as the

[39] See, for example, Marcus Hund, 'ASEAN Plus Three: Towards a New Age of Pan-East Asian regionalism? A Skeptic's Appraisal' (2003) 16(3) *The Pacific Review* 383–417.

[40] Rodolfo C. Severino (former ASEAN Secretary General), 'The ASEAN Way and the Rule of Law' (Speech delivered at the International Law Conference on ASEAN Legal Systems and Regional Integration, University of Malaya, Kuala Lumpur, 3 September 2001).

[41] Samantha Besson, 'Sovereignty in Conflict' in Colin Warbrick and Stephen Tierney (eds.), *Towards an International Legal Community* (London: British Institute of International and Comparative Law, 2006), 131–90, 148–9.

primary form of the state's power of coercion to one that is meant to constrain or limit the state's absolute exercise of authority.

From a theoretical perspective, the idea of the rule of law paralleled the development of the concept of sovereignty. Sovereignty was first understood as 'absolute' or an absence of legal and political limits to authority. It developed into a notion that sovereignty is generated through a form of social contract between the ruler and the ruled. This latter development addresses the need to safeguard the governed from abuse of state power through separation of powers and respect for fundamental freedoms. Viewed from Western historical tradition, sovereignty as constitutive of the state came about as a process of centralization of political power where law became the tool of ruling, but also an effective restraint against the tyranny of rule.[42]

The philosophical idea that the state and law are mutually identical has led to a conception of the rule of law as a set of verifiable formal criteria by which a particular state legal system has to be judged. A conception that underscores the universal application of the rule of law (without some separate criteria as to the law's contents) stresses the formal elements enabling law to be capable of guiding the behaviour of its subjects by allowing them to know and plan in advance the legal implications of their actions. From Hayek, Raz, Fuller and Unger comes an agreement that the law should possess at least five fundamental characteristics: that law should be prospective, general, clear, public and relatively stable.[43] This conception based on formal legality can be consistent with most regimes, regardless of their political systems. It could be as capable of maintaining authoritarian regimes as sustaining liberal democracies. Conversely, a thicker conception of the rule of law incorporates, in addition to formal rules, the law's 'morality', which in the European tradition originally derived from natural law. This more substantive conception includes values of democracy, justice and human rights, which imbue the law with popular legitimacy and ethical standards.[44]

In international law, the traditional conception of the rule of law presupposes the existence of international law as a substitute for power politics or

[42] Brian Z. Tamanaha, *On the Rule of Law: History, Politics, Theory* (Cambridge: Cambridge University Press, 2004), 7–46 and 96–7.

[43] Ibid.93–4.

[44] See, for example, Lon L. Fuller, *The Morality of Law*, revised edn. (New Haven: Yale University Press, 1969); Ronald Dworkin, *Law's Empire* (Cambridge: Harvard University Press, 1986).

the sovereign powers of states, in some aspects of functional cooperation. In this view, the dual character of the state's sovereignty is recognized, both its internal or external competencies, to determine the ultimate validity of the law. The recognition given to international law is said to flow from the voluntary acceptance of the state, the state's consent, and from the international community of states as a whole.[45] In this view, the states are still considered the main actors in international law.

The notion of state sovereignty as the ultimate source of legal authority in a given territory or jurisdiction has, however, been increasingly challenged. Globalization and the emergence of a supranational legal order in the EU have challenged the two basic tenets of sovereignty – the concepts of territorial integrity and voluntary principle underlying international law. New types of law have emerged that no longer depend on the voluntary acceptance of states but are imposed for the good of humanity or to avert humanitarian disaster.[46] New sources of laws are coming not from the traditional domain of law, the unitary state, but from a range of international organizations or non-state actors.[47] These phenomena are changing the significance of national and international boundaries in general and, in particular, the patterns of legal relations.[48] These have given rise to debates as to whether the sovereign authority of the state is weakened as a result of this encroachment on the state's lawmaking capacities.[49]

Globalization has brought new forms of law and authority which challenge even the formal conception of the rule of law. There is an increasing trend towards 'deformalization' of international law. This has been brought by an explosion in international rule-making particularly in commercial transactions and the rise of 'private global authority' that is increasingly the source of international rules and adjudication.[50] The use of these international economic rules, however, has been based on norms and customs,

[45] State consent is the primary basis of international law. See, for example, Ian Brownlie, *Principles of Public International Law*, 7th edn. (Oxford: Oxford University Press, 2008), parts I and II.

[46] Colin Warbrick and Stephen Tierney (eds.), *Towards an 'International Legal Community'?* (London: British Institute of International and Comparative Law, 2006), 1–4.

[47] See, for example, Anne-Marie Slaughter, *A New World Order: Government Networks and the Disaggregated State* (Princeton: Princeton University Press, 2004) for her work on networks of governmental experts operating across borders and in various international organizations.

[48] William Twining, *Globalisation and Legal Theory* (London: Butterworths, 2000), 8–10.

[49] This point will be fully explored in Chapter 2.

[50] Claire Cutler, Virginia Haufler and Tony Porter (eds.), *Private Authority and International Affairs* (Albany: State University of New York Press, 1999), 4–5. See also Brendan

called the 'law merchant', which are mostly dependent on the application of informal standards and rules. Problems of consistency, coherence and clarity are evident in the application of economic rules or norms which are applied on an *ad hoc* and individual basis. The implementation of international law is likewise problematic where its interpretation and application could vary from one jurisdiction to another or where, in the case of powerful states, compliance could be dependent on expediency.[51]

The public aspect of the rule of law is also being challenged. Newer forms of international adjudication, whether judicial or nonjudicial, avoid or restrict publicity. This raises questions about the transparency and accountability of international governance institutions and their activities. Even in the field of human rights where the interpretation and enforcement of international standards have suffered from much deviation or challenge, the use of non-formal and nonjudicial mechanisms are increasingly being explored or resorted to in resolving human rights issues.[52]

In the context of EU, the rule of law has taken a distinctive turn – a rather radical departure from classical international law – incorporating both aspects of formal legality and substantive values of democracy and human rights. The development of a constitutional legal order anchored in the principle of supremacy of Community law enabled the EU to assume a state-like quality with regard to the rule of law. The discussion in the following chapters will show the construction of the EU as a hybrid polity and thus the possibility of reproducing state-like rule of law in regional integration. Within the EU, the combination of laws and institutions – which are formal or informal, hard or flexible, national or supranational – has made it possible to expand the function of the rule of law from an instrument for achieving economic integration to a broader form of restraint upon, and mechanism of accountability for, EU authorities.

The EU thus presents an alternative model of an international society that it is not solely based on the supremacy of the state and guaranteed autonomy of its institutions. While the process has entailed giving up some aspects of

Edgeworth, *Law, Modernity, Postmodernity: Legal Change in the Contracting State* (London: Ashgate Dartmouth, 2003).

[51] Tamanaha, *On the Rule of Law*, 131.

[52] See David Kinley, 'Human Rights, Globalization and the Rule of Law: Friends, Foes or Family?' (2002) 7 *University of California, Los Angeles, Journal of International Law and Foreign Affairs* 239–64. See also John Ruggie, United Nations Special Representative of the Secretary-General on Business and Human Rights, *Protect, Respect and Remedy: A Framework for Business and Human Rights* (Report to the UN Human Rights Council 7 April 2008, UN Doc. A./HRC/8/5).

state sovereignty, this has not been regarded as 'weakening' the state. On the contrary, it has been observed that it has been possible for the EU to enhance the collective action of its members externally but also strengthen individual capacities of member states.[53] Other projects of regional integration by developing countries such as the Mercado Comun Del Sur (MERCOSUR) in South America (established in 1991 through the Treaty of Asuncion) and the African Union (established in 2001 through the Constitutive Act of the African Union) have increasingly found certain aspects of the EU's mechanism for integration relevant in establishing regional institutions. Despite the EU's problems, both past and during the current economic crisis, ASEAN has a lot to learn from the European experience in developing the rule of law as a viable framework for regional cooperation.

1.5 What Can Rule of Law Mean in ASEAN Integration?

From the inception of the EU, the rule of law has been recognized as a significant element in constructing the EU. The deepening of regional integration has been credited in large part to integration through law, by means of implementing the rules provided in EU treaties, the grant of rule-making powers to competent organs in the Union, and through judicial interpretation and expansion of treaty provisions.[54] An economic union has not only been made possible through the European polity but also established a certain degree of political union among the member states and the expansion of individual human rights protection within a single market. This is a model that, despite its flaws including the exit of the United Kingdom from the Union, remains relevant to developing regions like Southeast Asia where the need for peace, prosperity and respect for rights is of pressing concern for governments and their peoples.

When we think of rule of law as an element in the project of European integration, it is clear that multiple versions or definitions are implicated. The classical (or minimalist) version which emphasizes the architecture and processes for the creation of law at the national level[55] are transposed

[53] Neil MacCormick, *Questioning Sovereignty: Law, State and Nation in the European Commonwealth* (Oxford: Oxford University Press, 1998), 133.

[54] Giorgio Gaja, Peter Hay and Ronald Rotunda, 'Instruments for Legal Integration in the European Community – A Review' in Mauro Cappelletti, Monica Seccombe and Joseph Weiler (eds.), *Integration Through Law* (Berlin: Walter de Gruyter, 1986), 113–60, 115–42.

[55] See the eight principles of legality underlying the rule of law in Fuller, *The Morality of Law*, 33–94. See also Joseph Raz's account of rule of law in 'The Rule of Law and Its Virtue', *The Authority of Law: Essays on Law and Morality* (Oxford: Clarendon Press, 1979), 210–29.

to the supranational level, but so too are the more expansive versions of rule of law which emphasize the attainment of a wide range of normative goals, including economic growth, human rights, and distributive justice.[56] These are very clearly entwined in the post-1989 wave of democratic and legal reforms in Central and Eastern Europe, which were aimed at, inter alia, mobilizing legal rules and legal institutions nationally to accelerate states' accession to the EU and integration within the global economic order. One of the questions posed in this book is whether a similar entwining of the formalist and substantive aspects of rule of law discourse and design will emerge as part of the deeper integration in ASEAN.

ASEAN comprises a region where rule of law practices generally vary in each member state and is also generally perceived to be weak, from both the standpoint of the rule of law adopted by financial institutions and the United Nations. Pursuant to the World Bank criteria which measure the rule of law according to the extent 'agents have confidence in or abide by the rules of society, and in particular the quality of contract enforcement, property rights, the police, and the courts, as well as the likelihood of crime and violence', countries in ASEAN, excluding an exceptionally compliant Singapore, have scores below the 70th percentile ranking, with six countries – Vietnam, Philippines, Indonesia, Laos, Cambodia and Myanmar – all falling below the median rank.[57] Poor governance and corruption have been identified as major roadblocks to development in Southeast Asia.[58] Systemic corruption

[56] For a classical version of a substantive conception of rule of law as a means of achieving liberty, see John Rawls, *A Theory of Justice* (Cambridge, MA: Harvard University Press, 1971), 230–45. For more recent elaborations implicating normative ends of rule of law see, for example, Michael J. Trebilcock and Martina Mota Prado, *What Makes Poor Countries Poor* (Cheltenham: Edward Elgar, 2011), 41–80; Thomas Carothers, 'The Rule of Law Revival' (1998) 77(2) *Foreign Affairs* 95–106; Amartya Sen, *Development as Freedom* (New York: Alfred Knopf, 1999); World Justice Project, *What is the Rule of Law*, http://worldjusticeproject.org/what-rule-law

[57] Comparison of data on the 10 members of ASEAN on the rule of law in 1998, 2003, 2006 and 2007 at World Bank, *World Wide Governance Indicators* (2016), http://info.worldbank.org/governance/wgi/index.aspx#home. Laos, Cambodia and Myanmar received the lowest percentile ranking which is less than 25th percentile while Singapore has the score above 90th percentile. Malaysia, Brunei and Thailand obtained scores between 50th and 60th percentile. See also Daniel Kaufmann, Aart Kraay and Massimo Maztruzzi, 'Governance Matters VII: Aggregate and Individual Governance Indicators 1996–2007' (Policy Research Working Paper No. 4652, World Bank, 24 June 2008).

[58] Donald E. Weatherbee, 'Governance in South East Asia: The Good, The Bad and the Ugly' in Yoichiro Sato (ed.), *Growth and Governance in Asia* (Honolulu: Asia Pacific Center for Security Studies, 2004), 4–14; Clay Wescott, 'Combating Corruption in Southeast Asia' in John Kidd and Frank-Jürgen Richter (eds.), *Fighting Corruption in Asia, Causes, Effects and Remedies* (Singapore: World Scientific Publishing, 2003), 237–40. See also Vito Tanzi,

is a major problem with many countries in the region perceived as among the most corrupt countries in the world.[59]

The fragile rule of law condition in transitional democracies in the region – Thailand, Indonesia, Philippines, Malaysia, Cambodia and, lately, Myanmar – has slowed down and, in many instances, undermined the democratization process in those countries. Massive electoral fraud and violence mar the political landscape in those countries and exacerbate existing societal conflicts and divisions. Weak and corrupt judiciaries, poor access to justice, the ascendancy or strong influence of the military in civil governance, persistence of summary or extrajudicial killings and low capacity of accountability institutions are only among the most visible manifestations of the weakness of rule of law in the region. This has allowed unchecked or unaccountable state power, enable 'state capture' by particular groups or interests and diminish confidence by the people in the democratic and judicial processes.

The absence or weakness of the rule of law has also been identified as causing or abetting impunity and thus the persistence of grave human rights abuses in the region.[60] ASEAN states are continuously cited for failing to protect, or inadequately protecting, the human rights of their citizens and for their utter contempt for, or indifference to, popular democratic governance.[61] Before the restoration of electoral democracy in 2015, Myanmar was cited as a 'pariah state' by most Western countries having flouted, by force and violence, the democratic will and fundamental rights of its people. The socialist countries of Vietnam and Laos continue to suppress democracy and human rights activism as 'anti-government propaganda', while democratic Thailand, Indonesia and the Philippines

'Governance, Corruption and Public Finance: An Overview' in Salvatore Schiavo-Campoe (ed.), *Governance, Corruption and Public Management* (Manila: Asian Development Bank, 1999), 1–21.

[59] The 2015 survey of Transparency International (TI) Corruption Perception Index shows significant improvement of ASEAN countries in the last 5 years. However, most member countries with their respective scores, Myanmar (22), Laos (25), Cambodia (21), Vietnam (31), Philippines (35), Indonesia (36), Thailand (38) and Malaysia (50) are in or below the median score. Only Singapore (85) belongs to the ranks of most clean countries. Transparency International, *Corruption Perceptions Index 2015*, http://www.transparency.org/cpi2015

[60] See Office of the High Commissioner for Human Rights, 'Impunity and the Rule of Law' in *Cambodia – 20 Years on from the Paris Peace Agreements* (21 October 2011) www.ohchr.org/EN/NewsEvents/Pages/Cambodia-20yearsonfromtheParisPeace.aspx, 44–61; Southeast Asian Press Alliance, *Overview of Impunity Related Incidents in 2012 in Southeast Asia*, www.seapa.org/?p=4003

[61] See Human Rights Watch, *World Report 2016*, www.hrw.org/world-report/2016

use extrajudicial methods in response to ethnic dissent, criticisms of government or in restoring security and order. The more affluent countries of Singapore and Malaysia may have lifted the living conditions of their people, but they have also maintained a select class of persons enjoying economic and political privilege while imposing tight security and legal controls on political expression by the broader population.

The manner by which ASEAN states observe the rule of law in varying degrees and shapes speaks volumes about the rule of law itself. The rule of law is not a 'one-size, fits all' prescription to all that ails society or one that can readily be exported from one place to another. The concept of the rule of law is as contested as those of democracy and justice, whose meaning depends on the intended purpose and who controls it. A simple expedient idea that it is aimed at substituting or managing discretionary power with some form of rules is indeed a salutary attribute of the rule of law and one that is desirable especially when seen from the chaos, unpredictability and violence where brute force rules.

Regional integration demands the rule of law not only as an instrument to provide stability and predictability in economic relations but also as a means to establish a coherent and stable framework for guiding the relations of member states, particularly in resolving issues or disputes among members. The EU may be experiencing its worst economic problem at the moment, with stagnant growth and several EU members such as Greece and Spain experiencing economic crisis, but regional mechanisms and political leadership exist to tackle the problem. Regional integration has also shown the capacity to affect rule of law practices in member states. As will be discussed in succeeding chapters, the EU has made it possible to develop a type of state-like rule of law as a framework for integration, and also provided the means to bolster rule of law within its new members with weak rule of law traditions. The minimum criteria for membership in the EU require that states provide protection and necessary conditions to achieve the substantive rights of its citizens; states also need to provide the framework and mechanisms how citizens can receive redress for breach of their rights and to demand accountability for the state's actions or inactions that contravene their constitutional duties.

This book seeks to explain the dynamics of rule-making in ASEAN and the prospects for the development of the rule of law in the processes of integration. This is an interdisciplinary study of the rule of law involving the politics of rule-making in regional integration. It is an exploration of rather than a definitive formulation of the rule of law. It is an area that has, in the last 5 years, only been recently systematically explored with regards to ASEAN, perhaps due to the regional organization's origins as a loose association operating on informal and non-binding arrangements. ASEAN, until after the adoption of the AFTA and ASEAN Charter, has not had intensive cooperation among member states founded on definitive, clear and enforceable agreements. There is, however, a plethora of scholarship on the rule of law within individual member states in ASEAN and comparisons of states using some criteria based on the rule of law.[62] The shift in ASEAN's strategic focus for regional integration has stimulated research on legal and institutional developments in ASEAN. Earlier works interrogate the binding or non-obligatory nature of ASEAN economic agreements, or the emerging legal framework for regional dispute settlement among member states.[63] The past 2 years have seen the production of comprehensive and empirical works particularly the series of publications through Cambridge University Press's 'Integration through Law: The Role of the Rule of Law in ASEAN Integration'.[64] What this suggests is that there

[62] See for example Randall Peerenboom, *Asian Discourses of Rule of Law: Theories and Implementation of Rule of Law in Twelve Asian Countries, France and the U.S.* (London: Routledge Curzon, 2004), which compares rule of law based on thin and thick conceptions representing formalistic or substantive theories of the rule of law.

[63] Paul J. Davidson, 'The ASEAN Way and the Role of Law in ASEAN Economic Cooperation' (2004) 8 *Singapore Yearbook of International Law* 165–76; Andrew Harding, 'Strengthening ASEAN Integration: Lessons from the European Union's Rule of Law' (Paper presented at the Conference on the Legal Aspects of Regional Integration: the EU and ASEAN Compared, Centre for European Studies, Chulalongkorn University, Bangkok, 19 February 2001); Paul J. Davidson (ed.), *ASEAN: The Evolving Legal Framework for Economic Cooperation* (Singapore, Times Media, 2002); Mary Hiscock, 'Changing Patterns of Regional Law Making in Southeast Asia' (1995) 39 *Saint Louis University Law Journal* 933–50; Purificacion Quisumbing, 'An ASEAN Perspective on the Legal and Institutional Aspects of the Community: 'Emerging Legal Framework of ASEAN' in Purificacion Quisumbing and Benjamin Domingo (eds.), *EEC and ASEAN: Two Regional Community Experiences* (Paper presented at the *Proceedings of the ASEAN Seminar on the EEC Experience on Regional Integration*, Manila, 5–8 January 1983), 69–88.

[64] Cambridge University Press publications in 2015 and 2016. See, for example, Jean-Claude Piris and Walter Woon, *Towards a Rules Based Community: An ASEAN Legal Service* (Cambridge: Cambridge University Press, 2015); Robert Beckman, Leonardo Bernard, Hao Duy Phan, Tan Hsien-Li and Ranyta Yusran, *Promoting Compliance: The Role of Dispute Settlement and Monitoring Mechanisms in ASEAN Instruments* (Cambridge: Cambridge University Press, 2016); Jon S.T. Quah (ed.), *The Role of the Public Bureaucracy in Policy Implementation in Five ASEAN Countries* (Cambridge: Cambridge University Press, 2016); Simon Chesterman, *From Community to Compliance?: The Evolution of Monitoring Obligations in ASEAN* (Cambridge: Cambridge University Press, 2015); Stefano Inama and Edmund W. Sim, *Rules of Origin in ASEAN: A Way Forward* (Cambridge: Cambridge University Press, 2015).

is a scope to consider the prospects for the development of rule of law norms and processes at the regional level within ASEAN.

The main argument being made in this book is that for rule of law to be a relevant concept to evaluate how it assists in promoting integration among politically diverse countries, rule of law needs to be seen from a functional perspective. This means looking at how well law and legal institutions perform certain functions, or how they constrain discretion or arbitrary power in a particular setting. In evaluating the development of ASEAN's rules-based regime, this requires asking how ASEAN's institutions perform within rules or are bounded by rules? What are these rules and for whom these rules should be applied? Through this construction, rule of law here is conceived not simply as having the characteristics of either formal or substantive elements but one that is rooted in the history and political experiences of ASEAN member states. The rule of law in ASEAN integration needs to be viewed from its wider context, of regionalism and globalization, and from the internal political dynamics in member states which are brought to bear in the processes of regional integration.

Through a comparative approach, this book further argues that, despite the fundamental differences in history and motivations for integration, and current economic and political challenges such as the persistence of economic problems and migration issues that have created policy divide among members, the EU is a dynamic model whose technique of combining varied legal and institutional forms has been influential for other regional groups. Other regional integration projects share similar issues and challenges to those of the EU, although in varying degrees and scale. The African Union, Southern African Development Community (or SADC), and MERCUSOR have adopted certain features of EU integration and this suggests that the EU is still a relevant model, though not a template, for ASEAN.

To elucidate the main theme of this book, four interrelated questions will be discussed:

1. Does regional integration promote the development of the rule of law?

   This work explores whether the rule of law is indeed a byproduct of regional integration. If so, what is the function and nature of the rule of law in regional integration? Subsequent chapters explain the conditions which give rise to the formation of regional integration and strategic choice of framework for integration. This involves exploring the domestic causes or interests of member states and external factors. The interplay of these factors produces variations in the nature and institutional forms of different regional projects. Chapter 2 discusses in detail the impact of globalization as a key element in the formation of regional projects and its effect on member states' motivation for integration. The chapter then looks into how globalization has brought about contradictory processes and generated new techniques in developing the rule of law at national and regional levels.

2. Under what conditions does the rule of law develop during regional integration?

   This work identifies factors that make it possible for the rule of law to develop during integration and how these factors interact with legal and institutional mechanisms of integration. This work discusses in brief the origins of the rule of law, both as a theoretical construct and as an historical experience, and how this evolves when regional integration takes place. In Chapter 3, we identify factors and processes in the EU – as the most advanced form of regional integration – that made it possible for the development of a state-like rule of law through supranational constitutional developments and hybrid institutional arrangements. The chapter tackles the limits and challenges of the rule of law in the EU and the way it has coped with issues of compliance, sovereignty claims and enlargement, issues that are common to ASEAN and other regional projects. It also looks into how the EU 'transplanted' its style of rule of law to new members with weak traditions of rule of law. Chapter 4 discusses in brief the trends in other regional projects of integration, such as the African Union and its subregional groups, and some of the legal mechanisms and techniques they have borrowed from the EU.

3. Is there a particular type or model of the rule of law that is most appropriate to regional integration?

   In this sense, is the EU, the most advanced form of regional integration, a relevant and viable model for other regional projects, particularly those comprising developing countries? The different economic and political conditions that underlie the formation of regional integration may preclude a uniform conception of a regional rule of law. As a political project, member states still exert primary influence, if not control, of the processes of regional integration. Chapters 5–7 show that rule of law traditions bear heavily on the character of regional rule of law especially in the context of ASEAN and its member states. Locating the rule of law based on the practices of ASEAN member states is thus an important part of this research. Chapter 5 discusses the divergence and convergence of ideas and practices relating to the rule of law in all ten member countries of ASEAN. The diversity of practices in member states suggests that the formation of a 'regional' rule of law, if it occurs, will be through consensus and accommodation of varying practices.

4. What is the nature and function of the rule of law in ASEAN's legal and institutional framework?

   Chapters 6 and 7 discuss recent developments in ASEAN. They examine in detail the ASEAN Charter, the development of legal and regulatory framework in the three pillars and ASEAN's dispute resolution mechanisms, in determining the prospects for rule of law in an ASEAN context. These developments are viewed from the perspective of increasing non-state participation and civil society advocacy in the region – and how this may act as a 'third force' in influencing the process of developing the rule of law in ASEAN. A key question that needs to be addressed is: are there opportunities for the relaxation of sovereignty principle in ASEAN that may pave the way for institutional autonomy, as well as provide for broader or more inclusive participation in regional integration processes?

This book concludes in Chapter 8 that ASEAN integration opens up spaces for the rule of law to grow. The legal and institutional framework brought about by integration initiatives – the ASEAN Charter, the ASEAN Blueprints and a range of trade, economic and other agreements signed among member states and with external partners – have ushered in institution-building, rule creation and a path towards a more stable and coherent framework for regional cooperation. The economic demands of regionalism and globalization have pushed ASEAN to adopt legally binding agreements, as well as to use new techniques of law creation and implementation – such as 'soft' agreements, scorecards and other forms of peer pressure. Other opportunities for the rule of law have also been opened up through opportunities for engagement with non-state actors and civil society to participate in ASEAN processes, and the prospects of making human rights matter in ASEAN.

Rule of law formation in ASEAN, however, is likely to remain statist in nature with inviolability of state sovereignty as the overarching framework of regional integration. While globalization has driven initiatives for regional economic integration, state-building and security remain the core basis of broader regional cooperation. There is increasing push and pace in developing rule of law as an element in economic integration, but this is not going to be the case for political and security concerns of the organization. The persistence of traditional security issues and emergence of new internal and external challenges create a dilemma for members: they encourage a shift towards a more comprehensive approach to security, including looking at more effective and stable mechanisms for regional dispute settlement, and also strengthen states' desire for control and flexibility in dealing with political issues. This is reflected in the state of the largely unused formal dispute mechanisms on the one hand, and the increasing role or 'intervention' of ASEAN or individual members in political or security issues affecting member states on the other.

ASEAN has recognized the importance of rule of law for realizing the much-heralded ASEAN Community and in bringing about peace, prosperity and stability for its members. But unlike the EU where there is stronger political commitment and a common rule of law tradition among many members, developing the rule of law within ASEAN will be gradual and requires softer tactics of promotion, socialization and generating results and confidence. We are unlikely to see the kind of accession criteria used in the EU – a 'take it or leave it' conditionality for new members required to undertake wholesale political and legal reforms as the price of admission. A long history of colonization, internal conflict and underdevelopment has produced countries in Southeast Asia with varied and uneven economic, political and legal systems, as well as a rule of law culture among many elites and political actors that favours 'unrestrained' state powers and the normative construction that this implies.[65] Mutual encouragement and learning – not sanctions or compulsion – is the way forward to further encourage ASEAN member states to commit to rule of law promotion and reform at the regional and national level. This would entail positive motivation for member states through a good, if not modest, showing of the fruits of integration reforms in terms primarily of economic benefits or a secure and stable environment in the region.

[65] See Martin Krygier, 'The Rule of Law: Legality, Teleology, Sociology' in Gianluigi Palombella and Neil Walker (eds.), *Relocating the Rule of Law* (Oxford: Hart Publishing 2008), 45–69; Martin Krygier, 'Rule of Law' in Michel Rosenfeld and András Sajó (eds.), *The Oxford Handbook of Comparative Constitutional Law* (Oxford: Oxford University Press, 2012), 233–49, 234 and 240–2.

2

Conceiving the Rule of Law in ASEAN Integration

2.1 Introduction

As the rule of law becomes a much-heralded virtue of regional integration, this book asks exactly what rule of law means in this context. Does the concept of rule of law serve any analytical purpose to explain the developments in ASEAN integration? Indeed, the key question that is posed in this chapter is whether the rule of law poses a challenge to the ASEAN Way – and vice versa, or whether the rule of law – or a culture of rule of law can be fostered, in spite of the ASEAN Way.

A starting hypothesis in this book is that regional integration drives the rule of law. This is shown in how the EU has in fact generated rule of law at the regional level and affected rule of law development in member countries. In this chapter, we discuss how both processes of regional integration and globalization impact on ASEAN integration and how rule of law may develop in this context. As we shall see in succeeding discussions, ASEAN's path to integration has been informed in many ways by globalization. This is a significant divergence from the process in the EU where regional integration was conceived foremost from historical necessity to avert war through economic and political integration.[1] In the case of ASEAN, the impact of globalization was to provide the motivations and the tools of integration that are consistent with ASEAN's and member countries' prevailing values and normative systems. The enter-twining of the political and economic in the EU – which is largely absent in ASEAN – has made it possible to embrace the idea of supranationalism and constitutionalism that were key to a formal and state-like rule of law in the Europe.

What are the conditions or factors in globalization and regional integration that promote the rule of law or a particular type of rule of law? How is the rule of law formed in these two processes? How are the nature

[1] See, for example, Michelle Cini and Nievez Pérez-Solórzona Borragan, *European Union Politics* (Oxford: Oxford University Press, 2013), 59–71.

and capacities of the state affected by the processes of globalization and regional integration and whether the two complement each other or act in discrete ways? Although globalization and regional integration may be seen as antagonistic phenomena, the convergence of these two processes in ASEAN has the potential to change its political and legal culture and thus moderate the restrictive impact of its core values of sovereignty and non-intervention. Given the wide diversity of rule of law practices among the 10 member states of ASEAN, fostering the rule of law in regional relations as well as in their domestic practices however can be a complex process. This chapter seeks to provide a framework to better understand how rule of law is in current practices in ASEAN and how it may be transformed in the future.

2.2 The Emergence of Regional Integration and Theoretical Discourses on Integration

Regional integration arrangements can be said to have come in two waves. One is the origin for the term, when the EU or its precursor, the European Coal and Steel Community (ECSC), and later the European Economic Community (EEC) were established in 1951 and 1957, respectively. The second wave came mostly in the 1980s with the emergence of regional integration arrangements, mostly characterized as free trade agreements. This heralded the period of 'new regionalism'[2] where new regional projects were characterized by deeper forms of integration with the building of new forms of institutions with broader political, social and cultural objectives. The most notable regional projects formed during the period include the deepening of European integration through the formation of the Single European Market, the creation of the North American Free Trade Area (NAFTA), the establishment of MERCOSUR in Latin America and the formation of the Asia-Pacific Economic Cooperation (APEC). In Africa, regional integration started to gain momentum also during this period with the formation of various Regional Economic Communities (RECs) which have economic integration as their primary objectives.

In Southeast Asia, the response to regional integration was initially slow and perceived to exist only on paper. This is partly due to the fact that Asian countries have long benefited from an open multilateral trading system

[2] See Mina Mashayekhi, Lakshmi Puri and Taisuke Ito, 'Multilateralism and Regionalism: The New Interface' (Paper presented at the United Nations Conference on Trade and Development, Geneva, UNCTAD/DITC/TNCD/2004/7, 2005).

rather than inter-regional trade, and partly to the diversity in the political and economic situation of those countries.[3] The only regional trading arrangement formed in Asia was the ASEAN Preferential Trading Area (ASEAN PTA) in 1977 which remained dormant until the revitalization of economic cooperation in ASEAN after the financial crisis in 1997–8. The aftermath of the 1997 crisis saw the formation of the ASEAN Free Trade Area (AFTA), the East Asia Free Trade Area (EAFTA), the South Asian Association of Regional Cooperation (SAARC) and other subregional groups like the Greater Mekong Area (GMA) and growth triangles or regions formed among states in Southeast Asia. The Pacific has seen even slower and looser regional cooperation, the Pacific Island Countries Trade Agreement (PICTA) and the Pacific Islands Agreement on Closer Economic Relations (PACER) having started to gain traction only in recent years.[4]

Globalization has influenced the formation of regional integration initiatives. However, the relationship between globalization and regional integration underscores the contradiction inherent in the processes of globalization.[5] Integration and fragmentation, expansion and contraction, cooperation and competition are all contradictory processes and effects generated by globalization.[6] The relationship between regional integration and globalization is also ambiguous, even from a strictly economic perspective.[7] One view sees regional integration as being at odds with globalization and with multilateral arrangements in general. Regionalism has been perceived as a reaction against the excesses or uncertainty of globalization.[8] The failure of the multilateral trading system to level the

[3] Robert C. Hine, 'Regionalism and the Integration of the World Economy' (1992) 30(2) *Journal of Common Market Studies* 115–24, 115–16.

[4] PICTA is composed of 11 countries in the Pacific – Cook Islands, Fiji, Kiribati, Nauru, Niue, Papua New Guinea, Samoa, Solomon Islands, Tonga, Tuvalu and Vanuatu – while PACER includes New Zealand and Australia.

[5] James H. Mittelman, 'The Dynamics of Globalization' in James H. Mittelman (ed.), *Globalization: Critical Reflections* (Boulder: Lynne Rienner, 1996), 1–19.

[6] See, for example, James N. Rosenau, 'The Complexities and Contradictions of Globalization' (1997) 96(613) *Current History* 360–4; Jonathan Friedman (ed.), *Globalization, the State and Violence* (Walnut Creek: AltaMira Press, 2003).

[7] William Coleman and Geoffrey Underhill, 'Introduction: Domestic Politics, Regional Economic Co-operation, and Global Economic Integration' in *Regionalism and Global Economic Integration: Asia, Europe and the Americas* (London: Routledge, 1998), 1–16, 2–3.

[8] Adam Lupel, 'Regionalism and Globalization: Post-Nation or Extended Nation?' (2004) 36(2) *Polity* 153–74, 159.

playing field among participating countries has been cited as an important reason for the proliferation of various regional projects.[9]

We can argue that regionalism or regional integration seeks to mediate the dialectical relationship between national and global processes and structures through a strategy that minimizes the negative impact of globalization and maximizes its benefits, as well as bringing domestic interests into the regional agenda. Regionalism reflects the paradox of globalization as it 'both shields domestic society from, and integrates it into, the global division of labour'.[10] Most developing countries which are at the periphery of the international trading system face the dilemma of joining a multilateral trading system dominated by developed countries, the centre. Regional integration partly shields them from this unfair competition. In recent years, however, competition has also come from other developing nations as foreign direct investment becomes the common strategy for achieving economic development.

The other perspective views the two phenomena as consistent, because globalization has the capacity to foster deeper liberalization, expand markets and prepare domestic corporations for global competition. Regional integration, as part of the broader process of regionalism, is seen as a strategy to ensure greater participation by developing countries in the world trading system through the adoption of neoliberal economic policies that open up domestic markets.[11] It allows the formation of free trade areas and customs unions, and trade in goods and services as well as the formation of preferential trading areas among developing member countries.[12] The WTO recognizes the coherence of regional trading arrangements with multilateralism.

We can say that ASEAN tends to follow this latter perspective and in fact exhibit many features of globalization. ASEAN's economic integration

[9] Richard Pomfret, 'Blocs: The Threat to the System, and the Asian Reactions' in Bijit Bora and Christopher Findlay (eds.), *Regional Integration and the Asia-Pacific* (Melbourne: Oxford University Press, 1996), 13–24, 21–2.

[10] Mittelman, 'The Dynamics of Globalization', 11.

[11] Paul Bowles, 'Regionalism and Development after (?) the Global Financial Crises' (2000) 5(3) *New Political Economy* 433–55, 434–5.

[12] General Agreement on Tariffs and Trade, Marrakesh Agreement Establishing the World Trade Organisation, Marrakesh, 15 April 1994, in force 1 January 1995, 1867 UNTS 190; 33 ILM 1153, art. XXIV(4)–(10); General Agreement on Trade in Services, 15 April 1994, Marrakesh Agreement Establishing the World Trade Organisation, Annex 1B, 1869 UNTS 183, 33 ILM 1197 (GATS), art. V; Differential and More Favourable Treatment, Reciprocity and Fuller Participation of Developing Countries, 28 November 1979, GATT Doc L/4903, BISD (26th Supp) (1980) (Enabling Clause).

strategies are outward-looking in building an attractive site for production and investments from within and outside of the region. ASEAN's architecture has also adopted similar legal and institutional arrangements generated by globalization. However, it should be borne in mind that ASEAN is also a product of long historical and political processes that aim to enhance and complement the state-building purposes of member states. The formation of ASEAN in 1967 and the years before the Asian Financial Crisis (AFC) paralleled and supported the consolidation of state-building in Southeast Asian states by fostering regime stability and freedom from intervention.[13] We can therefore argue that in ASEAN's case, regional integration is a form of defensive reaction to globalization from member states. It is a mechanism to secure a position in the international trading system against other countries or regional groups, and a way to defend the position of dominant groups within the member states. Global competition is potentially detrimental to domestic interests, particularly where states have a strong interventionist role in their economies. The shift from economic interventionism to market liberalism does not eliminate the role of the state in a market-led economy. Many ASEAN states, for instance, still exert strong roles in their economies owing to powerful coalitions of political and economic elites in those economies.[14] Thus to a considerable degree, ASEAN is perceived to be the 'regional expression' of domestic coalitions.[15]

2.2.1 A Eurocentric Discourse on Regional Integration

Theoretical discourses on regional integration have mirrored closely the historical developments in the EU and in this sense it is 'Eurocentric'. The term 'regional integration' started with the conceptual tools to describe the development of the EU in its early stages to explain the process of economic and political integration in Europe, including the development of legal integration. Two dominant conceptual approaches – neo-functionalism and intergovernmentalism – have emerged to present competing explanations as to who the main drivers of integration are.

[13] Discussed in more detail in Chapter 5.

[14] See Antoinette R. Raquiza, *State Structure, Policy Formation and Economic Development in Southeast Asia: The Political Economy of Thailand and the Philippines* (New York: Routledge, 2012), 7–10; Garry Rodan and Caroline Hughes, *The Politics of Accountability in Southeast Asia: The Dominance of Moral Ideologies* (Oxford: Oxford University Press, 2014), 30–3.

[15] Etel Solingen, 'Southeast Asia in a New Era: Domestic Coalitions from Crisis to Recovery' (2004) 44(2) *Asian Survey* 189–212.

Neo-functionalism developed in the 1950s from the functionalist approach to give prominence to the role of non-state actors and supranational institutions. Pioneered by Ernest Haas, neo-functionalism proceeds from the same premise as the functionalist approach but asserts the non-unitary character of the state and stresses the major role of economic and political elites in the process.[16] Neo-functionalism sees integration as a process generating spillover effects from one economic or technical sector to other areas of political significance and that, as a result, integration would become self-sustaining. It involves the process of gradual reduction of authority of national governments in favour of supranational institutions. The stagnation in European integration in the 1970s, however, caused adherents of neo-functionalism to question its relevance and brought a renewed focus on the centrality of the states in regional integration. Ernest Haas even officially announced its obsolescence in 1975, observing that an incremental logic of spillover had ceased to describe decision-making choices of regional actors and regional policy outcomes owing to what he described as a 'condition of turbulence' in world politics.[17]

The stagnation of integration initiatives in the 1970s and the reassertion of state power in European Community decision-making culminated in the adoption of the so-called 'Luxembourg veto' and gave rise to the discourse on 'intergovernmentalism'. This concept emphasizes that states, rather than supranational institutions, are the key instigators of regional integration.[18] This theory is premised on the centrality of states as actors in international relations, the role of power-bargaining and preferences among states and the relative gains of states proceeding from their preferences in pursuing their own interests.[19] It gained prominence during the period of deeper integration in the 1980s which featured the adoption of the Single European Act in 1986 and the holding of the Intergovernmental Conferences (IGCs) up until the ratification of the Maastricht Treaty in 1993.

In the 1980s, the dominance of supranationalism and intergovernmentalism as the focus for studying regional integration was questioned and

[16] Ernest Haas, *Beyond the Nation State: Functionalism and International Organization* (Stanford: Stanford University Press, 1964).

[17] Ernest Haas, 'Turbulent Fields and the Theory of Regional Integration' (1976) 20(2) *International Organization* 173–212, 174–8.

[18] Andrew Moravcsik, 'Preferences and Power in the European Community: A Liberal Intergovernmental Approach' (1993) 31(4) *Journal of Common Market Studies* 473–524.

[19] Ibid.; Michael Huelshoff, 'Domestic Politics and Dynamic Issue Linkage: A Reformulation of Integration Theory' (1994) 38(2) *International Studies Quarterly* 255–79, 257–9.

challenged by new schools of thought. The theories to emerge from this assume the EU as a given, not so much concerned on systems transformation but rather focus on the institutions, policymaking and implementation.[20] The institutionalists put emphasis on the institutions of governance and a wider range of actors involved at all levels of lawmaking and decision-making. A focus on the institutions resulted in giving EU a character of a unique polity wherein it possesses features of a national state[21] or in describing it as a system of multilevel governance. EU studies arising from this genre either followed the rational choice model or drew from international relations theories of historical institutionalism and constructivism.[22] The divide between the rationalists and constructivists is particularly evident as the former is concerned about the process of decision-making as determined by the pursuit of interests of primary actors while the latter stresses the primacy of norms, ideas and values in shaping or reshaping of preferences and identities in the institutions and processes of integration.[23] Other conceptions about the EU put emphasis on particular factors affecting the processes of integration such as the importance of non-state actors,[24] the linkage between domestic and regional politics or the development of the global economy as a major force in European integration.[25]

2.3 How Have Regional Integration and Globalization Influenced the Rule of Law?

The relationship between regional integration and rule of law has mostly been discussed and theorized in the EU where the two are seen as having a reciprocal relationship. As will be discussed in more detail in Chapter 3, regional integration was the vessel through which the rule of law was established at the regional level which in turn provided the engine to facilitate

[20] James Caporaso, 'Regional Integration Theory: Understanding our Past and Anticipating our Future' (1993) 5(1) *Journal of European Public Policy* 1–16, 6–7.

[21] Alec Stone Sweet and Wayne Sandholtz (eds.), *Integration, Supranational Governance and the Institutionalization of the European Polity* (Oxford: Oxford University Press, 1998), 1–25.

[22] See generally Mark A. Pollock, 'Theorizing the European Union: International Organization, Domestic Polity, or Experiment in New Governance?' (2005) 8 *Annual Review of Political Science* 357–98, 361–4.

[23] Paul Craig and Gráinne de Búrca, *EU Law: Text, Cases, and Materials*, 3rd edn. (Oxford: Oxford University Press, 2003), 6–7.

[24] See, for example, Robert O. Keohane, *After Hegemony: Cooperation and Discord in the World Political Economy* (Princeton: Princeton University Press, 1986).

[25] Huelshoff, 'Domestic Politics and Dynamic Issue Linkage', 260.

integration in the face of commitment issues by member states. From an instrumentalist function in creating a common market economy, the rule of law progressively transformed the EU as a constitutional legal order that constrained discretion of member states, protected citizens from the excesses of market forces and generated individual and collective rights.[26]

'Legal integration' is the concept that is used to denote the development of legal rules and norms that are applicable in all member states. The Community law, or the *acquis communitaire*, consists of body of laws developed through the EU that are directly demandable and enforceable in any member state. It also presupposes the supremacy of Community law and principles against which national laws have to conform. How legal integration developed, and its impact on the broader scheme of regional integration, has also followed from the main theoretical constructs discussed above. All of these theories highlight the role of a powerful and activist regional court, the European Court of Justice (ECJ) established in 1952, in taking an active role in pursuing integration during the period of disintegration or faltering in the formative period of the EU.

Following the neo-functionalist perspective, legal integration is explained as a process that developed through spillover and caused a 'virtuous circle' that constantly produced and reproduced users of and demand for EU law.[27] This approach highlights the role of private actors in triggering judicialization, or the process whereby the ECJ emerged as authoritative interpreter of EU laws, rules and principles and consequently became a key driver of regional integration.[28] An intergovernmentalist perspective informs some theories of 'principal agent'; by this it means that the principal, the member states, has engaged the agent, the ECJ, to help member states overcome dilemmas of commitment and collective action and thus assist them in governing – through judicial supervision – the EU and the member states themselves.[29] One perspective also suggests that the reason

[26] Paul Craig, 'Constitutions, Constitutionalism and the European Union' (2001) 7(2) *European Law Journal* 125–50.

[27] Alec Stone Sweet, 'Judicialization and the Construction of Governance' (1999) 31 *Comparative Political Studies* 147–84; Alec Stone Sweet and Thomas Brunell, 'Constructing a Supranational Constitution: Dispute Resolution and Governance in the European Community' (1998) 92 *American Political Science Review* 63–81.

[28] Anne-Marie Burley and Walter Mattli, 'Europe Before the Court: A Political Theory of Legal Integration' (1993) 47 *International Organization* 41–76.

[29] See generally Geoffrey Garrett, 'The Politics of Legal Integration in the European Union' (1995) 49 *International Organization* 171–81; Mark Pollack, *The Engines of Integration: Delegation, Agency, and Agency Setting in the European Union* (Oxford: Oxford University

why states permit the courts to exercise more authority is that the courts help them solve problems arising from incomplete contracting and that the ECJ's rulings are in accord with the interests of major EU countries such as Germany and France.[30]

Another important theory to emerge on legal integration was to present an equilibrium between the role of member states and supranational actors. Weiler fashioned the mechanism of 'exit' and 'voice', derived from game theory, to provide a framework for explaining the process of constitutionalization and consequent lock-in, or foreclosure of exit from EU by the member states.[31] This theory proposes that the legal transformation of EU becomes more acceptable to member states as they exercise more control in the decision-making process. Voluntary exit of members is foreclosed as voice is given in the form of control in legislation making. Two factors were identified that foreclosed exit from the EU – the constitutionalization of the Community legal structure and the system of legal and judicial guarantees.[32] Brexit however has shown that the EU legal regime has its own constraints or limits in terms of addressing all potential pressing political issues.

2.3.1 Globalization: Uncertainties and Possibilities in the Rule of Law

While there is consensus that regional integration is beneficial to rule of law, views are divided on how globalization impacts the rule of law. Undoubtedly, the modern era of globalization has ushered an explosion of law, both at the national and international domains. This is particularly noticeable in the economic area where various forms of rules and norms occur that range from state-sponsored statutes, obligatory rules and court decisions to international norms such as model laws, international standards drawn by private organizations and rulings from international judicial or nonjudicial tribunals. Collectively known as 'global law', these rules have arisen through the diffusion of the lawmaking process in multiple sectors of society which are independent of nation-states and have

Press, 2003); Giandomenico Majone, *Dilemmas of European Integration: The Ambiguities and Pitfalls of Integration by Stealth* (Oxford: Oxford University Press, 2005).

30 Geoffrey Garrett, 'International Cooperation and Institutional Choice: The European Community's Internal Market' (1992) 46 *International Organization* 556–69.

31 Joseph H. Weiler, 'The Transformation of Europe' (1991) 100(8) *Yale Law Journal* 2403–83.

32 Ibid., 2407–8.

grown out of transglobal commercial contracts or the *lex mercatoria* ('law merchant').[33] Globalization of law is not, however, equivalent to globalization of the rule of law; in this latter area, we do not have an emerging consensus. The effect of globalization on the rule of law is largely seen in globalization's impact on state sovereignty, where the rule of law has found its expression.

There are generally three views on globalization's effects on state sovereignty which are premised on the state's lawmaking capacities. The 'hyperglobalist' predicts the ultimate demise of the state. In this account, the logic of commerce and capital is driving the political obsolescence of the state as the global economy is becoming less tied to and reliant upon territorial borders within which to conduct economic activity and the states loses its ability to control or regulate these activities.[34] The 'sceptic' maintains the centrality of the state and argues that there is nothing exceptional about the current levels of interdependence at the global level. Sassen, for example, maintains that the state remains the 'ultimate guarantor of the rights of global capital, that is, the protection of contracts and property rights'.[35] The third category, the 'transformationalist', acknowledges the unprecedented change caused by globalization but, unlike the hyperglobalists, asserts that the process remains uncertain and contested. In this view, globalization is continuously transforming state sovereignty in relation to a globalizing world economy.[36] A consequence of this sovereign transformation has caused a shift in the 'dispersion and dissolution of powers of governance in institutions in civil society as well as the economy' or 'a move away from government to governance'.[37] To Jayasuriya, this transformation is ushering a transition from political constitutionalism to a kind of economic constitutionalism which sees sovereignty increasingly being fragmented and distributed across a range of nonpolitical institutions.

33 See Gunther Teubner, '"Global Bukowina": Legal Pluralism in the World Society' in Gunther Teubner (ed.), *Global Law Without a State* (Brookfield: Dartmouth, 1997), 3–28, 1–5.

34 See, for example, Susan Strange, *The Retreat of the State* (Cambridge: Cambridge University Press, 1996) who observes, taking the global financial economy in particular, the increasing power of nonpolitical actors in the global system which has diminished the state's responsibilities and capacity in the market economy.

35 Saskia Sassen, *Globalization and Its Discontents* (New York: The New Press, 1998), 197.

36 David Held, Anthony McGrew, David Goldblatt and Jonathan Perraton, *Global Transformations: Politics, Economics and Culture* (Stanford: Stanford University Press, 1999), 1–8.

37 Kanishka Jayasuriya, 'Globalization, Sovereignty, and the Rule of Law: From Political to Economic Consitutionalism?' (2001) 8(4) *Constellations* 442–60, 443–4.

The above perspectives on globalization and state sovereignty do not offer a concrete and overall pattern of the development of the rule of law under globalization or an explanation for how either weakening or strengthening the state could possibly transform the rule of law either in the context of the state or in the international legal order. There are two main propositions describing general trends in the impact of globalization on the rule of law. The Hayekian view sees globalization and the rule of law as sharing a reciprocal relationship, meaning that globalization encourages adoption of stable and predictable rules necessary for the enforcement of contracts and the protection of property rights.[38] Adherents of this view suggest an unwavering faith in globalization's capacity for 'spillover' and eventual strengthening of the rule of law in other spheres of private and public life. The observance of the rule of law in the economic sphere is believed to expand to social and political rights, which happened in the case of the United States and the EU.[39]

An opposing view asserts that the rule of law has not been helped by globalization. The hoped-for spillover arising from the intensification of the use of rules in the economic domain into the public sphere has so far been confined to the experiences of Western developed countries.[40] Unlike mostly developed Western economies, many other countries lack constitutional or political space that would guarantee the autonomy of an independent judiciary, the institution that could allow the expansion of legal reasoning into other areas of law. A key objection lies in the nature and character of forms of law developed under the rubric of globalization. Scheuerman argues that there is little evidence to suggest that internationalization of capital is strengthening traditional conceptions of the rule of law. On the contrary, the evolving informal and discretionary legal regime erodes the classical notion of the rule of law which is grounded in such normative rules as being general, public, prospective and stable and is fundamentally inconsistent with a minimally defensible conception of the rule of law.[41] A growing body of economic rules is shunning the formal, public,

[38] William Scheuerman, 'Economic Globalization and the Rule of Law' (1999) 6(1) *Constellations* 3–25, 4–5.

[39] This is the view subscribed to by economists and policymakers in international financial institutions like the World Bank and other academics and nongovernment organizations. See Gordon Silverstein, 'Globalization and the Rule of Law: "A Machine that Runs Itself?"' (2003) 1(3) *International Journal of Constitutional Law* 427–45, 428–9.

[40] Ibid., 430–42.

[41] William Scheuerman, 'Economic Globalization and the Rule of Law', 3.

predictable and stable systems of law in favour of discretionary, informal and open-ended system of law and flexible private self-regulation.[42]

The attention given to the use of 'soft law' within international relations would seem to support the less optimistic view on globalization's impact on the rule of law. Soft laws, which are characterized by lesser degrees of obligation, precision and delegation, tend to preserve the sovereignty of member states. Through its non-binding and flexible nature, soft law allows states to weaken their commitments and possibly their compliance under the treaties or agreements. Where states ardently guard their sovereign powers, soft laws provide the tool through which states could commit to agreements and lessen sovereignty costs through forms that are non-binding, imprecise or do not delegate extensive powers.[43] It is the area of delegation, either of decision-making or enforcement, which provides the greatest source of 'unanticipated sovereignty costs' and where states hesitate to give in, particularly where they assert ultimate control over legal authority in the courts and domestic institutions.[44]

However, the use of soft laws should not in itself be regarded as entirely undesirable. Not only does it have the capacity to be a springboard for the development of formal, precise and enforceable law through repetitive practices and socialization, but also soft law offers many benefits of its own.[45] It presents an attractive option for states who are reluctant to diminish their sovereign powers or unwilling to accept the 'uncertainties' that high obligation, precision and delegation could bring into domestic policies and issues. For international organizations with varying values and interests and degrees of power among member states, soft law affords member states the chance to forge more acceptable agreements or compromise, especially regarding politically sensitive issues. Another advantage of a softer law regime is its capacity to facilitate 'learning' of matters that are new or alien to the organization or its members. Over time, soft law may evolve into harder law. In many instances in international relations, softer law can have a powerful effect or even be superior to and more desirable than hard law.[46]

[42] Ibid., 6–19.

[43] Kenneth Abbot and Duncan Snidal, 'Hard and Soft Law in International Governance' (2000) 54(3) *International Organization* 436–41.

[44] Ibid., 438.

[45] Ibid., 434–8.

[46] Ibid., 447–8 and 451–2, citing the Helsinki process forged between Western Europe and the United States on one side and the Soviet Union on the other, over the latter's desire to stabilize military and political relations with the former and thus establish economic relations.

Although states are given room to manoeuvre or to resist compliance, softer law nevertheless provides opportunities for private non-state actors, particularly nongovernmental organizations, to invoke 'non-legally binding but highly elaborated' documents to demand compliance from governments.[47] Several issues involving human rights and in recent years, the environment, have been constituted in soft forms due to their high sensitivity and the unwillingness or reluctance of states and other private non-state actors to turn commitments into hard obligations. Some of these loose declarations have been developed into hard treaties or conventions or have become valuable tools for advocacies. Soft law may not be invoked as 'law'. It supports similar normative discourse, however, and legitimizes the issues raised in the instruments and could become the basis of initiating change in the political processes.[48]

These developments have shown that assessing the impact of globalization on the rule of law has to take into account the role of non-state actors and informal or unofficial processes in decision-making, rule-making and implementation in international or regional domains. The focus of the study should not be confined to how states are strengthened, weakened or transformed. An important research task is to determine how states respond to various external and internal challenges. Of particular significance to Southeast Asian states is the way states respond to their challenges to their authority or legitimacy, and how and to what extent they respond to challenges by individuals and civil society groups which present opposing or alternative views of state or regional governance. To what extent has globalization aided in galvanizing or suppressing public discourse or the articulation of new ideas that unsettle official state 'ideology', and how do states respond to this at the level of state and regional governance? These are the crucial questions that have become more significant for the rule of law under globalization.

2.4 The Rule of Law: As Constraint and As Enabler

Having discussed the phenomenon of regional integration and globalization, we proceed to consider the rule of law, a concept that has become 'uncertain' due to the range of meanings it has acquired for different aims and contexts. The purpose of this section is to explain the emergence of the concept of rule of law as an incident of Western liberal states and whether

[47] Ibid., 452.
[48] Ibid.

this course is peculiar to them. Revisiting the historical genesis of the rule of law should give us a concrete and broader appreciation for the concept and not to be locked in or made to choose between its formal and substantive definitions.[49] According to Martin Krygier, both of these conceptions have given the rule of law an 'anatomical' meaning where certain elements are essential to judge the rule of law's existence or absence.[50]

The formal conception pertains to the process and procedure by which law is promulgated and is not concerned with the content or morality of the law. It emphasizes the elements of generality, autonomy and predictability of legal norms.[51] Several attributes are also listed in judging the validity of the law – generality, clarity, promulgation, consistency, non-retroactivity, noncontradictory rules, and that law should not require impossible conditions.[52] Conversely, the substantive conception recognizes that apart from the formal aspects certain values or principles are considered to be part, if not essential attributes, of the rule of law, and by which laws should comply. The contents of the law must be looked at in order to determine whether they satisfy the rule of law; formal rules and procedures should be made to enforce moral rights.[53] Both conceptions of the rule of law particularly emphasize the role of autonomous judicial institution or a form of judicial review to ensure that government institutions act within the bounds of their authority.

The ambiguities involved in conceptualizing the rule of law and the difficulties associated with ascribing it to different types of political systems have led to the recent typology of 'thin rule of law' and 'thick rule of law'.[54] A thin conception generally puts stress on the formal or instrumental aspects, or features that any legal system must possess to function effectively as a system of laws regardless of whether the legal system is democratic or non-democratic, capitalist or socialist state. A thick rule of law incorporates the former conception but includes other elements such as economic arrangements, forms of government and conceptions of human rights.[55] The thin–thick rule of law dichotomy could be useful framework

[49] Jonathan Rose, 'The Rule of Law in the Western World: An Overview' (2004) 35(4) *Journal of Social Philosophy* 457–70.

[50] Krygier, 'The Rule of Law: Legality, Teleology, Sociology'.

[51] Raz, 'The Rule of Law and Its Virtue', 210.

[52] Fuller, *The Morality of Law*, 33–94.

[53] Ronald Dworkin, *A Matter of Principle* (Oxford: Clarendon Press, 1990), 11.

[54] Randall Peerenboom, 'Varieties of Rule of Law, An Introduction and Provisional Conclusion', *Asian Discourses of Rule of Law*, 2–13.

[55] Ibid.

for describing a range or combination of rule of law practices in different political systems and is closer to a contextual understanding of the rule of law.

In this book, it is argued however that a sociological account of the rule of law should be the starting point of inquiry in examining the development of rule of law practices in non-Western countries. Through this account, we know how a linear model of the development of state system came to be in the Western context, that is not observed in ASEAN countries, where law has played a role in monopolizing and centralizing the 'business of ruling'[56] and also a means of regulating the exercise of state authority.[57] What is relevant in this account to ASEAN, however, is the law's function in forming and sustaining a centralized public authority. Although the normative character of the state has been much emphasized, particularly in the context of Western countries, an understanding of the state's centralizing function situates the rule of law in a more concrete and broader perspective.

The centralizing function of law accounts for the significant variance in the practice of the rule of law in Southeast Asian states by comparison with liberal democratic states in the West. Cohesion and the strengthening of institutions of power – vis-à-vis civil society power – underlie rule of law practices in ASEAN states and this has impelled states to treat law as 'enabling' than 'limiting'.[58] This was the practice of past authoritarian regimes and is also characteristic of highly centralized states in ASEAN. In contrast, Western states are generally characterized by limits on and fragmentation of state power. Restraint on state power requires that arbitrary government action is prevented. The rule of law tames this so-called 'brute power', hence the classical liberal view presupposes that sovereign powers are circumscribed.[59] A shift from this centralizing theme towards restraint on state powers has proven to be a daunting test for newly liberalizing states in Southeast Asia. Factors affecting the reorientation of Southeast Asian states towards a 'limited state' show that these are both externally and internally driven as shown in its peculiar history and culture.

[56] Gianfranco Poggi, *The State: Its Nature Development and Prospects* (Stanford: Stanford University Press, 1990), 72–3.

[57] See Max Weber, *Economy and Society* (1968) cited in Karl Dusza, 'Max Weber's Conception of the State' (1989) 3(1) *International Journal of Politics, Culture, and Society* 71–105, 75–6.

[58] See, for example, Jothie Rajah, *Authoritarian Rule of Law: Legislation, Discourse and Legitimacy in Singapore* (Cambridge: Cambridge University Press, 2012).

[59] José María Maravall and Adama Przeworski (eds.), *Democracy and the Rule of Law* (Cambridge: Cambridge University Press, 2003), 8–10.

Moreover, the character of legal system needs to be understood beyond 'established' formal rules and institutions. In Chapter 5, we therefore propose a typology of law regime types that shows the fluctuating trends in law developments in Southeast Asian states.

2.5 Understanding Integration and Rule of Law in ASEAN

In Southeast Asia, the discourse on regional integration is a much more recent phenomenon, having taken off only after the AFC in 1997. As ASEAN integration remains to be in its formative stage, we define regional integration in its current state generally as a form of deeper commitment of member states to a range of economic, political and social matters that demand greater institutionalization of cooperative behaviour. As mentioned in Chapter 1, ASEAN regionalism has been a state-led political project since its inauguration in 1967 where internal security and political stability as a prerequisite to state-building has been the rationale for regional cooperation. Regional economic cooperation was minimal until the 1990s.

The idea of regional integration in ASEAN only surfaced when the AFTA was established in 1992, providing the springboard for new discussions on enhanced regional cooperation.[60] The economists were the first to mention 'integration', borne out of frustration over the ineffective implementation of past economic agreements such as the ASEAN PTA and the organization's trademark, the 'ASEAN Way'. They advocated the need for a comprehensive regional trade agreement and the necessity for binding rules and formal institutions. The social and political consequences of the Asian crisis in ASEAN member states exposed the limits, and eroded the salience, of the 'ASEAN Way' as the underlying principle of ASEAN regionalism.[61] The regionalism that emerged in the 1990s was clearly marked by a more expansive basis of cooperation which is reflected in new institution-building, harmonization of policies and norm creation. The decision by state leaders to pursue regional integration by building an ASEAN Community has greatly expanded the coverage of regional cooperation and extended to other areas or subjects that were 'off-limits' in the past. These include human rights, civil society participation and

[60] Eero Palmujoki, *Regionalism and Globalism in Southeast Asia* (New York: Palgrave, 2001), 4–5.

[61] Stephen Haggard, 'The Politics of the Asian Financial Crisis' (2000) 11(2) *Journal of Democracy* 130–44, 134–8.

cooperation in dealing with vulnerable sectors in society such as migrant workers, women and children.

Unlike the case of the EU, early attempts at analysing ASEAN did not promote 'integration'. The concept of 'cooperation' was used, mainly because of ineffective functional cooperation and the notable absence of binding rules and formal regional institutions. One study questioned the suitability of applying the concept of integration to an area 'which is not, as yet, historically delineated, and does not exhibit large-scale interdependence in many areas of mutual concern'.[62]

Solidum was the first scholar to use the concept of functionalism to determine whether functional cooperation in ASEAN may lead to incremental effects leading to integration. She suggested cooperation as the appropriate framework to describe and explain the motivations of political elites in Southeast Asia in establishing ASEAN.[63] The loose and flexible organizational setup in ASEAN pursuant to the Bangkok Declaration of 1967 clearly manifests that 'ASEAN is an instrument for cooperation, not integration.'[64] However, Solidum believes that if integration involves in the final phase the sharing of values, habits and expectations among peoples of discrete units in such a way that a social and psychological foundation is built for a transnational society, then cooperation may contribute to the building of mutual understanding and confidence until the peoples involved in the integration process share the same institutions and values in a political community.[65] Solidum's work has strongly influenced state leaders, policymakers and academics about the importance of sharing of norms, values and practices and the socialization of leaders and elites as key strategy in providing the building blocks for deeper cooperation among member states.[66]

[62] Hugh Byrne, *The Classic-Functional Approach to Regional Integration: The Association of South-East Asian Nations (ASEAN) – A Case Study* (Ph.D. Dissertation, Sydney: University of New South Wales, 1980), 13.

[63] Estrella D. Solidum, *Towards a Southeast Asian Community* (Quezon City: University of the Philippines Press, 1974).

[64] Estrella D. Solidum, 'An ASEAN Perspective on the Decision-Making Process in the European Community' in Quisumbing, EEC and ASEAN, 129.

[65] Solidum, *The Politics of ASEAN*, 2.

[66] Jörn Dosch, 'The Post-Cold War Development of Regionalism in East Asia' in Fu-Kuo Lin and Philippe Régnier (eds.), *Regionalism in East Asia: Paradigm Shifting?* (New York: Routledge Curzon, 2003), 30–51, 33–4; See also Amitav Acharya, 'Culture, Security, Multilateralism: The "ASEAN Way" and Regional Order' (1998) 19(1) *Contemporary Security Policy* 55–84, 56.

While legal integration in the EU has been an integral component of regional integration, the concept has been absent in ASEAN. There have been attempts, however, to provide a framework for ASEAN legal cooperation.[67] Integration, in general, has been defined as a process by which national states transfer parts of their autonomy to a common institutional framework in order to allow for common rules or policies.[68] Legal integration, from the point of view of the EU, is the process by which a binding supranational system of the rule of law has been established among the members of the union.[69] These definitions clearly involve a voluntary transfer of aspects of sovereignty to a supranational institution. This is not the case for ASEAN, which rejected supranationalism. Yet there is now increasing interest in examining ASEAN's legal development, primarily by testing the binding nature of ASEAN's recent legal agreements and the new regional dispute mechanism.[70]

ASEAN lacks legal integration owing to the absence of binding rules and agreements. Formal binding rules have played a minimal role in the development of ASEAN, despite greater initiatives at increased economic cooperation.[71] As will be discussed at length in later chapters, the development of more precise and detailed language and binding dispute mechanisms is gaining ground in ASEAN economic integration, but is virtually absent in the other two Community pillars, the ASEAN Political and Security Community and the ASEAN Socio-Cultural Community.

There had been two main strands in the study of law within ASEAN until the constitution of the ASEAN Community. An earlier theme in ASEAN legal study emphasizes culture as the basis for explaining ASEAN's proclivity for loose and informal mechanisms.[72] ASEAN's aversion to legal

67 See, for example, Purificacion V. Quisumbing, 'Problems and Prospects of ASEAN Law: Towards a Legal Framework for Regional Dispute Settlement' in R.P. Anand and Purificacion V. Quisumbing (eds.), *ASEAN Identity, Development and Culture* (Manila: University of the Philippines Law Center and East–West Center Culture Learning Institute, 1981), 300–18, 313–15.

68 Dorette Corbey, 'Dialectical Functionalism: Stagnation as a Booster of European Integration' (1995) 49(2) *International Organization* 253–84, 253–4.

69 Jean-Yves Pitarakis and George Tridimas, 'Joint Dynamics of Legal and Economic Integration in the European Union' (2003) 16 *European Journal of Law and Economics* 357–68.

70 See, for example, Gerry Ferguson and Douglas Johnston (eds.), *Asia-Pacific Legal Development* (Vancouver: University of British Columbia Press, 2011); Piris and Woon, *Towards a Rules-Based Community*.

71 Mary Hiscock, 'Changing Patterns of Regional Law Making in Southeast Asia', 937–8.

72 Nobuyuki Yasuda, 'Law, Legal Culture and Regional Integration: Asian Perspectives' (APEC Study Center Discussion Paper Series No. 7, Graduate School of International Development, Nagoya University, 1996).

formalism has been traced from Asian traditional values of collectivism or communitarian behaviour and a preference for informal dispute resolution methods present among member states, as a means to preserve peace and harmony even in times of conflicts. It is believed to have served the basis of cohesion among an otherwise diverse group of nations and is reflected in the mechanisms of ASEAN.[73] The cultural factor in ASEAN has found compelling expression by official personages in the organization such as Singapore's former Prime Minister Lee Kuan Yew and Malaysia's former Prime Minister Mahathir Mohammad, who articulated the uniqueness of 'Asian values'.[74] Cultural relativism in the context of ASEAN became the banner under which member states attempted to challenge Western conceptions of liberal democracy and human rights. While the discourse of Asian values has lost traction in recent years particularly after the AFC, it has found its way, through subtle formulation, into ASEAN instruments articulating human rights in the region. However, there is no common formal legal culture among the member countries owing to the differences in legal systems reflecting different colonial influences and the pluralism of indigenous customs and practices.

The other view identifies ASEAN states' firm adherence on the principle of sovereignty. The inability of ASEAN to adopt formal and binding rules has also been blamed mainly on the strong adherence of member states to the principle of national sovereignty.[75] This conception presents one important explanation for ASEAN's reluctance to adopt formal legalism in intra-regional relations.

Since the adoption of the ASEAN Charter in 2007 that ushered in community building, increasing scholarship on regional rule-making and institutions has come about. A cross-disciplinary and comparative trend on studying ASEAN has emerged that situates ASEAN integration in wider political and economic context, nationally and globally.[76] Conceptual and practical dimensions of how law and institutions work in

[73] Ibid., 15–16.

[74] Michael D. Barr, *Cultural Politics and Asian Values: The Tepid War* (New York: Routledge, 2002), 4–8.

[75] Locknie Hsu, 'Towards an ASEAN Charter: Some Thoughts from the Legal Perspective' in Rodolfo Severino (ed.), *Framing the ASEAN Charter* (Singapore: Institute of Southeast Asian Studies, 2005), 45–52, 50. See also Mark Beeson, 'Sovereignty under Siege: Globalisation and the State in Southeast Asia' (2003) 24(2) *Third World Quarterly* 357–74, 358.

[76] Inama and Sim, *The Foundation of the ASEAN Economic Community*; Carlos Closa and Lorenzo Casini, *Comparative Regional Integration: Governance and Legal Models* (Cambridge: Cambridge University Press, 2016).

ASEAN at different levels and areas of governance show the potential in building a legal regime in regional cooperation and its impact on domestic legal systems and processes.[77]

2.5.1 *A Framework for Understanding the Relationship between Integration and the Rule of Law in ASEAN*

The salience of economic integration has allowed for the process of institutional and legal experimentation in ASEAN. ASEAN is a state-led regional project where sovereignty and nonintervention remain the central tenets of integration. However, the confluence of the global, regional and national/local has allowed for a peculiar pathway for the rule of law in the region. As rule of law practices have been contingent on politics, so is ASEAN's legal regime. In this sense, the approaches taken in this study come from several conceptual frameworks.

European integration has provided the inspiration, and not necessarily the exact template for ASEAN integration. The broad outlines for ASEAN architecture followed the earlier three-pronged Community model of EU's early stages but not the model of supranationalism and judicial review system. The political economy approach in international relations is still relevant in explaining the motivations for integration in ASEAN – that is the relationship of the regional with the global and local political economy, in shaping the dynamics of integration. As discussed earlier, this framework is increasingly acknowledged in the EU as the global economy expands and impacts on regional dynamics. As global pressure becomes strong, the push for regional integration increases; in most cases, however, this has been accompanied or complemented by broader multilateral initiatives. ASEAN integration for instance has from the beginning adopted an open regionalism with its ASEAN Plus initiatives that involve simultaneous forging of bilateral economic agreements with other countries.[78] Greater competition for foreign investments from other developing regions has prompted ASEAN states to constitute itself as a production and investment base. In recent years, it has not only succeeded in generating

[77] See Beckman *et al.*, *Promoting Compliance*; Chesterman, *From Community to Compliance?*; Inama and Sim, *Rules of Origin in ASEAN*; Kheng-Lian Koh and Nicholas Robinson, *ASEAN Environmental Legal Integration: Sustainable Goals?* (Cambridge: Cambridge University Press, 2016).

[78] There are a number of countries included in the ASEAN Plus arrangements such as China, Japan and South Korea (ASEAN Plus 3) and China, India, Japan, South Korea, Australian and New Zealand (ASEAN Plus 6).

foreign investments from outside the region but also increased the flow of intra-ASEAN investments.[79]

The rule of law as part of the process of ASEAN integration shadows this broader rationale for integration. The process described by transnational legal process theory is likewise useful in understanding the spillover from economic cooperation in fostering rule of law in ASEAN context. How rules are made by and for whom in ASEAN are key questions in determining both the nature and function of the rule of law. In this formulation, states and various non-state actors interact to make, interpret, enforce and internalize rules of international law.[80] The most important dimensions of this approach are the aspects of interaction, interpretation and internalization of rules among the various actors in the international system. These latter approaches show the dynamics of the diffusion of the sources of law and how norms are being developed and continuously shaped by actors and factors within and outside the state. The pervasiveness of state interdependence and the pluralism of values and interests existing in national and international spheres have continuously influenced, perhaps in equal measure, the development of international norms and their reception across states through the non-formal or 'soft' processes and mechanisms.[81] Through this perspective, it is possible for us to pragmatically evaluate how global and national processes, and ASEAN Way, interact and generate rules and institutions that may produce a distinctive rule of law practice in ASEAN or subsequently how it may affect those in member states.

Informal international lawmaking or 'In-Law'[82] is a growing phenomenon that reflects how law is socialized among different actors at the international level and observed to have intensified under the onslaught of globalization.[83] It has also generated different or alternative processes that depart from the 'formalities' of traditional international law rule-making. This concept is significant in ASEAN as it is through the informal

[79] ASEAN Secretariat and United Nations Conference on Trade and Development, *ASEAN Investment Report 2013–2014: FDI Development and Regional Value Chains* (Jakarta: ASEAN Secretariat, 2014).

[80] Harold Koh, 'Why Do Nations Obey International Law?' (1997) 106 *Yale Law Journal* 2599–659.

[81] Paul Berman, 'From International Law to Law and Globalization' (2005) 43 *Columbia Journal of Transnational Law* 485–556.

[82] Joost Pauwelyn, Ramses A. Wessel and Jan Wouters (eds.), *Informal International Lawmaking* (Oxford: Oxford University Press, 2012), 14–15.

[83] Claire Cutler, 'Globalization, the Rule of Law, and the Modern Law Merchant: Medieval or Late Capitalist Associations?' (2001) 8(4) *Constellations: An International Journal of Critical and Democratic Theory* 480–502.

processes, rather than the formal ones, that drive the development of its rules-based regime. It identifies three aspects – the output, process and actors, which work in nontraditional manner.[84] What is particularly relevant for ASEAN is the way it highlights 'cross-border cooperation between public authorities, with or the participation of private actors and/or international organizations' and the 'focus on regulatory networks which do not issue legally binding documents'.[85]

While effectiveness is the main driving attraction for In-Law – in that it reduces obstacles for cooperation – this strategy is also well-suited to ASEAN's legal culture of flexibility, informality and aversion to highly formal arrangements. ASEAN is careful in denoting its legal system as 'rules-based' rather than 'law-based', in which the latter connotes of more rigid legal application and enforcement. This system also lends nicely to member states' fear of parting their sovereignty and thus enables them to control the pace and direction of integration. As we will discuss in subsequent chapters, the combination of formal and informal legal regime in ASEAN suits the instrumentalist and aspirational character of the rule of law in ASEAN. We see that a rules-based is shaping up in the ASEAN Economic Community but is very less so in other pillars. In particular, we note that while landmark instruments or mechanisms have been adopted in the ASEAN Security and Political Community such as the establishment of the ASEAN Inter-governmental Commission on Human Rights (AICHR) and the ASEAN Human Rights Declaration, these are largely aspirational and have very low enforcement mechanisms.

Accountability is however a key issue of informal lawmaking which has been widely accepted as important indicator of rule of law.[86] How informal mechanisms and soft approach to integration may promote or diminish the rule of law will be analysed on how ASEAN uses these methods. In this book, we will look at ASEAN's institutions of governance and rule-making – in both its formal and informal aspects to determine to what extent rules are made and applied in its three Community pillars and in member states – in realizing the key objectives of integration.

The demand for coherence, predictability and enforceability of economic commitments in regional integration could lead to greater demand

[84] Pauwelyn *et al.* (eds.), *Informal International Lawmaking*, 14–21.

[85] Ibid., 21–2.

[86] Ibid., 23–8; Judith Bannister, Gabrielle Appleby, Anna Olijnyk and Joanna Howe, *Government Accountability: Australian Administrative Law* (Port Melbourne: Cambridge University Press, 2015), 15–17.

for lawmaking. In its early stage of integration, we can see an increasing pace in this area in ASEAN and member countries in the economic sector in the lead-up to December 2015, the date of formally instituting integration in the region. In subsequent chapters, we will discuss that ASEAN plays a facilitative and coordinative function in this regard – rather than through regional legislation or judicial enforcement as had happened in the EU – through such measures as harmonization, mutual recognition and technical trade facilitation that are done through a range of informal and formal processes at the regional and national levels. Important market legislation in member countries is also being driven by integration such as the passage of competition law that is nonexistent in many member countries prior to integration initiatives.[87] In this sense, functionalism may be able to explain the within sector spillover, or the triggers for greater formalization in the ASEAN Economic Community. Considering ASEAN's origin of very low level of formalization and institutionalization, integration has clearly driven this change.

2.6 Conclusion

The idea of restraint has become accepted as the conceptual idea of the rule of law. How to achieve it is a question for the different rule of law practices in member states. In practice, rule of law in ASEAN countries has developed as 'enabling', a product of its history of nation-state building. Globalization has provided the impetus for regional integration and brings with it a range of new tools that can fit any form of rule of law arrangement. Herein lies the perceived ambiguity of the impact of globalization on rule of law. ASEAN has remained a state-driven integration programme and it is through the lens of the state that rule of law proceeds in ASEAN's regional integration. This signifies that states, as the primary actors of integration, exert predominant control of ASEAN's processes and mechanisms. However, even ASEAN, which had developed its own brand of inter-state relations – the ASEAN Way – is no longer insulated from global developments in the rule of law. In fact, the principles of democracy, rule of law and human rights have been recognized collectively by member states and have found their way into ASEAN Charter.

[87] For example, the Philippines recently enacted the landmark Philippine Competition Act (21 July 2015), Republic Act No. 10667. This Act is designed to further the country's economic progress through improved market competition.

How ASEAN formulates, interprets and applies its rules is conditioned by what motivates member states in pursuing the project of integration. However, as a regional–international pursuit, integration needs not only ensure that commitments are complied with but also build itself as a credible and legitimate Community. Just as the ASEAN Charter can be regarded as a form of nascent regional constitution, so too is the rule of law in regional integration still in its embryonic stage. In the meantime, we can expect that rule of law promotion will be carried out the ASEAN Way. For this reason, it is worth considering, as we do in the following chapter, what aspects of regional integration design from the EU experience are relevant for ASEAN's coming shift to more substantive regional integration.

3

Beyond Supranationalism: The European Union as Inspiration for ASEAN Integration

3.1 Introduction

From a trade regime with a political objective of ending decades of war among neighbours, the EU has come a long way. It is now an almost fully integrated regional project that transcends the intergovernmental structure common among multilateral organizations. The EU has gone beyond interstate trade relations and now involves civil society in the development, change and transformation of the European polity, not solely on the basis of economic ties but on the basis of shared values based on respect for human rights, the rule of law and democratic principles. Yet the EU is not without its own fault lines. The Greek debt crisis, the United Kingdom's (UK) exit vote, disparities in economic and social development, erosion of cultural identity and the seeming undemocratic nature of regional governance are only some of the salient issues confronting the Union. These developments not only raise doubts about the long-term direction of European regional integration but also raise questions about whether it remains an 'ideal' model of regional integration for regional projects in other parts of the world.

To what extent is the EU integration model relevant to other projects of integration? This chapter discusses the reasons why studying the European model remains relevant for other regional projects. While the successes of the EU have inspired other regions, its significance rests not so much on what it has achieved – or in what it failed, but on the processes, institutions and values that have developed in the course of its evolution as an autonomous legal order. It was the establishment of the rule of law that was crucial to deepening integration in the EU. There are two points to be made in this chapter. The first point is to show how the rule of law has provided a framework for managing the problems of integration within the EU – that of compliance, sovereignty claims, pluralism and heterogeneity and popular demands for democracy; these are issues that are equally relevant to ASEAN and other regional projects. Second, it aims to show that beyond the aspects of supranationalism and constitutionalism, EU's hybrid institutional and legal architecture provides various techniques for managing diversity in its membership and expectations. The diverse range in membership came especially with its enlargement in Central and Eastern European (CEE) countries where a combination of hard and soft approaches was used in their transformation process.

3.2 The EU: From Market Rule to the Rule of Law

From an instrumentalist function for achieving the economic objectives of the Community, the rule of law has transformed the EU into a constitutional legal order.[1] Through rule of law, barriers to the free movement of factors of production and trade were progressively abolished that significantly solved the problem of compliance by member states. The judicial review mechanism in the European Court of Justice enabled the process of 'negative integration', where the Court invalidated measures or practices in member states that hinder the free flow of commerce.[2] Cases handed down from the 1960s to 1970s concern prohibitive and discriminatory measures by governments that restricted or hindered intra-Community trade and thus were struck down by the Court.[3] Positive integration, or the formulation of rules and regulations by Community organs, has in turn been helped as these became guided by the general principles of Community law.

The case of *Van Gend en Loos* v. *Nederlandse Administratie der Belastingen*, the earliest and single most important source of jurisprudence on the direct effect and supremacy of Community law, was a challenge against a Dutch customs authority's imposition of tariffs on imports.[4] Trade protectionist measures by governments on such grounds as public health and safety,[5] trading arrangements[6] and other such measures which

[1] Craig, 'Constitutions, Constitutionalism and the European Union'.

[2] Philip Alston, Mara Bustelo and James Heenan (eds.), *The EU and Human Rights* (Oxford: Oxford University Press, 1999), 451.

[3] Alec Stone Sweet and Thomas Brunell, 'The European Court and the National Courts: A Statistical Analysis of Preliminary References, 1961–95' (1998) 5(1) *Journal of European Public Policy* 66–97.

[4] *Van Gend en Loos* v. *Nederlandse Administratie der Belastingen* (Case 26/62) [1963] ECR 1. This is a preliminary reference case to the Dutch national court which made the referral to the ECJ over the imposition of tariffs on the import of urea–formaldehyde from Germany.

[5] *Case 8/74, Procureur du Roi* v. *Dassonville* [1974] ECR 837; *Case 120/78, Rewe-Zentral AG* v. *Bundesmonopolverwaltung für Branntwein (Cassis de Dijon)* [1979] ECR 649.

[6] Joined cases C-267/91 and 268/91, Criminal Proceedings against Bernard Keck and Daniel Mithouard [1991] ECR 1-6097 (Keck) where ECJ ruled that selling arrangements are not per se

are capable of hindering, directly or indirectly, actually or potentially, intra-regional trade were struck down as constituting trade restrictions. Since governments were hesitant to implement the terms of the treaties, the ECJ took the initiative for integration through expansive interpretation of treaty provisions and developing Community principles that could be invoked against the member state, by the Commission and by private companies and individuals. For instance, Article 28 on quantitative restrictions on imports was extensively interpreted by the Court to implement freedom of movement of goods despite member states' opposition.[7]

General principles of law have been fashioned from the economic case laws that became the legal foundation of the Union, and a significant stage in establishing the rule of law in European integration. For other regional projects, these principles of law could be powerful guides in steering integration even in their narrower economic agenda and in protecting the interests of states and their citizens. These principles also engendered the protection or generation of other rights that can be used to protect the individual from the acts of the Union or its member, or from the excesses of market forces. For instance, the Court will not sustain a challenge to a measure by a member state infringing on the freedom to provide services if such freedom would infringe on public policy which is constitutionally protected.[8]

The two most important principles are the doctrines on direct effect and supremacy that enabled the recognition and reception of Union law directly into national legal systems and the development of norms that became fundamental and inviolable in the Community system. Direct effect provides direct applicability of treaty provisions to individuals and member states without the necessity for domestic legislation or harmonization.[9] Supremacy provides unity and stability in the Community system

discriminatory if applied to all traders. For later refinements of the *Keck* formula, see Case C-254/98, *Schutzverband gegen unlauten Wetteberb* v. *TK Heimdienst Sass GmbH* [2000] ECR I-151; Case C-405/98, *Konsumentombudsmannen (KO)* v. *Gourmet International* [2001] ECR I-1795.

7 Alec Stone Sweet and Margaret McCowan, 'The Freedom of Movement of Goods' in Alec Stone Sweet, *The Judicial Construction of Europe* (Oxford: Oxford University Press, 2004), 138–9.

8 Case C-36/02, *Omega Spielhallen-und Automatenaufstellungs-GmbH* v. *Oberbürgermeisterin der Bundesstadt Bonn* [2004] ECR I-9609 (Omega), a case on the use of laser beam for gaming purposes that 'simulate homicide' and considered as an affront to human dignity.

9 *Van Gend en Loos*, Section B; see also Daniel Halberstam, *Constitutionalism and Pluralism in Marbury and Van Gend* (Public Law and Legal Theory Working Paper No. 104, University of Michigan Law School, March 2008), http://ssrn.com/abstract=1103253, 4–5.

that prevents member states from using their sovereign discretion to enact contradictory domestic laws and regulations that could defeat the objectives of the treaties. Through the supremacy doctrine, the Community legal order has achieved its unity and coherence.[10] As a corollary to the supremacy of Community law, the treaty came to be regarded as the Constitutional Charter of the Community based on the rule of law.[11]

There are two other general principles – that of proportionality and non-discrimination – that erected a barrier for possible abuse or excesses of Union acts or policies and ensure recognition of fundamental rights as general principles of law.[12] Proportionality was initially used to test the legality of a Community or member state action based on whether the measure is suitable or necessary to achieve the desired end and whether it imposes a burden on individuals that is disproportionate to the objectives sought to be achieved.[13] As a cornerstone of EU reforms, it is now applied to test the legality of restrictions by member states on the free movement of persons, services or goods by reasons of public policy, public health and other limits recognized by the treaties and has to be construed in relation to the principle of proportionality.[14] Subsidiarity requires that the Union takes action whenever such action cannot be sufficiently undertaken by member states and whenever an action is taken, such should not be more than necessary to achieve the objectives of the treaty, in accordance with the principle of proportionality.[15] Conversely, non-discrimination or equality has gained general applicability and became a fundamental principle for rights protection. It is recognized in its wider social dimension to include non-discrimination based on race, ethnicity, disability, religion, age and sexual orientation and the provision prohibits acts of discrimination and empowers the Union to take action against discrimination in its various forms.[16]

[10] Case 106/77, *Administrazione delle Finanze Stato* v. *Simmenthal SpA* [1978] ECR 629; Case C-213/89, *R* v. *Secretary of State for Transport, ex parte Factortame Ltd.* [1990] ECR I-2433.

[11] Case 294/83, *Parti Ecologiste 'Les Verts'* v. *Parliament* (1986) ECR 1339, 1365. See also Opinion 1/91 on the Draft Agreement relating to the creation of the European Economic Area (1991) ECR I-61079.

[12] Treaty Establishing the European Community, Maastricht, 7 February 1992, in force 1 November 1993, [1992] OJ C 224/6 (EC Treaty), art. 3(b) states that an action of the Community shall not go beyond what is necessary to achieve the objectives of the Treaty.

[13] Craig and de Búrca (eds.), *The Evolution of EU Law*, 372–3.

[14] EC Treaty, ex. art. 5, states the 'principle of subsidiarity' now art. 5 of the Consolidated Version of the Treaty on European Union, Maastricht, 7 February 1992, in force 1 November 1993, [2012] OJ C 326/15 (TEU).

[15] TEU, art. 5 (EC Treaty, ex. art. 3(b)).

[16] TEU, arts. 19(1) and (2) (EC Treaty, ex. art. 13).

We have shown that the rule of law developed to ensure that Community measures and Community powers were exercised within the bounds of the law, the treaties, and that member states respect and comply with their treaty obligations. This constitutional order confers rights and obligations upon member states, the regional organs and of individuals. It provides for both legal and democratic controls on the exercise of public power similar to that of liberal democracies and guarantees the protection of fundamental rights. While it cannot be regarded as a state of its own, the EU has emerged as a unique polity that has achieved a level of integration similar to that found only in full-fledged federal states. There is little room to doubt EU's constitutionalization – in their thin or thick meanings – or an idea of constitutionalism that embodies precepts of separation of powers, democracy, accountability and human rights.[17]

3.3 The Push-and-Pull Factors of the Rule of Law in European Integration

Although regional integration serves as the vehicle for the rule of law, we argue that the 'spillover' effect from economic activities to greater observance of the rule of law is not self-executing. There are several factors in the EU that set in motion the process of generating rule of law in the political sectors. These are factors that may be absent or missing in other regions, and this explains why that hoped-for spillover is not happening or merely confined to a specific sector. We can see in the EU that both the push factor, the aim of forging a unified Europe, and the pull factor are mostly internally generated. The pull factors – and the synergy created from them – have made it possible in continuously turning the wheel which fuelled the demand for integration. In this section, we tackle briefly the role of the courts, private groups or individuals and member states in fashioning the rule of law in European integration.

Much has already been said about the European Court of Justice which is regarded as the pillar of integration in the early stages of Community building. Composed of independent and highly regarded jurists, the ECJ developed from an economic court to a court of general jurisdiction and hailed as 'the motor' of regional integration.[18] It was originally intended as an

[17] See Berthold Rittberger and Frank Schimmelfennig, 'Explaining the Constitutionalization of the European Union' (2006) 13(8) *Journal of European Public Policy* 1148–67.

[18] See Renaud Dehousse, *The European Court of Justice* (London: Palgrave Macmillan, 1998), 35–8.

administrative 'checking' mechanism, an industrial court, to guard against possible excesses of the High Authority in the European Coal and Steel Community (ECSC, the precursor of the European Community) and to prevent such authority from encroaching on member states' sovereignties.[19] The ECJ fashioned general principle of laws from economic case laws by making purposive interpretation of treaties. Known generally as 'teleological interpretation', the Court construed treaty provisions in the light of the purpose or the spirit for which the provision or the treaty was made.[20] A frequent recourse by the Court to this dynamic mode of interpretation, particularly in articulating landmark decisions such as those in *Van Gend en Loos*, *Costa* and *Le Verts*, has promoted a transformation of Community law and in doing so also advanced the Community project.[21]

The ECJ has relied heavily on national courts for its supply of cases.[22] These cases emanated from national courts, in particular from the lower courts, and in cases pursued by individuals and companies.[23] Through a liberal construction of the ECJ on the use of Article 234 (ex. Article 177) in the EC Treaty, any courts or tribunal – without seeking first the judgment of the highest courts in member states – can suspend proceedings and seek an advice from the Court if the case raises questions of interpretation of Union law. It was through this procedure, also known as 'preliminary reference procedure' or case referral, that local courts directly receive Community law in national jurisdictions, circumscribe the cumbersome enforcement procedures in the treaties and become the agent for directly enforcing the treaty obligations of member states.[24]

[19] Hjalte Rasmussen, *On the Law and Policy of the European Court of Justice: A Comparative Study in Judicial Policymaking* (Dordrecht: Martinus Nijhoff, 1998), 5–43.

[20] See Albertina Albors-Lloren, 'The European Court of Justice: More than a Teleological Court' (1999) 2 *Cambridge Yearbook of European Legal Studies* 373–99, for a discussion of other methods used by the Court.

[21] Giulio Itzcovich, 'The Interpretation of Community Law by the European Court of Justice' (2009) 10 (5) *German Law Journal* 537–60, 555–9.

[22] Karen Alter, 'The European Union's Legal System and Domestic Policy: Spillover or Backlash?' (2000) 54(3) *International Organization* 489–518. EC Treaty, arts. 224 and 256 provide that the judgments of the ECJ shall be enforceable in accordance with national law of the Member State in which the judgment is carried out.

[23] Joseph H. Weiler, 'A Quiet Revolution – The European Court of Justice and Its Interlocutors' (1994) 26(4) *Comparative Political Studies* 510–34; Karen Alter, 'Who Are the "Masters of the Treaty"?: European Governments and the European Court of Justice' (1998) 52(1) *International Organization* 121–47.

[24] Karen Alter, *Establishing the Supremacy of the European Law* (Oxford: Oxford University Press, 2001), 4.

A consequence from this procedure was a mutually beneficial relationship developed between the ECJ and national courts. Described as 'inter-judicial dialogue', the process occurs as national courts first determine an issue of EC law which is necessary in resolving a dispute and then bring a referral to the Court and the Court in turn gives back its opinion on the matter.[25] It was not only through the cases but also through continuous social activities such as seminars, community visits and even dinners that the Court has engaged in institutional linkages with the national courts of member states.[26] National courts, particularly lower courts, have not only been merely fuelling cases or acting as passive recipients of the Court's rulings but also developed a practice of articulating their position on issues by sending preemptive opinions together with the preliminary references.[27] As a result from this dialogue, there was an overall strengthening of domestic judicial processes which served to boost the independence and competence of ordinary courts.[28]

The proliferation of preliminary reference cases in the courts from the 1960s has been correlated with the increase in intra-regional trade[29] and with the bigger member countries (Germany, France, Italy, Netherlands, Belgium and UK) sending the most number of referred cases.[30] Most of these cases involve individual litigants who invoked the applicability of some treaty provisions which member states violate by adopting contrary national measures or by delaying their implementation. A spillover effect of increased individual litigation in the EU has been made to encourage the proliferation of transnational activities of non-state actors seeking rights advocacy and advancing policy reforms for their domestic agendas. While litigation, including subsequent judicial decision, may not necessarily lead to policy changes,[31] the strategy of accessing the supranational court has

[25] Joseph H. Weiler and Ulrich Haltern, 'The Autonomy of the Community Legal Order: Through the Looking Glass' (1996) 37(2) *Harvard International Law Journal* 411–48, 420.

[26] Rasmussen, *On Law and Policy in the European Court of Justice*, 247.

[27] Stacy Nyikos, 'Strategic Interaction among Courts within the Preliminary Reference Process – Stage 1: National Court Preemptive Opinions' (2006) 45(4) *European Journal of Political Research* 527–50, 543–4.

[28] Vivien Ann Schmidt, *Democracy in Europe: The EU and National Polities* (Oxford: Oxford University Press, 2006), 70–1.

[29] Stone Sweet and Brunell, 'The European Court and the National Courts'.

[30] Ibid.

[31] Alter, 'The European Union's Legal System and Domestic Policy', 495.

helped in mobilizing interest or enabled marginalized groups to advance political agendas through the judicial process.[32]

We can see in this context that procedural justice expressed particularly through access to the courts demonstrates the importance of the formal rule of law in checking the powers of supranational institutions as well as that of member states in regional governance. When used as a means, rather than as an end in itself, procedural rule of law can have far-reaching impact as a way to protect and further develop individual rights and to achieve the purposes of integration. Thus, it may not be surprising that European citizens rank such procedural rights as equality before the law and the right to legal protection against discrimination above the right to vote.[33] The practice of referral has however varied in each member state and shows that domestic political factors determine to a large extent the decision to refer.[34] For example, courts in the UK were not predisposed to referring cases despite its size and its modern legal system, especially when compared to smaller states such as Belgium and the Netherlands. The UK has the highest referral however on anti-discrimination where there is strong domestic institutional support from the trade unions and the Equal Opportunities Commission.[35] In short, if citizen participation in the Union process is to be encouraged, their participation cannot be confined to the tedious, narrow and often expensive judicial litigation.

Aside from the courts and the public, member states' acceptance of Court decisions has been paramount in supporting the rule of law. The court rulings could have been rendered ineffectual had not the member states themselves respected and adhered to the decisions. There are various explanations given for member states' acceptance of the decisions. It suffices to mention here that the integrating quality of those decisions also served the interests of member states by promoting the objectives of the treaties, providing credibility to the common market and solving the enforcement problem inherent in classical international law.[36] Even the UK,

[32] See Rachel Cichowski, *The European Court and Civil Society: Litigation, Mobilization and Governance* (Cambridge: Cambridge University Press, 2007).

[33] Eurobarometer OP No. 47 (1997), 1 in Carol Harlow, 'Access to Justice as Human Right: The European Convention and the European Union' in Philip Alston *et al.* (eds.), *The European Union and Human Rights* (Oxford: Oxford University Press, 1999), 187.

[34] Jonathan Golub, 'The Politics of Judicial Discretion: Rethinking the Interaction between National Courts and the European Court of Justice' (1996) 19(2) *West European Politics* 360–85.

[35] Stone Sweet and Brunell, 'The European Court and the National Courts', 88–9.

[36] Dehousse, *The European Court of Justice*, 142–5.

which is reticent about further integration, let alone judicial integration, has shown general acceptance of and obedience toward Community law.[37] Despite criticism of its 'creeping competency' or the process of expanding its jurisdiction through judicial activism,[38] the Court's authority and decisions have been respected. ECJ's judicial independence had been inscribed in the treaties from the very beginning, which means that member states themselves assured the Court's independence. Moreover, the Court has always demonstrated its independence and championed the Community interests, that is, the objectives of the treaties, rather than a particular interest of a member country.[39]

The issue of sovereignty has been at the heart of the most persistent challenge to a regional rule of law in the EU, as in other regional projects such as ASEAN. Most of the confrontational postures have come from the highest or constitutional courts in member states. The highest courts in France, Germany, Denmark, Poland, Hungary and Czechoslovakia had put up resistance to the Court's rulings on direct effect and supremacy. It was only in 1989, or more than 20 years later from the formulation of the supremacy doctrine, that France through its *Conseil d'Etat* finally relented and accepted the supremacy of Community law.[40] While Germany was the first to recognize the supremacy of European law over subsequent national law enactments, its Constitutional Court is also a staunch advocate for putting restraints on the Court's seemingly uncontrollable exercise of judicial expansion.[41] In the *Maastricht* case,[42] the German Constitutional Court upheld the treaty but warned against any judicial expansion of the ECJ that goes beyond the limits conferred by the German Constitution. In the same constitutional challenge involving the ratification of the Maastricht Treaty

[37] For further discussion, see Damian Chalmers, 'The Much Ado about Judicial Politics in the United Kingdom: A Statistical Analysis of Reported Decisions of United Kingdom Courts Invoking EU Law 1973–1998' (Harvard Jean Monnet Working Paper 1/00, Harvard Law School, 2000).

[38] Rasmussen, *On Law and Policy in the European Court of Justice*, 14 and 62.

[39] EC Treaty, art. 253 (formerly Treaty Instituting the European Coal and Steel Community, Paris, 18 April 1951, in force 23 July 1952, 261 UNTS 140, art. 32(b), and Treaty Establishing the European Economic Community, Rome, 25 March 1957, in force 1 January 1958, 298 UNTS 11, art. 167).

[40] Alter, *Establishing the Supremacy of the European Law*, 156. For many years prior to 1989, France had been in direct confrontation with the ECJ, even rendering decisions invalid that were incompatible with treaty provisions or in repudiation of the direct effect of directives.

[41] Karen Alter, *Establishing the Supremacy of the European Law*, 116.

[42] Cases 2BvR 2134/92 and 2159/92 of 12 October 1993, *Manfred Brunner and Others* v. *The European Union Treaty* [1994] 1 CMLR 57.

in Denmark, the Danish Supreme Court likewise asserted its judicial prerogative to determine whether a Community measure has exceeded the transfer of sovereignty and declared that it retains the ultimate power of constitutional review over Community acts.[43]

We can say therefore that a common legal culture – or at least a close affinity among the members' legal tradition – had helped build the rule of law in the EU. The political commitment by the political elites in at least four major referring countries – Germany, Italy, France and the UK – was instrumental in sustaining the project of integration and the rule of law in EU's early period.[44] A common rule of law tradition is a state, however, not preexisting in the CEE countries, and a condition that must be fulfilled as a precondition for Union membership. The Accession criteria mandate that 'the candidate country has achieved stability of institutions guaranteeing democracy, the rule of law, human rights and respect for and protection of minorities, the existence of a functioning market economy as well as the capacity to cope with competitive pressure of market forces within the Union' and the ability to take on obligations of membership including adherence to the aims of political, economic and monetary union.[45] The Madrid European Council 1995 further requires structural adjustments in the fulfilment of these conditions such as appropriate administrative and judicial structures.[46] The Treaty of Accession for new member states binds the applicant to the *acquis communitaire* – the Constitution of the EU, the European Atomic Energy Community Treaty and practically all other acts adopted by the Union prior to accession.[47]

Two issues have arisen as a consequence of EU's supranational–constitutional architecture. Democracy deficit and sovereignty fears, the former asserted by the people and the latter by member countries, have emerged as two critical issues that impact on the legitimacy and salience of the regional project. This means that the EU needs to respond and balance these two interests to hold the construct together. We can add as

[43] Case I-361/1997, *Carlsen* v. *Prime Minister Rasmussen* [1999] ECR I-49; [1999] 3 CMLR 854.

[44] Schmidt, *Democracy in Europe*, 70–1.

[45] Also known as the 'Copenhagen criteria', promulgated by the EU Copenhagen Council at EU Copenhagen Council, 21–2 June 1993, http://ue.eu.int/ueDocs/cms_Data/docs/pressdata/en/ec/72921.pdf

[46] Madrid European Council, Presidency Conclusions, 15–16 December 1995, http://ue.eu.int/ueDocs/cms_Data/docs/pressdata/en/ec/00400-C.EN5.htm

[47] See, for example, Treaty of Accession of Bulgaria and Romania, Luxembourg, 25 April 2005, 1 January 2007, OJ L 157, 21.6.2005, EC 2005 No 2 (Cm 6657), art. 2.

third issue the limits of a highly rules-based system in 'policing' its member states in faithfully complying with their treaty obligations. It has been argued that the Greek crisis manifests the lack of adequate institutional and regulatory controls in the aspect of the monetary union that allowed the national government to hide its true financial position.[48] It can also be argued however that a wholesale acceptance of rules could lead to failure where rules are made without regard for existing sociopolitical conditions in receiving states.

3.4 The EU as a Hybrid System and Challenges of Expansion

The EU architecture is a result of legal and institutional innovations from member states' practices and traditions and also from a clear vision to progress. Clearly, there was a vision that political integration or the political aims are as equally important as its economic purposes. The innovation to adopt supranational institutions meant that there are some trade-offs, that is giving up a part of their sovereign powers, in return for achieving a vision of a unified Europe. However, expectations arising from this vision became varied and mixed as a consequence of enlargement of membership. The evolution of the EU as a hybrid polity shows these innovations and also the imperatives of managing new challenges and expectations.

While the EU is mostly known – perhaps outside of Europe – for its 'supranational' character, the Union is, and operates, as a hybrid polity, one that is not as yet fully conceptualized.[49] There exist multiple spheres in EU where authority is being exercised – the supranational, national, regional and local – such that it is now increasingly difficult to conceive of sovereignty as the exclusive attribute of statehood but easier to consider the possibility of shared and divided sovereignty.[50] It is in the hybrid nature of the Union where the most pressing challenges of the Union inhere: the sovereignty claim of member states and democratic legitimacy, and also in the variable and often highly complex nature of its processes and institutions. The Union

[48] Shelby Woods, 'The Greek Sovereign Debt Crisis: Politics and Economics in the Eurozone' (PhD Dissertation, Washington: University of Washington, 2012).

[49] Adam Czarnota, 'Barbarians Ante Portas or the Post-Communist Rule of Law in Post-Democratic European Union' in Wojciech Sadurski, Adam Czarnota and Martin Krygier (eds.), *Spreading Democracy and the Rule of Law?: The Impact of EU Enlargement for the Rule of Law, Democracy and Constitutionalism in Post-Communist Legal Orders* (Dordrecht: Springer: 2006), 283–97, 291.

[50] Michael Keating, 'Plurinational Democracy and the European Order' in Sonja Riekmann, Monika Mokre and Michael Latzer (eds.), *The State of Europe, Transformation of Statehood from a European Perspective* (Frankfurt: Campus Verlag, 2004) 196–216, 203–4.

possesses exclusive competence in many areas of economic governance but shares competence with members in the common foreign and security policy (CFSP) and freedom, security and justice (FSJ). The extent to which Union law has penetrated national jurisdictions, estimated at almost 75 per cent of laws in member states,[51] is suggestive of the depth of integration.

The supranational framework of governance in the EU is exercised in four major institutions – the European Council, European Commission, European Parliament and the European Court of Justice – each with their own areas of competence representing the executive, legislative and judicial powers similar to those in democratic nation-states. There are also other independent institutions such as the Court of Auditors (which serves as financial fiscalizer of the Community) and an Ombudsman (which is empowered to deal with complaints by individuals against regional organs and member states). While there is no strict separation of powers provided by the treaties, regional institutions function in such a way as to observe the principle of checks and balance.

Union governance functions however through a system of 'multilevel governance'. This system is characterized by 'the existence of overlapping competencies among multiple levels of governance and the interaction of political actors across those levels'[52] and elucidates the role of non-state and private actors in the regional process but maintains the salient, if altered, role of member states.[53] This is manifested in key areas of policy-making, decision-making and implementation which are shared by different institutions in complex mechanisms of co-decision, cooperation and consultation. The co-decision powers among the institutions operate to promote cooperation or sharing of powers and to provide an immediate checking function upon the other institution.

An illustration of multilevel governance is demonstrated in legislation making in the EU:

> The European Parliament which is directly elected through universal suffrage jointly exercises legislative and budgetary functions with the European Council and exercises functions of political control and consultation.[54]

[51] Schmidt, *Democracy in Europe*, 62.

[52] Gary Marks, Francois Nielsen, Leonard Ray and Jane Salk, 'Competencies, Cracks, and Conflicts: Regional Mobilization in the European Union' in Gary Marks (ed.), *Governance in the European Union* (London: Sage, 1996), 40–63, 41.

[53] See Gary Marks and Liesbet Hooghe, 'Contrasting Visions of Multi-Level Governance' in Ian Bache and Matthew Flinders (eds.), *Multi-Level Governance* (Oxford: Oxford University Press, 2004), 15–30, 18–20.

[54] TEU, art. 14.

It also has the power to elect the President of the Commission and exercise political oversight to the Commission by voting on a motion of censure or to set up a Committee of Inquiry to investigate alleged contravention or maladministration of Union law or to require the Commission to answer questions.[55] The Commission, an independent body whose membership is appointed by member states, is, by treaty, the only institution to initiate legislative proposals.[56] However, both the Council and the Parliament have the power to request the Commission to undertake any studies which are desirable in attaining the objectives of the treaties and to submit appropriate proposals.[57] In reality, a significant number of initiatives originate in the Parliament and Council but also from the Economic and Social Committee (ESC), the Committee of Regions (CoR) and other local subnational authorities, private interest groups and expert groups. Member states and other Unions institutions such as the Court the European Central Bank (ECB) can also make proposals for the adoption of legislation. Moreover, consultation among the three institutions has been formally provided in the treaties and would allow common agreements or arrangements and to conclude 'inter-institutional agreements' (IIAs) which could be of a binding nature.[58]

3.5 Flexibility and the Soft Approach to Integration in the EU

The hybrid nature of the Union, in terms of its institutional structure and governance, is underlined by a pluralist legal order. The previous sections of this chapter point to the rule-based regime in the Union which was driven by the institution of the judicial process. We now discuss the other side of the Union that operates through 'politics' and driven by the intergovernmental dimension of cooperation and by its complex institutional arrangements. The Union is accompanied by a process that shows heterogeneity not only in terms of member state participation but even as to the impact and outcomes of common policies.[59] The differences in the capacities and status of member states have brought about strategies that could promote 'Unity in diversity' in the Union. Flexibility has been in the nature of European integration, and this has come to the fore with Eastern enlargement.

55 Ibid., arts. 17(7), 226 and 230.

56 Ibid., art. 17(2).

57 Ibid., arts. 241 and 225.

58 Ibid., art. 295.

59 Svein Andersen and Nick Sitter, 'Differentiated Integration: What Is It and How Much Can the European Union Accommodate?' (2006) 28(4) *Journal of Integration* 313–30.

There are various approaches used in managing diversity or differences in the EU that can be relevant to ASEAN. The first approach is through 'differentiated integration' which is now considered to be of the highest importance for the future path of Union integration.[60] This strategy aims to solve the problem of deadlock inherent in heterogeneous membership and the pursuit of deeper integration.[61] The term has been applied to the variable participation in time, space and subject matter of member states in European integration and corresponds to such forms of integration as 'multi-speed', 'variable geometry' and '*à la carte*'.[62]

Multi-speed integration refers to the agreement of member states to pursue common policies and actions but not simultaneously, while variable geometry pertains to a mode of integration which allows permanent separation of a core of countries within an integrative unit. The first case is illustrated by the allowance of temporary derogations in the treaties by new members in the internal market or the allowance of time frames in attaining the convergence criteria for the Economic and Monetary Union (EMU). The second form is shown in the area of defence, peace-keeping and crisis management, where some member states are allowed to participate in deeper forms of integration.[63] Conversely, *à la carte* allows member states permanent derogations from specific policy areas by allowing them to 'opt out' in specific areas such as the EMU, *Schengen*, social policy and defence for such countries like the UK and Denmark.[64]

The second approach is that of 'enhanced cooperation' that allows interested member states to proceed with deeper integration within the institutional structure in the single market, justice and home affairs and foreign policy.[65] It is a measure of last resort to be authorized by the Council when it can be established that the objectives of such cooperation cannot be attained within a reasonable period by the Union and on the approval of

60 Position of the Irish Presidency for the Dublin European Council 1996.

61 Jan-Emmanuel De Neve, 'The European Onion? How Differentiated Integration is Reshaping the EU' (2007) 29(4) *European Integration* 503–21, 504–8.

62 Angelos Sepos, Differentiated Integration in the EU: The Position of Small Member States' (Working Paper No. 17, Robert Schuman Centre of Advanced Studies, European University Institute, 2005), 1–6.

63 Ibid., 4–5.

64 Ibid., 5.

65 Treaty of Amsterdam Amending the Treaty on European Union, The Treaties Establishing the European Communities and Certain Related Acts, Amsterdam, 2 October 1997, in force 1 May 1999, [1997] OJ C 340/1, part 1, arts. 6–13; *Treaty of Nice Amending the Treaty on European Union, the Treaties Establishing the European Communities and Certain Related Acts*, Nice, 26 February 2001, in force 1 February 2003, [2001] OJ C 80/1, part 1, arts. 1–2.

member states. One example in this scheme is to authorize a framework for 'permanent structured cooperation' to enable those member states which have higher military capabilities to establish closer defence and military cooperation.[66]

Informality and consensus are equally important aspects of EU policy-making and decision-making. It has been shown that consensus has been more the rule than the exception in the history of Community decision-making and data on legislation-making from 1994 to 2002 shows that 81 per cent of legislation was passed through informal consensus.[67] As already mentioned, major policy reforms are deliberated and negotiated by member states through the IGCs and the practice started with the adoption of the Single European Act in 1986.[68] Secret meetings and deliberations are a feature of the IGCs through which member states negotiate for revisions to the treaties. As a venue for political bargaining among member states, the IGC has been formalized into two modes of revision. Under the 'ordinary revision procedure', the proposal could serve to either increase or reduce Union competence while the 'simplified revision procedure' allows amendment to the internal policies and action but shall not increase the competence of the Union.[69] Moreover, the mechanism for drawing up inter-institutional agreements (IIAs) has become a prominent feature of Union governance and is primarily based on informality and consensus-making.[70]

Another notable form of informal arrangement in the EU is through the 'jungle of committees' that are responsible in drafting, adopting and implementing Union legislation. Known as 'comitology', this informal mechanism began in the 1960s to efficiently manage the delegation of the implementation of agricultural policy and also to ensure control by member states, and has expanded in many sectors of Union policy-making.[71] The term is now broadly used to describe other processes whereby committees and experts assist the workings of Union institutions from the drafting

[66] TEU, art. 42(6).

[67] Dorothee Heisenberg, 'The Institution of "Consensus" in the European Union: Formal versus Informal Decision-Making in the Council' (2005) 44 *European Journal of Political Research* 65–90, 71–3.

[68] Also known as the Treaty Establishing the European Community (EC Treaty), the first major treaty revision since the Treaty of Rome 1957.

[69] TEU, arts. 48(2)–(6).

[70] Sonja Riekman, 'The Cocoon of Power: Democratic Implications of Interinstitutional Agreements' (2007) 13(1) *European Law Journal* 4–19, 5–6.

[71] Thomas Christiansen and Beatrice Vaccari, 'The 2006 Reform of Comitology: Problem Solved or Dispute Postponed?' (EPIASCOPE 20006/3, European Institute of Public Administration, 2006),www.eipa.nl/cms/repository/eipascope/Scop06_3_2.pdf

of legislation proposals to adoption and implementation of Union legislative acts.[72] Under the treaty, the committee of permanent representatives (COREPER) prepares the work of the Council and is mainly responsible for the proposal and adoption phases in the Council.[73] In the Commission, there are four categories of specialized committees – advisory, management, regulatory and regulatory with scrutiny.[74] The committees, estimated to be more than 2,000, are run by the Commission but their membership is named by member states. As of 2003, it is estimated that more than 50,000 people are involved in the Commission's expert groups, which are mainly responsible for drafting policies and legislation and increasingly the Commission's frequently used mode of consultation.[75]

The system of comitology has been credited for its role in making Union governance more efficient, as it became responsible for finalizing most proposals without the need for ministerial negotiations. But its complexity and the expertise required for its membership makes the system a highly bureaucratic and technocratic mechanism which is only accessible to a few. It was observed that the work of some committees had been shrouded in utmost secrecy, the committees were unknown, the areas they work on were mostly informally formed and the names of committee members were kept confidential.[76] In response to demands for transparency and accountability, the Commission has allowed the publication of committee documents and created a registrar for committees and expert groups for the general public to access called the Comitology Register,[77] as well as making a promise to release names of experts and their qualifications, particularly after it was accused by civil society groups of bias to industry groups and experts.[78]

72 Corporate Europe Observatory, 'Lobbying the European Union by Committee' (Corporate Europe Observatory Briefing Paper, July 2007), http://archive.corporateeurope.org/lobbyingbycommittee.html

73 TEU, art. 240(1).

74 Europa Glossary, *Comitology*, http://europa.eu/scadplus/glossary/comitology_en.htm

75 Corporate Europe Observatory, 'Lobbying the Union Committee', 1; Yiorgos Vassalos, 'Secrecy and Corporate Dominance: A Study on the Composition and Transparency of European Commission Expert Groups' (Brussels: Alliance for Lobbying Transparency and Ethics Regulation in the European Union, 2008).

76 Corporate Europe Observatory, 'Lobbying the Union Committee', 2–8.

77 European Commission, *Comitology Register*, http://ec.europa.eu/transparency/regcomitology/index_en.htm

78 *Commission to Target Expert Groups in Transparency Drive* (26 March 2008) EurActiv, www.euractiv.com/section/public-affairs/news/commission-to-target-expert-groups-in-transparency-drive/

The use of informal soft mechanisms in the EU has implications for the development of the rule of law in new member states which are in the process of transition towards law-based regimes. Flexibility, which is rooted more on discretion than on stability and predictability, has the capacity to undermine the constitutional or normative character of the EU brought about by the instability and continuous shifting of institutional mechanisms resulting from such practices.[79] With enlargement, secret negotiations were instrumental in assessing compliance with the accession criteria of new member states. In the context of CEE countries, the use of informal regulation could reinforce the pattern of informal operations existing in these societies borne out by decades of mistrust to public authorities.[80] It had been observed that the soft approach has also tended to privilege the intergovernmental and executive powers, which caused institutional imbalance at the expense of the Parliament and exacerbated problems of democratic control and accountability.[81]

As the issues that have been generated by flexibility have shown, law has to come inevitably to manage or contain the issues of institutional imbalance and also to give form to expressions of popular democracy. Informality and flexible approaches to integration are therefore an outcome of the multidimensional modality in the Union that interacts with the autonomous legal field. Largely, it seeks to resolve 'sovereignty claims' of member states vis-à-vis a centralized supranational legal authority steering integration.[82] It also seeks to address competing visions of those who favour deeper integration and those who espouse a more restrained or limited form.

3.5.1 Complementarity and Tension between Soft Law and Hard Law

The use of soft law in the EU is a fairly recent phenomenon influenced by developments in international relations and has been experimented on for

[79] Gráinne de Búrca, 'The Institutional Development of the EU: A Constitutional Analysis' in Craig and de Búrca (eds.), *The Evolution of EU Law*, 55–81.

[80] Czarnota, 'Barbarians *Ante Portas* or the Post-Communist Rule of Law', 296.

[81] Heisenberg, 'The Institution of "Consensus" in the European Union', 82–4.

[82] Andrew Glencross, 'Federalism, Confederalism and Sovereignty Claims: Understanding the Democracy Game in the EU' in Rebecca Adler-Nissen and Thomas Gammeltoft-Hansen (eds.), *Sovereignty Games: Instrumentalizing State Sovereignty in Europe and Beyond* (New York: Palgrave, 2008), 105–26, 108–10.

a wide area of Union governance.[83] It has been deployed particularly in the fields of social policy, employment and gender equality where member states want more flexibility in attaining policy objectives. A wide array of soft methods have been employed such as the Commission's 'action programmes' to promote gender equality in the workplace, through the open method of coordination (OMC), adoption of the non-legally binding Community Charter of the Fundamental Rights of Workers of 1989 and the use of mechanisms such as codes of conduct, frameworks, resolutions, communications, declarations, guidance notes and circulars.[84] The use of soft law in approximating the *acquis* was also seen as a 'necessary evil' that enabled the EU to maintain its own governance system and also to maintain stability in CEE countries.[85]

The practice of using soft law has largely complemented – or supplemented – the use of hard law in Union governance. In evaluating EU's experience, we can say that it is the function of the rules, rather than their form, that defines whether they are 'rule of law compliant'. The use of this measure is intended principally to 'assist' member states to effectively comply with their obligations by giving them necessary flexibility to suit rules for local implementation. The use of OMC method in social policies is a clear example of this function that employs innovative method of monitoring compliance through the use of diverse mechanisms such as fixing guidelines for the Union combined with timetables, quantitative and qualitative indicators and benchmarks, drawing national and regional action plans and conducting periodic peer review organized as mutual learning processes.[86] While the OMC was not itself formalized in the treaty, Lisbon made an implicit acknowledgement of its growing function in the Union and the possible extension of the method to wider areas by providing that directives, though legally binding, shall leave to the national authorities the choice, form and methods of their implementation.[87] The OMC strategy is also aimed as a voluntary intergovernmental method of coordination that involves a decentralized approach to be in line with the

[83] Emer O'Hagan, 'Too Soft to Handle? A Reflection on Soft Law in Europe and Accession States' (2004) 26(4) *Journal of European Integration* 379–404, 380–2.

[84] Eurofound, *Soft Law* (12 June 2007) www.eurofound.europa.eu/areas/industrialrelations/dictionary/definitions/softlaw.htm

[85] O'Hagan, 'Too Soft to Handle?', 384–5.

[86] Madrid European Council, Presidency Conclusions, 15–16 December 1995, http://ue.eu.int/ueDocs/cms_Data/docs/pressdata/en/ec/00400-C.EN5.htm

[87] Consolidated Version of the Treaty on European Union, Maastricht, 7 February 1992, in force 1 November 1993, [2012] OJ C 326/15, art. 288.

principle of subsidiarity and to involve the active participation of social partners and civil society.[88]

The use of soft law offers many benefits that makes it an attractive policy preference and not merely as a second-best option for hard law. It brings about efficiency as complex legislation is avoided, affords flexibility in changing circumstances and promotes mutual learning of norms where internalization of hard law may be difficult.[89] The ECJ has also dealt with soft law in such a way that though unenforceable and could not generate rights and obligations in judicial proceedings could nevertheless be used as supplementary aid to the interpretation of hard law.[90] Soft law, while not legally binding, carries persuasive force that could influence member states to voluntarily do things that they might not do if in the form of hard obligation.

Conversely, soft law could undermine or weaken the constitutional legal system and the authoritative institutions, the Commission and the ECJ, safeguarding its coherence. The Commission itself has expressed grave reservations over its effectiveness and the incompatibility of OMC with Community method.[91] A more specific objection is focused on its ambiguous effectiveness on social policy, particularly on such areas as poverty reduction and social exclusion, which are crucial issues for new member states in Eastern Europe.[92] Formalizing the use of 'framework directives' in the Treaty of Lisbon aims to solve the inherent contradictions in the use of soft law. The provision attempts to 'harden' soft law while retaining its flexible nature. As a middle ground between the two forms of law, the provision also recognizes the capacity for soft law and hard law to coexist and affect similar domains and actors.[93] Whether Lisbon resolves the

[88] Treaty of Lisbon Amending the Treaty on European Union and the Treaty Establishing the European Community, Lisbon, 13 December 2007, in force 1 December 2009, [2007] OJ C 306/1.

[89] David Trubek, Patrick Cottrell and Mark Nance, '"Soft Law", "Hard Law", and European Integration: Toward a Theory of Hybridity' (Research Paper No. 1002, University of Wisconsin Legal Studies, 2004), 3–4.

[90] Luca Barani, 'Hard and Soft Law in the European Union: The Case of Social Policy and the Open Method of Coordination' (Webpapers on Constitutionalism and Governance Beyond the State No. 2, ConWEB, 2006), www.wiso.uni-hamburg.de/fileadmin/sowi/politik/governance/ConWeb_Papers/conweb2-2006.pdf, 22–3.

[91] Vassalos, Yiorgos, 'Secrecy and Corporate Dominance: A Study on the Composition and Transparency of European Commission Expert Groups' (Brussels: Alliance for Lobbying Transparency and Ethics Regulation in the European Union, 2008), 4.

[92] O'Hagan, 'Too Soft to Handle?', 391–5.

[93] Trubek *et al.*, '"Soft Law", "Hard Law", and European Integration'.

issue of the use of soft law through the middle ground, the use of soft law in the Union has its apparent vices and virtues and therefore has a divided constituency.

The evolving function of soft law and that of flexibility in the EU poses a challenge to the classical conception of the rule of law that is based on aspects of generality, predictability, clarity and certainty. Previous discussions have clearly indicated the development of the European legal order along the classical line and how it has in fact deepened and broadened Union integration. The hybrid nature of the European polity, however, points to a different face of the EU, the soft part, which is driven by the demands of politics – at the level of member states – and also increasingly by its citizens. There are many benefits of the use of soft law including the possibility to address the democratic deficit in the Union through mechanisms that engender meaningful deliberation and consultation. The combination and coexistence of these seeming contradictory features of the Union suggest a different and evolving form of the rule of law in the EU that has critical relevance to other projects of regional integration.

3.5.2 A Soft Solution to Democracy Challenges in the EU

The problem of democratic deficit is inexorably interlinked with legitimacy and underlies the tension that runs through the constitutional and political, the hard and soft core of the EU. The ambiguity in defining EU democracy – or its lack of state-like democratic features – will serve to reinforce not only the growing demand to limit the competency but also the constitutional autonomy of the Union. Recent reforms and treaty amendments have meant to provide political solutions which could potentially improve democracy but clash with the Union's established constitutional autonomy. The debate over what 'democracy deficit' means, particularly when there is no agreement in the first place about what democracy is in the peculiar political environment in the Union, has not been settled.[94] It is also debatable whether such deficit exists at all.

On the negative view, the perception of democratic deficit merely arises when the Union is seen as an entity different from an intergovernmental organization. There is no deficit when seen exclusively from the intergovernmental character of the Union itself, which was never intended to be

[94] Dorian Jano, 'Understanding the "EU Democratic Deficit": A Two Dimension Concept on a Three Level-of-Analysis' (2008) 14(1) *Politikon: The IAPSS Journal of Political Science* 61–74, 58–62.

democratic and works primarily through intergovernmental institutions under direct or indirect democratic control of member states' citizens,[95] because the regulatory technocratic nature of EU does not necessarily have to conform to democratic standards.[96] The 'standard version' of the existence of democracy deficit is focused on the institutional aspect that points to the increase in executive powers and corresponding loss of control by national parliaments as a result of the transfer of competencies to the Union. The reduction of national parliamentary control has not been adequately compensated by the authority of the European Parliament, whose powers remain relatively weaker in relation to other Union institutions.[97] Another source of deficit is traced from the functioning of Union institutions in the secretive and non-deliberative procedures in the Council or the Commission or from the lack of information and excess of delegation[98] which raises questions of the transparency, accountability and legitimacy of supranational institutions.

Democracy deficit has likewise been sourced from the breakdown of general public support in the EU or the lack of European-wide '*demos*'.[99] In this view, the Union has grown without due regard to the democratic substructure that underlines a democratic polity. The Union is seen as lacking significant European-wide discourse, being too distant from the people, and, lacking demos, the legitimacy of the Union will remain contested.[100] This became evident in the 1990s following the Danish rejection

[95] Andrew Moravcsik, 'Why the European Community Strengthens the State: International Cooperation and Domestic Politics' (Center for European Studies Working Paper No. 52, Harvard University, 1994); Andrew Moravcsik, 'In Defense of the "Democratic Deficit": Reassessing the Legitimacy of the European Union' (2002) 40(4) *Journal of Common Market Studies* 603–34.

[96] Giandomenico Majone, 'Europe's "Democratic Deficit": The Question of Standards' (1998) 4(1) *European Law Journal* 5–28.

[97] Dimitris Chryssochoou, 'Democracy and the European Polity' in Michelle Cini (ed.), *European Union Politics*, 2nd edn. (Oxford: Oxford University Press, 2007), 359–374, 361–3. See also Weiler, 'The Transformation of Europe', 2415.

[98] Crombez, Christophe, 'The Democratic Deficit in the European Union: Much Ado about Nothing?' (2003) 4(1) *European Union Politics* 105–17.

[99] Jano, 'Understanding the "EU democratic deficit"', 60–2; Simon Hix and Andreas Follesdal, 'Why There is a Democratic Deficit in the EU: A Response to Majone and Moravcsik' (European Governance Paper No. C-05-02, 14 March 2005), www.connex-network.org/eurogov/pdf/egp-connex-C-05-02.pdf

[100] See Stephanie Sifft, Michael Bruggeman, Katharina Kleinen-von Königsloöw, Bernhard Peters and Andreas Wimmel, 'Segmented Europeanization: Exploring the Legitimacy of the European Union from a Public Discourse Perspective' (2007) 45(1) *Journal of European Public Policy* 127–55; Mette Jolly, 'A Demos for the European Union?' (2005) 25(1) *Politics* 12–18.

of the Maastricht Treaty in 1992, the *petit oui* in France and Dutch no vote for the EU Constitutional Treaty in 2005, the low voter turnout in 1994 European elections and public dissatisfaction with difficulties associated with EMU convergence in 1996.[101] The Greek crisis and Brexit signal yet again the growing disaffections with the EU. If there were a crucial lesson to be learned from these experiences, it is that the narrowing of the gap between the EU and its citizens also demands a firmer basis of political discourse at the grass roots.

The various solutions proposed to improve democracy and polity building in the Union have therefore corresponded to many of the aspects of democracy deficit discussed earlier. The Treaty of Lisbon seeks to become 'more democratic, more transparent and more efficient',[102] and aims to address both the institutional and social bases of democracy deficit. Institutional solutions are aimed at improving the powers of the Parliament such as the election of the Commission President,[103] expanding its co-decision procedure and consultative role for the internal market and also for the area of FSJ[104] and increasing the transparency and accountability of the functions of Union institutions like the Council meeting in public in performing its legislative function. Through the principle of subsidiarity, it is hoped that the social bases of democracy deficit can be addressed. Aside from the mandate of national parliaments in taking part in revising the treaty and in inter-parliamentary cooperation,[105] direct and indirect forms of political participation are guaranteed to citizens of the Union through its institutions and initiatives aimed at improving the quality of discourse and representation of European political parties and elections.[106]

Civil society participation has been guaranteed in policy-making through mechanisms such as the White Paper on European Governance in 2001 which aims to provide effective and transparent consultation through such measures as adopting a reinforced culture of consultation and dialogue,

[101] Pippa Norris, 'Representation and Democracy Deficit' (1997) 32(2) *European Journal of Political Research* 273–82, 276–77.

[102] *From the Treaty of Nice to the Treaty of Lisbon* (February 2014) Living Heritage: Parliament & Europe, www.parliament.uk/about/living-heritage/evolutionofparliament/legislativescrutiny/parliament-and-europe/overview/from-the-treaty-of-nice-to-the-treaty-of-lisbon/

[103] TEU, art. 17(7).

[104] On the right to be informed or consulted, see TEU, arts. 70, 71 and 74; on terrorism measures, see ex. art. 75; on asylum, see art. 78; on immigration, see art. 79.

[105] TEU, art. 12.

[106] Ibid., arts. 9 and 10.

adopting a code of conduct of consultation that sets minimum standards and developing extensive partnership arrangements.[107] Giving the Charter of Fundamental Rights a legal value in the Treaty of Lisbon, albeit with the exception of domestic courts in Poland,[108] will give more protection and rights to individuals in the EU against excessive use of Union and member states' powers and could therefore enhance the Union's popular legitimacy.

3.6 Conclusion

The history of the EU is also a history of the development of the rule of law. The rule of law in the EU has provided a solution to the problems of compliance and enforcement that eluded classical international law. It provided an effective restraint to the exercise of Union powers or to excesses of government authority and generated greater protection for individual rights. There are limits however to constitutionalization and this is shown in the twofold resistance to Union authority – from the member states which see an erosion to their sovereignty and from the European citizens themselves who perceive the Union as a remote and complex entity. The CEE enlargement which added greater diversity and pluralism in the Union has brought into sharp focus the tension between the constitutional legal regime and political expression of sovereignty and popular democracy.

Given the unique history and distinctive politics in the EU, it is hard to make a hasty conclusion that the Union is or has to be a model for other projects of regional integration. However it shows that the rule of law, even within its constraints, could offer a potential for change. The rule of law, though still conditioned by politics, has the capacity to generate new rules, mechanisms and institutions, as well as new behaviour. The 'EU model' of the rule of law has shown this capacity for generation and more often with unintended consequences. This model has been built on the basis of the autonomy of its institutions and also that these institutions are able to function with flexibility through various informal and soft mechanisms that coexist with formal and rigid rules. There are various aspects of the hybrid character of the EU that could serve as model or points of learning to other projects of regional integration.

107 Vassalos, 'European Governance: A White Paper'.

108 Protocol on the Application of the Charter of Fundamental Rights of the European Union to Poland and to the United Kingdom, Lisbon, 13 December 2007, in force 1 December 2009, [2008] OJ C 115/313.

Regional integration is a condition that presents similar challenges to all other programmes, though perhaps in varying degrees and importance for others. The relative success of integrating the CEE countries into the Union through the combination of authoritative legal measures and flexibility and socialization shows the capacity of developing the rule of law in jurisdictions having very little rule of law traditions. Diversity presents an immense obstacle to regional integration but the EU model has shown that a combination of legal, institutional and political criteria could potentially narrow the discrepancy of rule of law practices in member countries.

For ASEAN, the main challenge at the moment is how to build the integrity of its institutions. ASEAN was built on a foundation of loose institutions and developed a culture in regional relations that is not based on hard and enforceable commitments, which only tend to reinforce the former. Given that it has shown its dislike to supranational and judicial bodies, ASEAN has to work within the narrow confines of its legal and institutional framework. Is it then possible to strengthen ASEAN's intergovernmental institutions? The answer is yes. It means that ASEAN has to go beyond the 'ASEAN Way' and the first step is that it has to trust its own institutions by using them and to make these institutions actually work. Taking a lesson from the EU, various strategies to deploy and combine the soft and political approaches with institutional mechanisms to integration can address problems of commitment and enforcement of member states. There are many other areas in EU's hybrid system that could be explored to tailor to ASEAN's diversity or its core value of sovereignty, at least in addressing ASEAN's commitment problem in the sphere of economic cooperation. The basic commitment that member states in ASEAN have to resolve however is their political will to pursue regional integration.

4

Limiting Sovereignty and the Limits of Judicial Authority in Regional Integration

4.1 Introduction

The previous chapter discussed the achievements of the EU in fostering the rule of law and also in making the rule of law, through the process of constitutionalization, the foundation of regional integration. The European constitutional order is a work in progress and with endless debates about its nature explained by diverse theories, the rule of law in the Union defies fixed categorization and therefore 'modelling'. We look into the experiences of other regional projects in Latin America and in Africa to show how the EU has served as inspiration in making rule of law an integral part of Community building. These experiences demonstrate how they have reinterpreted – and not simply adopted – certain aspects of the EU in their own path to foster economic and political integration. Their examples – as in ASEAN – show that their strategies to integration are as much dictated by the imperative to find the best-fit solutions to complex problems they face at the regional and local levels.

Both Africa and Latin America have a relatively longer history on regional integration than the ASEAN. Regional projects in these two regions were launched or revitalized since the early 1990s. Like ASEAN, these initiatives were driven by economic globalization and strongly underpinned by state building imperatives to consolidate the nation-state, eliminate conflicts and chronic poverty and achieve economic development.[1] Similarly, these regional groupings have diverse membership in terms of economic, political and legal systems. We also discuss how major regional blocs in Africa and Latin America have diverged with

[1] See United Nations of the High Representative for the Least Developed Countries, Landlocked Developing Countries and Small Island Developing States, *Least Developed Countries Factsheet 2013*, http://unohrlls.org/custom-content/uploads/2013/09/LDC-Factsheet-2013.pdf. There are 49 countries categorized as LDC, with 14 in Asia and the Pacific, 1 in Latin America and the Caribbean and 34 in Africa. LDCs in Southeast Asia are Laos, Cambodia, Myanmar and Timor Leste.

ASEAN in the way they construct their own normative and institutional framework and develop rule of law as a component of integration. The divergence in rule of law approaches in different regions reflects the extent to which sovereignty is held by states, and shows how they perceive and tailor their responses to economic and political challenges in their respective regions. The variation in the outcomes of rule of law practices in the MERCOSUR and African integration also reflects domestic practices and norms that condition these results.

4.2 Using the EU Model: Diffusion and Reinterpretation of the Rule of Law

We have pointed out in Chapter 2 that rule of law in regional integration is contingent on function, meaning that rules and institutions follow the functions of or motivations for integration. Once a decision on function has been made, decision-makers are faced with various options – either to adopt from the menu of existing instruments and mechanisms, modify or innovate from current practices or come up with novel approach, based on what is perceived as appropriate to their requirements. The EU architecture is itself an innovative idea fashioned from the confluence of desired integration goals and existing shared values and norms. In this chapter we show that diffusion of the idea of the rule of law framework in the EU to other regional projects is conditioned by both the function of market integration and domestic politics. Diffusion is not wholesale adoption but involves the process of continuous interpretation not only by the decision or policy-makers but also by the users of rules and institutions.[2] Aside from their formal mandated roles, these actors – in the state and non-state sectors in a particular region – are influenced by their own backgrounds and the way they interact and socialize among themselves and with those outside of the group.[3]

External influence may also provide the stimulus for the diffusion of rules and norms.[4] This can come in varied forms – from emulation on the part of the receiver to subtle or overt pressure for change by the external

[2] Michael Zürn, André Nollkaemper and Randall Peerenboom (eds.), *Rule of Law Dynamics: In an Era of International and Transnational Governance* (New York: Cambridge University Press, 2012), 8–11.

[3] Jeffrey W. Cason, *The Political Economy of Integration: The Experience of Mercosur* (New York: Routledge, 2011), 17.

[4] Amichai Magen and Leonardo Morlino (eds.), *International Actors, Democratizations and the Rule of Law: Anchoring Democracy?* (New York: Routledge, 2009), 28.

source. The extent to which rules and norms are adopted and internalized is dependent on the interaction between the degree of pressure of external source and the receiver's capacity for acceptance. The EU, through its officials or agents, has been a form of external stimulus for other regional groups. The EU has been used as both a model and inspiration for establishing the common market as a strategy to overcome global and domestic economic pressures.[5] It has largely remained an inspiration however for others in terms of its legal and institutional framework used in Community building. Domestic capacity, which includes such factors as wide differences in legal and political systems, leadership role and domestic elite support for institutional change, determine to a large extent the decision on the form of institutional arrangement needed to support integration. As we show in the following discussions, transplantation does not necessarily result in diffusion of rules and norms in the absence of domestic conditions to guarantee or ensure their application.

In the two case studies that will be presented – that of the MERCOSUR and AU – we show the degree to which the EU framework of the rule of law has been emulated or adapted in these regional projects and the consequential outcomes. What is highlighted in this chapter is the adoption of the Union's key strategy of community building through market integration and the role of an autonomous dispute or judicial resolution mechanisms in solving integration issues. MERCOSUR however was constituted as an intergovernmental organization while the AU adopted many aspects of EU's hybrid system of supranational and intergovernmental governance architecture.

4.3 African Integration and Sovereignty with Responsibility

Africa's integration initiatives are based on strong economic and political aspirations that provided an immense push for members to commit to a more relaxed interpretation of sovereignty. In the aftermath of devastating wars in the 1990s in countries such as Liberia, Somalia, Sierra Leone, Congo and Rwanda that saw the abject failure of the international community to prevent mass atrocities, a continent-wide consensus emerged to redefine sovereignty. Not only is sovereignty a right of every independent state to exercise, it is also one that attaches responsibility. The concept of 'sovereignty with responsibility' therefore seeks to strike a balance between the

[5] See, for example, Salvador Rivera, *Latin American Unification: A History of Political and Economic Integration Efforts* (Jefferson: McFarland, 2014), 169.

right of member states to safeguard their territorial integrity and their responsibility to respect and protect the dignity and human rights of the people within the continent.[6] Coupled with huge external pressure from the international community,[7] the initiative for a continent-wide regional bloc in 2001, the African Union (AU), was moved largely by domestic pressures to address chronic problems of conflict and underdevelopment.[8] It is also underpinned by African nationalism and solidarity – an expression of Pan Africanism – to develop its own capacities and to provide an African solution to its problems.[9]

The AU was established in 1999 through the Sirte Declaration among the Heads of States and Governments of the Organization of African Unity (OAU) and was formally created through the Constitutive Act of the AU (Constitutive Act) which entered into force on 26 May 2001.[10] The founding of the AU also affirmed the establishment of the African Economic Community (AEC) as its flagship initiative for a continent-wide market economy. The AEC is unique in that it serves as an umbrella for other sub-regional economic communities called the RECs or Regional Economic Communities. Owing to the proliferation of RECS in every region in Africa with multiple and overlapping memberships causing a complex entanglement of political commitments and institutional requirements that undermines regional integration itself,[11] the AU recognized only eight RECs as the 'building blocks' for realizing a continent-wide economic area.[12] The three major RECs – COMESA, SADC and EAC – have agreed

6 In relation to art. 3 of the Constitutive Act of the African Union, Lomé, Togo, 11 July 2000, in force 26 May 2001, OAU Doc CAB/LEG/23.15.

7 Mammo Muchie, Phindile Lukhele-Olorunju and Oghenerobor Akpor (eds.), *The African Union Ten Years After: Solving African Problems with Pan-Africanisms and the African Renaissance* (Pretoria: Africa Institute of South Africa, 2013), 3.

8 See Organisation of Africa Unity, *Lagos Plan of Action for the Economic Development of Africa: 1980–2000* (Addis Ababa: Organisation of African Unity, 1980).

9 Constitutive Act of the Union 2001, art. 3(a). Pan-Africanism has been articulated as the struggle for social and political equality and the freedom from economic exploitation and racial discrimination.

10 There are currently 54 countries which ratified the Constitutive Act of the Union 2001, see list at African Union Commission, *Ratification Table: African Charter on Human and People's Rights*, www.au.int/en/sites/default/files/992achpr.pdf. It was born out of the OAU which was established in 1963.

11 Peter Draper, Durrel Halleson, and Philip Alves, 'SACU, Regional Integration and the Overlap Issue in Southern Africa: From Spaghetti to Cannelloni?' (Trade Policy Report No. 15, South African Institute of International Affairs, 2007), 7.

12 The eight RECs are: ECOWAS, Common Market for Eastern and Southern Africa (COMESA), Economic Community of Central African States (ECCAS), Southern African

to create a single free trade area covering 26 countries or more than half of the AU membership.

Through a wide consensus to construe sovereignty principle liberally, it was possible for the AU to adopt an ambitious programme for comprehensive regional integration spanning political and socioeconomic integration of the continent[13] and including the establishment of a common defence policy.[14] The right of intervention, which is a direct breach to the traditional notion of sovereignty, became recognized as an exception. Thus it has become possible for the AU to exercise this option to intervene in cases of grave circumstances involving war crimes, genocide and crimes against humanity, from a request from a member state to restore peace and security,[15] and in 'serious threats to legitimate order to restore peace and stability'.[16] AU's intervention has so far ranged from diplomatic, as in Zimbabwe and Kenya, to peacekeeping, in Sudan, and military intervention, in Burundi and the Comoros.[17]

AU's choice for its institutional design has been influenced to a high degree by the EU. Domestic elites or policy-makers were encouraged by EU's successes and also by EU's material support and influence including the role of EU's agents in drafting the AU Constitution.[18] The hybrid architecture of the AU follows the main institutions of executive, legislative and judicial governance. The AU has a Pan African Parliament envisioned in the long run as the lawmaking organ of the Union, with powers to propose draft laws to the Assembly and to have consultative and oversight functions.[19] The African Commission functions in similar ways as the EU Commission, not only being designated as Secretariat of the Union but also

Development Community (SADC), Community of Sahel Saharan States (CEN-SAD), East African Community (EAC), Intergovernmental Authority on Development (IGAD), and Arab Maghreb Union (UMA) at African Union Commission, *Regional Economic Communities*, www.au.int/en/organs/recs

13 Constitutive Act of the Union 2001, art. 3(c).

14 Ibid., art. 4(d).

15 Ibid., arts. 4(h) and (j).

16 Protocol on Amendments to the Constitutive Act of the African Union, Addis Ababa 3 February 2003, Maputo 11 July 2003, not yet in force, art. 4(h).

17 See Tim Murithi, 'The African Union's Transition from Non-Intervention to Non-Indifference: An Ad Hoc Approach to the Responsibility to Protect?' (2009) 1 *Internationale Politik und Gesellschaft* 90–106.

18 See Tobias Lenz, 'Spurred Emulation: The EU and Regional Integration in Mercosur and SADC' (2012) 35(1) *West European Politics* 155–73, 162–7.

19 See Draft Protocol to the Constitutive Act of the African Union Relating to the Pan-African Parliament, Fifth Meeting of Government Experts, Addis Ababa, 9–17 May 2011, not yet in force.

to undertake executive functions.[20] There is a clear predominance however of intergovernmental organs responsible for policy and decision-making, implementation of agreements, authorization of sanctions against member states[21] and enforcement of judicial decisions.[22] These are the Assembly of the Union, Executive Council, Commission, Specialized Technical Committees and Permanent Representative Committee. In addition, the African Peace and Security Architecture (APSA) was established and consequently the formation of the Peace and Security Council (PSC), which is mandated as the central mechanism to manage and respond in a timely manner any crisis or conflict situation on the continent.[23]

4.4 Judicialization and the Prospects of the Rule of Law in African Integration

The establishment of judicial oversight is one of the most ambitious programmes in the AU that is in many respects patterned after the EU – considering weak judicial institutions, or generally of national institutions, in the continent.[24] The establishment of regional judicial bodies in the AU and at subregional levels preceded the formation of the Union which took place in the 1990s when AOU leadership, aware of the impact of globalization and the increasing trend towards regional integration, aimed to replicate an EU on African soil.[25] Three subregional courts or tribunals started to function in the early 2000s – *Economic Community of West African State* (ECOWAS) Community Court of Justice in 2001, EAC Court of Justice in 2001 and SADC Tribunal in 2005. A continent-wide judicial organ, the African Court of Justice, was provided for in the Abuja Treaty of 1991 but renamed the African Court of Justice and Human Rights (ACJHR) in 2008.[26]

20 African Union Commission, *Commission*, www.au.int/en/commission.

21 Constitutive Act of the Union 2001, art. 23.

22 Protocol on the Statute of the African Court of Justice and Human Rights, Sharm El-Sheikh, 1 July 2008, OAU Doc Assembly/AU/Dec. 196 (XI), arts. 46(4) and (5).

23 See Protocol Relating to the Establishment of the Peace and Security Council of the African Union, Durban, 9 July 2002, in force 26 December 2003, OAU Doc Assembly/AU/Dec. 3(I).

24 Said Adejumobi and Adebayo Olukoshi (eds.), *The African Union and New Strategies for Development in Africa* (New York: Cambria Press, 2008), 332.

25 See Rachel Murray, *Human Rights in Africa: From the OAU to the African Union* (Cambridge: Cambridge University Press, 2004), 31.

26 Treaty Establishing the African Economic Community, Abuja, Nigeria, 3 June 1991, in force 12 May 1994, (1991) 30 ILM 1241, art. 7. Pursuant to the decision during the African

The ACJHR, which remains non-functioning to date, is envisioned as the first international court to be constituted with jurisdiction to try both state responsibility and individual accountability.[27] It is intended to be merged with the existing African Court on Human and Peoples Rights (ACHPR) and will have a criminal chamber to try international law crimes such as genocide, crimes against humanity, war crimes, crimes on unconstitutional change of government, piracy, terrorism, mercenarism, corruption, money laundering, trafficking in persons, trafficking in drugs, trafficking in hazardous wastes, illicit exploitation of natural resources, crimes of aggression and inchoate offences.[28] The decision by the AU to constitute the ACJHR is seen as 'countervailing' measure against international pressure for Africa to prosecute state leaders and officials who are suspected of involvement in crimes against humanity or of war crimes.[29] Many member states believe that the indictment of African leaders in the International Criminal Court is selective and a form of overt interference in the continent's political affairs.[30] 'We support the fight against impunity, we do not support impunity, we are not even against the Criminal Court . . . We are against the way justice is being rendered because . . . it looks as if this ICC is only interested in trying the Africans', said former AU Commission chairman Jean Ping.[31] There is also a question of resources in establishing a criminal court, a key argument that has been used to merge the African

Union Summit of Heads of State of Governments on 1 July 2008 and is covered by the Protocol on the Statute of the African Court of Justice and Human Rights 2008.

27 Kristen Rau, 'Jurisprudential Innovation or Accountability Avoidance? The International Criminal Court and Proposed Expansion of the African Court of Justice and Human Rights' (2012) 97(2) *Minnesota Law Review* 669–708, 670.

28 Draft Protocol on Amendments to the Protocol on Statute of the African Court on Justice and Human Rights, Legal/ACJHR-PAP3(II) Rev.5Reve. 4 EX.CL/846(XXV) Annex 5.

29 Imelda Deinla, 'Fostering Rule of Law in African Integration' (Paper presented at the 35th AFSAAP Conference 'Africa: Peoples, Places and Spaces', Canberra, 26–8 November 2012). See also Chacha Bhoke Murungu, 'Towards a Criminal Chamber in the African Court of Justice and Human Rights' (2011) 9(5) *Journal of International Criminal Justice* 1065–75.

30 Although three members have actually requested ICC indictment in the case of Condo, Uganda and Central African Republic. Since 1999, the AU has continuously passed resolutions not to implement the ICC's arrest warrant against Bashir and requested deferral of the proceedings involving Sudan and Kenya. Some members however vowed to arrest Bashir while others defied the ICC order; see Malawi's decision to host the 15–16 July 2012 AU Summit, see Al Jazeera, *Malawi Cancels AU Summit over Sudan's Bashir* (9 June 2012) www.aljazeera.com/news/africa/2012/06/20126974132905285.html

31 In 'African Union refuses to arrest Gaddafi', www.globalpost.com/dispatches/globalpost-blogs/africa-emerges/african-union-refuses-arrest-gaddafi, viewed on 25 June 2012.

Court and the African Court of Justice.[32] Conversely, the ACHPR which became operational in 2006 was established pursuant to the Protocol to the African Charter on Human and Peoples' Rights (African Charter).

The following sections discuss the nature of and developments in the ACHPR and in the two subregional judicial organs in Africa and the way these institutions have affected or developed rule of law practices in the region. The three case studies presented here show how wide diversity in political and legal systems, economic underdevelopment and persistence of conflicts determine the success or failure of rule of law strategies in poor or developing countries.

4.4.1 The African Court of Human and Peoples' Rights: Rule of Law and Human Rights

At present, it is only possible to get a glimpse of a functioning continent-wide judicial organ through the ACHPR in its role of upholding rule of law in the context of human rights protection in Africa. The ACHPR has both judicial and advisory functions, has a complementary mandate with the African Commission on Human and Peoples' Rights (African Commission) and has jurisdiction to hear cases or disputes involving the African Charter on Human and Peoples' Rights, its Protocol and human rights instruments ratified by member states.[33] States and non-state parties are entitled to initiate proceedings in the Court, such as the ACHPR, African Intergovernmental Organization, accredited Nongovernmental Organizations (NGOs) and individuals.[34] However, only countries that made specific declarations to receive complaints by NGOs and individuals are permitted to file cases directly with the Court. As of September 2015, there are 53 signatories to the protocol establishing the ACHPR and 11 ratifications.[35]

[32] For a historical review of the decision on merger, see Dan Juma, 'Lost (or Found) in Translation? The Anatomy of the New African Court of Justice and Human Rights' (2009) 13 *Max Planck United Nations Yearbook* 267–306, 276.

[33] Protocol to the African Charter on Human and Peoples' Rights on the Establishment of the African Court on Human and Peoples' Rights, Ouagadougou, June 10 1998, in force 25 January 2004, OAU Doc OAU/LEG/EXP/AFCHPR/PROT (III), arts. 2–4. It is composed of 11 judges appointed by member states.

[34] Ibid., art. 5. Under art. 34(6) of the Protocol, the Courts' competence to receive complaints from NGOs and individuals applies only to those ratifying states making a declaration to be bound by such competence.

[35] African Union Commission, *Ratification Table: African Charter on Human and People's Rights*, www.au.int/en/sites/default/files/992achpr.pdf

That the ACHPR does not operate on its own but needs to work with other political institutions to be effective is emblematic of the structural foundation of the rule of law. In understanding the operations of the ACHPR, it is important to know the dynamics of its relationships with the AU Assembly and African Commission which are the main organs tasked with promoting and protecting human rights in the continent. The PSC could be added to this triumvirate as the central mechanism to manage and respond to major conflicts in the region, which often involve large-scale human rights abuses. The African Commission is an autonomous quasi-judicial body that can issue recommendations to the AU Assembly and has the standing to file complaints before the Court.[36] Members of both the Court and the African Commission are appointed by Heads of States and the institution's budgets are determined by the Union.[37] Neither organ has independent enforcement mechanism and relies on the AU Assembly to implement or make effective their recommendations or decisions. In the case of the Court, it will submit an annual report to the AU Assembly on those states that did not comply with its orders or decisions, while the AU Executive Council monitors enforcement on behalf of the Assembly.[38]

The African Commission's role in rule of law development in the context of human rights promotion and protection cannot be underestimated. It has the power to file complaints of human rights violations against states before the ACHPR and to accept and rule on communications. In the latter role, it clarifies human rights norms at the national, regional and international levels and gives recommendations. For example, it considered the Zimbabwean government's regulation for accreditation of journalists drawn from both international law and regional norms in the Americas in recommending the repeal of the regulation.[39] The African Commission has so far shown preference for communications than in filing complaints with only one case filed. Conversely, it has decided 196 communications

[36] See Rules of Procedure of the African Commission on Human and People's Rights, Banjul, 26 May 2010, in force 18 August 2010, rule 3.

[37] African Charter, arts. 30 and 31; Protocol to African Charter 1998, arts. 13 and 14.

[38] Protocol to African Charter 1998, arts. 29 and 30.

[39] Considering the Advisory Opinion of the Inter-American Court of Human Rights on the question of registration of journalists in Costa Rica, in Communication 297/05, *Scanlen and Holderness* v. *Zimbabwe* [2009] AHLR 289 (African Commission on Human and Peoples' Rights, 2009).

out of 400 received but only 10 countries implemented, fully or partially, its recommendations.[40]

The relationship between the African Commission and ACHPR is based on complementarity and cooperation. Both regional organs are also faced with institutional and legal constraints. In the absence of initiatives by the African Commission, very few cases could reach the African Court. It is only through the African Commission that indirect individual access to the African Court can be made because only six countries made the declaration to receive NGO and individual complaints (Ghana, Burkina Faso, Malawi, Mali, Tanzania, and in April 2012 Rwanda).[41] Aside from financial dependency to the AU Assembly, the African Commission's decision-making is also constrained by the politics of member countries the majority of which have proclivity towards long-run political solutions. The AU's political organs largely ignored the African Commission and its recommendations and at times have deplored its actions.[42] It is not surprising that of the 44 cases filed before the ACHPR, only one had been filed by the African Commission while all the rest were initiated by individuals and private groups. It was also largely 'invisible' in times of major human rights crises such as in Sudan, Somalia, Rwanda and Sierra Leone.[43] Conversely, the Court itself has not shown an inclination for judicial activism to broaden access of NGOs and individuals in the absence of action by the African Commission and member states. It has repeatedly dismissed individual access cases[44] and precludes the possibility for individual challenge against violation of substantive rights guaranteed under the African Charter.

The Libya case,[45] however, has opened a new era for cooperation between the African Commission and the ACPHR that can potentially enhance

[40] International Service for Human Rights, *African Commission on Human and Peoples' Rights, Marking the 30th Anniversary of the African Charter*, www.ishr.ch/document-stuff/.../1393-regional-focus-hrmq1-2012

[41] See African Union Commission, *Ratification Table: African Charter on Human and People's Rights*, www.au.int/en/sites/default/files/992achpr.pdf

[42] See Andreas Stensland, Walter Lotze and Joel Ng, *Regional Security and Human Rights Interventions: A Global Governance Perspective on the AU and ASEAN* (Oslo: Norwegian Institute of International Affairs, 2012), 34–42.

[43] The African Commission's budget was reduced by the AU in 2011 at a time when it was pursuing the case against Libya.

[44] See Application No. 001/2011, *Femi Falana* v. *African Union* (African Court of Human and Peoples' Rights, Judgment of 26 June 2012).

[45] Application No. 004/2011, *African Commission on Human and Peoples' Rights* v. *Great Socialist Peoples' Libyan Arab Jamahiriya* (African Court of Human and Peoples' Rights, Order for Provisional Measures of 25 March 2011).

judicial oversight on the continent. This is the first case when the African Commission filed a complaint and where the African Court also issued an unprecedented provisional measure by its own requiring Libya to 'refrain from any action that would result in the life or violation of physical integrity of persons'.[46] This case is path-breaking in the African court system for an indirect access originally submitted to the African Commission by an Egyptian NGO, the Egyptian Initiative for Personal Rights (EIPR) and two foreign NGOs, Human Rights Watch and the International Centre for the Legal Protection of Human Rights (INTERIGHTS). The Libya case was followed by the Court's decision against Tanzania,[47] which is considered the first ever case decided on the merits. In this latter case, the ACHPR declared that the government violated the African Charter by disallowing non-party members or independents from participating in national and local elections.

The indifference to judicial processes by the political organs of the AU shows the political barrier to the rule of law. The AU's lack of support to enforce the provisional order in the Libya case manifests the importance of political commitment by governments and elites to make judicial institutions an authoritative mechanism to resolve disputes. The AU Assembly, despite the escalation of violence against civilians in Libya, refrained from making any criticism and the Court's decision did not even merit mention during the Extraordinary Session of the Assembly on 25 May 2011.[48] As the unfolding events showed, the AU's political roadmap had been rejected or brushed aside by competing forces in Libya and by other regional players and precipitated the United Nations Security Council's authorization of the use of force by international coalition. Both the African Commission's complaint and the Court's provisional order could have provided the legal justification for AU intervention authorized in the Constitutive Act and may have thwarted the full military intervention that was so feared from Western powers.

[46] Ibid.

[47] Application 009/2011 and 011/2011, *Tanganyika Law Society and the Legal and Human Rights Centre and Reverend Christopher Mtikila* v. *the United Republic of Tanzania* (African Court of Human and Peoples' Rights, Judgment of 14 June 2013).

[48] Declaration on the State of Peace and Security in Africa, Addis Ababa, 25 May 2011, OAU Doc EXT/Assembly/AU/Decl/(01.2011); See also Rachel Murray and Debra Long, *The Implementation of the Findings of the African Commission on Human and Peoples' Rights* (UK: Cambridge University Press, 2015), 145–6.

4.4.2 *The Demise of the SADC Tribunal: Political Decision Trumps Judicial Activism*

The formation of the Southern African Development Community in 1980 was originally meant as a counterbalance to South Africa's economic hegemony in the region and initially rejected economic integration based on liberal market economy, preferring a balance trade strategy based on technical and economic cooperation.[49] In 1992, SADC was revitalized for regional integration committed to addressing underdevelopment and peace and security issues. It aims to promote economic liberalization and eventual formation of an economic union, similar to the EU, and commits to the values of human rights, democracy and the rule of law.[50]

As an intergovernmental organization, SADC established a tribunal that is many respects patterned on the European Court of Justice. Its competence is an exact reproduction of ECJ's – 'to ensure the adherence to law in the interpretation and application of the Treaty'[51], has broad jurisdiction[52] to hear disputes between the states, between individuals and member states and between individuals and the Community,[53] provision for preliminary reference procedure from national courts or tribunal, which is an almost textual reproduction of the preliminary ruling provisions under Article 177 of the EEC Treaty.[54] This is not a coincidence given the material support for funding and technical assistance provided by the EU and the pressure to attain credibility and legitimacy from the international community.[55]

The SADC Tribunal had a short-lived existence from 2005 up to its eventual dissolution in 2012. This case clearly reflects the pitfalls of replicating legal and institutional designs in a domestic setting where little domestic capacity and political support exist for its proper functioning.

49 G.G. Maasdorp, 'Economic and Political Aspects of Regional Cooperation in Southern Africa', 95–6.

50 SADC's forerunner was the Southern African Development Co-ordination Conference (SADCC) and its 15 member countries are: Angola, Botswana, Lesotho, Malawi, Mozambique, Swaziland, Tanzania, Zambia, Zimbabwe, Madagascar, Seychelles, Democratic Republic of Congo, Namibia and Mauritius.

51 Treaty of the Southern African Development Community, Windhoek, Namibia, 17 August 1992, in force 30 September 1992 (1993) 32 ILM 116, art. 16.

52 Protocol on Tribunal and the Rules of Procedure Thereof, SADC Protocol on Tribunal and the Rules of Procedure Thereof, Windhoek, 7 August 2000, in force 14 August 2001, art. 14.

53 Ibid., arts. 15 and 18.

54 Ibid., art. 75(1)–(2), Protocol on Tribunal and the Rules of Procedure Thereof.

55 Lenz, 'Spurred Emulation', 166–7.

The Tribunal's experience shows the tension between law and politics in an environment where politics has always ruled and determined legal outcomes. The Tribunal and its supporters were clearly driven to make it work but it could not simply withstand the weight of member states' political decisions and expectations. After deciding 21 cases since it received its first case in 2007, the SADC Summit which is composed of members' heads of states suspended the Tribunal's operations in August 2010.[56] Prior to its suspension, the Tribunal rendered a variety of decisions that involve labour, commercial, human rights and deportation issues[57] and clearly an opportunity to develop a regional jurisprudence and a mechanism for justice for individuals against the arbitrary exercise of powers by states or agencies, particularly when municipal mechanisms offer no effective remedies.

The Tribunal's closure was precipitated by an increasingly activist court whose development and actions were not expected of and could not be tolerated by member states. Its development as a progressive court was nipped in the bud having permitted individual access for almost 80 per cent of its accepted cases and in instances where exhaustion of remedy at the member state level is ineffective.[58] It was also actively involved in disseminating information about the Tribunal and its work, and in encouraging discussion of its decisions, having produced the SADC Tribunal Review. The establishment of the Tribunal fuelled the beginning of a discourse on SADC integration and the evolution of a regional jurisprudence.[59]

The highly controversial ruling in *Mike Campbell (PVT) Limited and William Michael Campbell* v. *The Republic of Zimbabwe*[60] sealed the fate of the Tribunal. In that case, the Tribunal granted an interlocutory relief to the

[56] The Tribunal's first case was a labour complaint against the SADC Secretariat in *Ernest Francis Mtingwi* v. *SADC Secretariat*, Case No. SADC (T) 1/07 (SADC Tribunal, 2008); also cited in Oliver Ruppel and Francois Bangamwabo, 'The SADC Tribunal: A Legal Analysis of Its Mandate and Role in Regional Integration' (2008) 8 *Monitoring Regional Integration in Southern Africa Yearbook* 1–43, 3–4.

[57] List of decided cases at Southern African Development Tribunal, *Decisions*, www.sadc-tribunal.org/pages/decisions.htm. Most cases were filed against Zimbabwe but there are cases against SADC Secretariat, the SADC Parliamentary Forum and cases filed against Lesotho and Congo.

[58] *Mike Campbell (PVT) Ltd* v. *The Republic of Zimbabwe*, Case No. SADC (T) 2/07 (SADC Tribunal, 2007), 21, restated in *Bach's Transport (Pty) Ltd* v. *Democratic Republic of Congo*, Case No. SADC (T) 14/08 (SADC Tribunal, 2010).

[59] See (2011) 1 *Southern African Development Community Law Journal*, www.kas.de/wf/doc/kas_23107-1522-2-30.pdf?110721140849

[60] *Mike Campbell*. The case concerns the highly controversial policy of Zimbabwe to expropriate lands owned by its white population. Intervention by 77 other farmers was granted in

private applicant to prevent the Government of Zimbabwe from evicting the landowner from his land pending the determination of the main issue with the regional court. The Tribunal in *Campbell* also interpreted broad provisions of the SADC treaty on human rights, democracy and the rule of law. 'This means that SADC as a collectivity and as individual member States are under a legal obligation to respect and protect human rights of SADC citizens. They also have to ensure that there is democracy and the rule of law within the region.'[61] The Tribunal's decision in Campbell was clearly perceived as a 'threat' to sovereign prerogatives of member states. The dissolution of the Tribunal was not simply a move to shield Zimbabwe from embarrassment but a signal that many governments also fear that their national policies would increasingly be scrutinized and stricken down.[62] 'We have created a monster that will devour us all' is a remark attributed to Tanzanian President Jakaya Kikwete referring to the Tribunal.[63] While very few countries had spoken openly of their views, it is understandable that they would have been unsettled by the Tribunal's rulings, since many other African countries are beset with colonial land policies and may be contemplating similar affirmative measures.[64] In many ways, SADC member states did not foresee the consequences of their actions when they created an independent tribunal.

The Tribunal's short existence shows the promise and also the limits of developing an independent and activist regional court in Africa. Zimbabwe's actuations clearly show its bold stance against the Tribunal's decision. Not only it defied the order by prosecuting and evicting the applicant,[65] but also its ruler scoffed at the decision calling it 'nonsense and of no consequence'.[66] A direct confrontation ensued that led the Tribunal

---

Gideon Stephanus Theron v. *The Republic of Zimbabwe*, Case No. SADC (T) 02/08; 03/08; 04/08; 06/08 (SADC Tribunal, 2008).

[61] *Mike Campbell*, 3.

[62] Sasman, Catherine, *Kawana Defends SADC Tribunal Suspension* (15 July 2011) The Namibian www.namibian.com.na/index.php?id=28&tx_ttnews[tt_news]=84492&no_cache=1

[63] Christie, Sean, *Killed Off By 'Kings and Potentates'* (19 August 2011) Mail and Guardian, http://mg.co.za/article/2011-08-19-killed-off-by-kings-and-potentates

[64] See, for example, discussion on land issues in African Union, African Development Back and the UN Economic Commission for Africa, *Framework and Guidelines on Land Policy in Africa: A Framework to Strengthen Land Rights, Enhance Productivity and Secure Livelihoods* (Addis Ababa: AUC-ECA-AfDB Consortium, 2010), www.uneca.org/sites/default/files/PublicationFiles/fg_on_land_policy_eng.pdf

[65] *Campbell* v. *Zimbabwe Contempt of Court*, Case No. SADC (T) 11/08 (SADC Tribunal, 2008).

[66] *Mike Campbell* v. *Republic of Zimbabwe*, Case No. SADC (T) 03/09 (SADC Tribunal, 2009).

to issue a contempt order against Zimbabwe and forwarded it to the SADC Summit pursuant to Article 10 of the SADC Treaty. In response, the Summit rather than deciding on Zimbabwe's noncompliance instead effectively suspended the operations of the Tribunal by not reappointing four of its members and ordering a review of the Tribunal's jurisdiction by an independent expert, whose recommendations are also consequently ignored.[67] The Tribunal went into a collision course with Zimbabwe's leaders without the benefit of a 'dialogue' or facilitation, which isolated it further from the political decision-makers. Perhaps in hindsight, the Tribunal members may have underestimated the camaraderie of SADC leaders or their interests in defending their sovereignty.

4.4.3 ECOWAS Community Court of Justice and Judicial Diplomacy

With more than half of its members belonging to the category of least developed countries that are continuously beset by internal armed conflicts, ECOWAS is gradually transforming itself and considered one of the prime engines of regional integration in Africa.[68] Founded in 1975 through the Treaty of Lagos, ECOWAS was given a boost in 1993 by adopting the Revised Treaty of ECOWAS (or Treaty of Cotonou) to accelerate economic integration that will culminate in an economic union and to enhance political cooperation. Unlike SADC, the ECOWAS membership has readily embraced a broader perspective of sovereignty and acknowledged the need for 'partial and gradual pooling of sovereignties to the Community within the context of a collective political will'.[69] This treaty gave rise to the establishment of supranational organs such as the Community Parliament and the ECOWAS Community Court of Justice (ECCJ).[70]

[67] For legal arguments on the validity of suspension/dissolution of the Tribunal see Matyszak, Derek, 'The Dissolution of the SADC Tribunal' (Research and Advocacy Unit, 19 August 2011), www.idasa.org/media/uploads/outputs/files/the_suspension_sadc_tribunal_final.pdf

[68] ECOWAS members are Ghana, Burkina Faso, Cabo Verde, Cote d'Ivoire, Gambia, Ghana, Guinee, Guinea Bissau, Liberia, Mali, Niger, Nigeria, Senegal, Sierra Leone and Togolese Republic. Many ECOWAS member countries have suffered long years of civil wars and armed conflicts.

[69] Revised Treaty of the Economic Community of West African States, Cotonou, Benin, 24 July 1993, in force 23 August 1995, 2373 UNTS 233; (1996) 35 ILM 660, preamble.

[70] Other organs are: The Authority of Heads of States, Council of Ministers, Economic and Social Council, Executive Secretariat, Fund for Cooperation, Compensation and Development and Specialized Technical Commissions. They also provided an Arbitral Tribunal which is yet to be constituted.

Through Articles 6 and 15 of the Revised Treaty, the ECCJ has been set up as the main legal organ of the Community where its decisions are binding on member states, Community institutions, individuals and corporate bodies.[71] Similar to the SADC Tribunal, it has a broad mandate to interpret and apply the treaty and other instruments adopted by the Community, including principles of human rights,[72] to admit individual access and to provide for preliminary reference by national courts or individuals.[73] Like the SADC Tribunal, it has weak enforcement capacity being reliant on member states to implement decisions. In ECCJ's case, enforcement will be carried out by a 'competent' authority which will be determined by the member state.[74] The Court can also be seized of advisory opinions on any matter that requires interpretation of Community law. In 2001, the ECCJ was formally established, composed of seven independent judges, and sits in Abuja, Nigeria.

In contrast to the SADC Tribunal, the ECCJ has enjoyed continued support from the member states. This can be explained partly by the long years of civil wars and armed conflicts in many member states that precipitated vigorous calls for peaceful and legal framework for dispute resolution. These conflicts – often the aftermath of electoral contests, *coup d'état* or other unconstitutional changes in governments – had resulted in grave humanitarian crises and total breakdown of the rule of law.[75] To further strengthen its commitment to the rule of law, ECOWAS adopted the Protocol on Democracy and Governance that sets out member states' commitment to constitutional democracy based on popular representation and separation of powers.[76] The section on Constitutional

71 Ibid., art. 15(4).

72 Manisuli Ssenyonjo (ed.), *The African Regional Human Rights System: 30 Years after the African Charter on Human and Peoples' Rights* (Leiden: Martinus Nijhoff, 2012), 296.

73 Non-exhaustion of remedies on human rights cases has been affirmed by the Court, see *Etim Moses Essien v. Republic of Gambia and Another*, Suit No. ECW/CCJ/APP/05/05 (ECOWAS Court of Justice, 2007).

74 Supplementary Protocol A/SP.1/01/05, Accra, 19 January 2005, art. 24(4): 'All Member States shall determine the competent national authority for the purpose of receipt and processing of execution and notify the Court accordingly.'

75 See David Harris, *Civil War and Democracy in West Africa: Conflict Resolution, Elections and Justice in Sierra Leone and Liberia* (London: I.B. Tauris, 2011); Cordenillo, Raul and Kristen Sample (eds.), *Rule of Law and Constitution Building: The Role of Regional Organisations* (Stockholm: International Institute for Democracy and Electoral Assistance, 2014), 10.

76 Protocol on Democracy and Governance Supplementary to the Protocol Relating to the Mechanism for Conflict Prevention, Management, Resolution, Peacekeeping and Security, Dakar, 21 December 2001, in force 20 February 2008, ECOWAS Doc A/SP1/12/01.

Convergence Principles, similar to EU's Accession Criteria, enumerates key principles of democratic governance that each member state should adhere to by enacting in their constitutional and legislative framework[77] and provides for sanction in cases where democracy is abruptly ended or massive human rights violation occurs.[78]

Part of the ECCJ's endurance as an institution is the result of the diplomacy and caution that its members have displayed with respect to member states. It has turned itself into a pragmatic court while strengthening its judicial mandate progressively. The Court has engaged in a policy of dialogue and consultation with member states culminating in such achievements as recognition of individual access and competence to rule on human rights,[79] the formation of Judicial Council of the Community responsible for recruiting judges to the Court and the establishment of the Association of West African Judges to serve as a framework for mutual judicial exchange and cooperation in developing regional policies and jurisprudence.[80] It has also embarked on popularizing the Court through its sensitization programme to increase awareness of and access to the Court by ordinary people[81] and has engaged with other national courts.[82] It has worked with the ECOWAS Commission in devising its work plan and budget and also in finding ways to implement Court decisions.[83]

While the Court had given adverse decisions against member states, it has kept a relationship of amity with them, rather than one of confrontation and antagonism of the kind that had beset the defunct SADC Tribunal. This could be explained partly by the policy of engagement of the Court and also by the fact that it adopts caution and tact in the enforcement of its decisions. For example in responding to Nigeria's designation of its

77 Ibid., art. 1.

78 Ibid., art. 45.

79 Institute for Human Rights and Development in Africa, *Court of Justice of the Economic Community of West African States*, www.ihrda.org/court-of-justice-of-the-economic-community-of-west-african-states/

80 *ECOWAS to Establish West African Judges' Association* (12 July 2011) Ghana Business News, www.ghanabusinessnews.com/ecowas-to-establish-west-african-judges-association

81 Community Court of Justice – ECOWAS, *The ECOWAS Court Concludes Sensitization Programme in Member States*, www.courtecowas.org

82 See Community Court of Justice – ECOWAS, *Final Communiqué – 10th Anniversary*, www.courtecowas.org

83 See Daboya, Hon. Justice Awa Nana, Community Court of Justice, *ECOWAS: Summary of Activities for the Year 2011* (Activities Report, ECOWAS Community Court of Justice, 2011), www.courtecowas.org

national authority tasked to enforce the Court's decision, a long-overdue obligation of member states, the Court remarked:

> The Court acknowledges this act and would like to express its joy upon receiving the information, which comes at a time when the Court is celebrating its 10th anniversary. The Court wishes that the other Member States will emulate this example and honour their commitments to the Community.[84]

Since it commenced operation in 2001, the ECCJ has decided 92 cases composed of 47 rulings and 45 judgments as of March 2012.[85] More than half of the cases were initiated by individuals against member states, mostly against Nigeria, while nine cases concern suits by and among Community organs and personnel.[86] These cases concern mostly issues of human rights, labour rights and contractual obligations. The Court's jurisprudence has affirmed direct individual standing to sue on human rights violations without the requirement to exhaust local remedies[87] and the legal standing of an association to sue.[88] It has delivered landmark decisions on human rights such as the right against torture and inhuman punishment,[89] the right against slavery[90] and the right to education as an enforceable right.[91] In some of the cases decided against member states, the Court had also provided for compensation or reparations for the victims of human rights violations.

Conversely, the Court also gave a controversial decision in the case filed by Hissène Habré, a former Chadian dictator in the 1980s being indicted for crimes against humanity, who questioned the competence of

[84] Community Court of Justice – ECOWAS, *The Republic of Nigeria Designates the Competent National Authority Responsible for Implementing Decisions of the Court*, www.courtecowas.org

[85] Press release at All Africa, *West Africa: Ecowas Court Decides 92 Cases in Nine Years* (9 March 2012), http://allafrica.com/stories/201203110048.html

[86] See Community Court of Justice – ECOWAS, *List of Decided Cases from 2004 Till Date*, www.courtecowas.org

[87] *Etim Moses; Moussa Leo Keita* v. *The Republic of Mali*, Suit No. ECW/CCJ/APP/05/06 (ECOWAS Court of Justice, 2007).

[88] *National Coordination of Departmental Delegates of the Cocoa Coffee Sector* v. *Republic of Cote d'Ivoire*, Suit No. ECW/CCJ/APP/02/09 (ECOWAS Court of Justice, 2009).

[89] *Chief Ebrimah Manneh* v. *The Republic of the Gambia*, Suit No. ECW/CCJ/APP/04/07, Judgment No. ECW/CCJ/JUD/03/05 (ECOWAS Court of Justice, 2008).

[90] *Dame Hadijatou Mani Koraou* v. *The Republic of Niger*, Suit No. ECW/CCJ/APP/08/07 (ECOWAS Court of Justice, 2008).

[91] *Socio-Economic Rights and Accountability Project* v. *President the Federal Government of Nigeria and the Universal Basic Education Commission*, Suit No. ECW/CCJ/APP/12/07 (ECOWAS Court of Justice, 2007).

a national Senegalese court to try him.[92] The proceedings against Habré had been delayed by the ECOWAS decision that requires an 'ad hoc special procedure of an international character' for the purpose.[93] Despite the long delays in the proceedings, the Extraordinary African Chambers in the Senegalese Courts, the first AU-backed international criminal court, finally handed a decision convicting the former Chadian dictator for crimes against humanity, war crimes and torture.[94] In ways the ECOWAS decision showed its wisdom as both decision and the Chambers are hailed as triumph for the AU to try Habré 'on behalf of Africa' and for the African court to effectively deal with impunity.[95]

Despite its achievements, the ECCJ has to address the issue of enforcement to ensure its long-term relevance and legitimacy with the broader Community. The Court itself acknowledged poor implementation of its decisions as its greatest challenge.[96] Only three countries – Nigeria, Guinea-Conakry and Niger – have designated their national authority tasked to enforce the Court's decisions. As enforcement is dependent on national mechanisms, the Court has no power to enforce its own rulings except when the ECOWAS Authority of Heads of States decides to impose sanctions against that member state for failure to fulfil its obligations.[97] This option has not been used to enforce a Court judgment. Among the three countries (Gambia, Nigeria and Niger) that received an adverse decision from the Court, only Niger implemented the decision in *Hadijatou Mani Koraou* v. *The Republic of Niger* by paying the applicant 10 million CFA Francs on 17 March 2009 amidst the spectre of ECOWAS warning

[92] *Hissène Habré* v. *Republic of Senegal*, Judgment No. ECW/CCJ/JUD/06/10 (ECOWAS Court of Justice, 2010).

[93] Human Rights Watch, *Chronology of the Habré Case* (27 April 2015), www.hrw.org/news/2012/03/09/chronology-habr-case; Valentina Spiga, 'Non-retroactivity of Criminal Law: A New Chapter in the Hissène Habré Saga' (2011) 9(1) *Journal of International Criminal Justice* 5–23; All Africa, *Senegal: 'Belgium* v. *Senegal' – The International Court of Justice Hears Habré Dispute* (29 March 2012), http://allafrica.com/stories/201203290885.html

[94] *Habré*.

[95] African Union Commission, *AU Welcomes the Judgment of an Unprecedented Trial of Hissène Habré* (1 June 2016), http://au.int/en/pressreleases/30728/au-welcomes-judgement-unprecedented-trial-hiss%C3%A8ne-habr%C3%A9

[96] Nigeria Daily News, *ECOWAS Court Laments Implementation Challenges*, www.nigeriadailynews.com/latest-additions/32514-ecowas-court-laments-implementation-challenges.html

[97] ECOWAS Revised Treaty 1993, art. 77.

to suspend the country.[98] The designation of the Attorney General as Nigeria's implementing body could boost enforcement as Nigeria is the Community's biggest and arguably most influential member.

4.5 MERCOSUR Integration and Pathway to Regional Jurisprudence

The Mercado Comun del Sur[99] is an intergovernmental organization where flexibility and consensus is the mode of decision-making and policy-making. Member states have not seriously considered the establishment of a supranational judicial organ although there have been initiatives from some member states to consider the institution of an ECJ-style Mercosur Court of Justice.[100] The EU influence in MERCOSUR is considered minimal and where material dependence from EU is generally lacking. The lack of independent bodies has been blamed for the difficulties of drawing up common policies, the low level of implementation of policies and weakness of dispute resolution.[101] The Brazilian/Argentinian financial crisis in the early 2000s provided the push for the establishment of a neutral dispute resolution mechanism as a measure to provide a viable and more stable alternative than 'presidential diplomacy' that was the main mechanism used to settle inter-state economic disputes.[102]

The Protocol of Olivos 2002 established the Tribunal Permanente de Revision (Permanent Tribunal of Review or PTR) and formally instituted in 2004 with its seat at Asuncion, Paraguay. It is part of the three-step process for resolving disputes among members. The first two stages are direct negotiations of the parties or intervention of the Common Market Group,

98 Community Court of Justice – ECOWAS, *ECOWAS Community Court of Justice Press Release*, www.courtecowas.org/site/index.php?option=com_content&view=article&id=105%3Arepublicnigeria&Itemid=15&lang=en.The compliance also came at a time of political turmoil in Niger when then incumbent President Mamadou Tandja changed the constitution to allow him to extend his term of office.

99 MERCOSUR's membership includes Argentina, Brazil, Paraguay, Uruguay and Venezuela with Bolivia applying for full membership.

100 Raul Emilio Vinuesa, 'Enforcement of Mercosur Arbitration Awards Within the Domestic Legal Orders of Member States' 40 *Texas Journal of International Law* (2005) 425–42. See also Lenz, 'Spurred Emulation', 168.

101 See Celina and Ricardo Rozemberg, 'MERCOSUR: A Different Approach to Institutional Development' (Focal Policy Paper No. 05-06, Canadian Foundation for the Americas, March 2005), www.focal.ca/pdf/mercosur.pdf, 1–12.

102 Kevin Gallagher, 'Financial Crises and International Investment Agreements: The Case of Sovereign Debt Restructuring' (2012) 3(3) *Global Policy* 362–74.

if agreed by the parties or requested by a third state, and the second is when parties agree to the formation of an *ad hoc* tribunal. The PTR therefore can be accessed either as a court of appeal from the awards of the *ad hoc* arbitral tribunal or on the first instance upon the agreement of the parties.[103] PTR's primary function is very similar with that of the ECJ which is to ensure the uniform interpretation and application of MERCOSUR law but its nature is strikingly different. Although it is denominated as a 'Tribunal', it is an arbitral tribunal composed of arbitrators not judges and its rulings are in the nature of arbitral awards rather than decisions.[104] Its decisions are therefore binding only upon the parties. The PTR is likewise not a regular tribunal but operates on *ad hoc* basis. As the highest adjudicatory organ in MERCOSUR, it can only be accessed by the member states to the exclusion of individuals and its preliminary reference can only be made by the Supreme Court of member states. Enforcement of MERCOSUR decisions or awards depends on the unilateral action of member states that are parties to the case. In many cases, enforcement had taken place through informal negotiations.[105]

The pathway to legal integration in MERCOSUR is intended as a voluntary course by member states which retain tight control over the process. As enforcement is dependent on unilateral or negotiated implementation, compliance with MERCOSUR law follows a gradual process of internalization through harmonization or voluntary amendment of domestic rules or regulations. However, the PTR's articulation of MERCOSUR law as 'integration law' is being regarded as having the potential of developing fundamental principles similar to the development in the European Community Treaty.[106] In *Laudo* 1/2005, 8 December 2005 and *Laudo Complementario*, 13 January 2006, the PTR clarified the nature of MERCOSUR law as integration law and aided by reference to ECJ jurisprudence.[107] As integration law, MERCOSUR law is deemed superior over international law in the resolution of disputes and needs to have sufficient autonomy in relation to other branches of law, as this autonomy

[103] Daniel Pavón Piscitello and Jan Peter Schmidt, 'In the Footsteps of the ECJ: First Decision of the Permanent MERCOSUR-Tribunal' (2007) 34(3) *Legal Issues of Economic Integration* 283–93, 283–4.

[104] Ibid., 285.

[105] Vinuesa, 'Enforcement of Mercosur Arbitration Awards', 435.

[106] Piscitello and Schmidt, 'In the Footsteps of the ECJ', 288–9.

[107] Both arbitral awards pertain to the dispute between Uruguay and Argentina, *Prohibicion De Importacion De Neumaticos Remoldeados Procedentes Del Uruguay*.

favours the integration process.[108] At the same time, the PTR pointed out that MERCOSUR law 'aspires to develop into community law'. The process of development of MERCOSUR by the PTR might proceed along similar lines as that of EC law carried out by the ECJ.[109]

4.6 Conclusion

The idea that a stable and impartial mechanism for settlement of issues among members is important for a functioning common market is one aspect of EU institutional design that has been emulated, to greater or lesser extent, by other regional projects in Africa and South America. There is also a growing recognition among the different regional bodies discussed that legal integration is a necessary complement of economic integration. Diffusion however is a different matter which involves the process of internalization of rules and norms by regional and domestic institutions and actors. There is wide divergence in other regional projects as to the strategy needed to attain legal integration. A critical criterion for the success of regional courts, as shown in African courts, is the degree to which member states allow the autonomy and support to the institutions. How member states are willing to loosen their control of the process of integration – and consequently allow the development of autonomous legal order – is one unique characteristic of the EU that has not been completely internalized in other regional projects.

The process of transplantation of the EU model can be at best a symbolic gesture to gain international credibility – as shown by the SADC Tribunal – in the absence of domestic capacity and strong political commitment by political elites. However, as shown by the ECCJ, domestic capacity can be alleviated when there is political support; the internal dynamics of the court itself and the innovative ways it adopts are also essential to navigating the complex political behaviour of political actors. While extraordinary events like the humanitarian crises in Africa could be triggers for adoption of institutions and norms, a gradual and flexible approach towards legal coherence, as demonstrated in MERCOSUR, can be more durable as member states are given the opportunity to learn and build from their own experiences. Given that claims of sovereignty remains a cherished value in inter-state relations and in state-building

[108] Piscitello and Schmidt, 'In the Footsteps of the ECJ', 289.
[109] Ibid.

processes in other regions of the world, fostering rule of law has to rely on the political and soft approaches.

In conflict or post-conflict settings, competing interests and values vie for states' attention, priorities and resources. The lengthy and complex process that rule of law mechanisms entail also precludes actors and stakeholders from considering it as the appropriate and effective option of settling disputes. As in many cases, diplomacy and the use of political solutions, including the use of force, seem to be regarded as the more viable strategy for conflict settlement, or even to restore the functioning of rule of law. As the foregoing discussion has shown, rule of law initiatives in Africa such as norm creation and strengthening legal institutions are at best complementary to political settlement in creating conditions for peace and eventual restoration of the rule of law.

5

Rule of Law or Rule through Law in Southeast Asia

5.1 Introduction

A key lesson from the previous chapters is that individual rule of law practices by member states play a critical part in the institutional design and development of rule of law in the context of regional integration. This is particularly so in the way the model of supranational and autonomous regional organs is emulated or internalized by non-Western countries. In this chapter, we discuss the development of the rule of law in Southeast Asia from the individual historical contexts of member states to show the particularities and variety of rule of law practices in the region. The wide variation in the pathways to attaining statehood among ASEAN states – and hence of the role played by law in state building – is a fundamental consideration for how we evaluate the function of rule of law in individual ASEAN countries. We are more interested in the process rather than in the 'what is' and in identifying elements that cause a change in or a break from legal developments of member states. A particular focus in this chapter is the way salient political developments contributed in major constitutional and legal changes and the impact they have on the institutions of power.

How institutions of power are constrained by legal institutions, how major political disputes are authoritatively settled through law and how law is applied to, privileges or discriminates one group over the others are the main questions in this chapter. We argue in this chapter that the better way to understand these questions is not to lump states in the 'either or' categories of rule of law and rule by law. Instead, we examine to what extent law has developed as a function of ruling or the development of the 'law regime'. We also introduce the term, 'rule through law', to better describe how the functioning of laws is determined by the dynamics of state and society. In Southeast Asia, formal rules have paradoxical meanings, not only because particular groups can thwart their functioning or use them to serve particular interests but also because society itself is steeped in the tension between modernity and tradition. Hence, we are also interested in how the elites – in particular, the ruling elites – are subject to law and the degree of political control over the population. If rule of law is instituted at the regional level, who could its objects, and subjects, be? If its object is in, at least, the facilitation of economic integration, necessarily its subjects are not merely 'regional' players but mostly nationals of member states who will be participating in or would most likely be affected by new rules of market integration.

5.2 Origins of the Law Regime in Southeast Asia: Colonialism, the Postcolonial State and 'Rule by Law'

One of the assumptions in this work is that the development of the state systems in Southeast Asia was conditioned by the process of nation-state building in the postcolonial era. It is argued that the development of the 'rule of law' followed the unifying and centralizing function of the new nation-state. The state had been formally constituted after colonialism in terms of territorial boundedness and centralized authority which superseded precolonial concepts of territoriality based on loyalties and ethnicity.[1] Although endogenous state systems were observed in several locations in precolonial period, these nascent states were organized or revolved around royal or charismatic authority while outlying provinces or districts were largely autonomous and replicating the centre in authority and functions.[2] In many instances, the precolonial states had been fluid rather than absolute, loosely organized with no clearly defined territorial boundary, and central authority rarely had firm control of the periphery.[3]

[1] Acharya, *The Quest for Identity*, 32–3.

[2] See G. Carter Bentley, 'Indigenous States of Southeast Asia' (1986) 15 *Annual Review of Anthropology* 275–99. For a discussion on the *mandala* system, see Oliver W. Wolters, *History, Culture and Religion in Southeast Asian Perspectives*, revised edn. (Ithaca: Cornell Southeast Asia Program, 1999), 21–3; the 'theatre state' in Clifford Geertz, *Negara: The Theatre State in Nineteenth-Century Bali* (Princeton: Princeton University Press, 1981), 124; and concept of 'galactic polity' in Stanley J. Tambiah, *World Conqueror, World Renouncer: A Study of Buddhism and Polity in Thailand Against a Historical Background* (Cambridge: University of Cambridge Press, 1976). For the role played by warfare in precolonial state formation, see D.G.E. Hall, 'South-East Asian Proto-History' in *A History of Southeast Asia*, 4th edn. (New York: St Martin's Press, 1986), 12–46; Michael Charney, 'Warfare in Early Modern Southeast Asia: Introduction' (2004) 12(1) *South East Asia Research* 5–12.

[3] David Joel Steinberg, *In Search of Southeast Asia* (Sydney: Allen and Unwin, 1987), 4–5; Tony Day, 'Ties that (Un)Bind: Families and States in Premodern Southeast Asia' (1996) 55(2) *The Journal of Asian Studies* 384–409, 395.

The appearance of the phenomenon of 'rule by law' particularly the period in the 1960s and early 1980s in Southeast Asian states, often understood as the opposite of the rule of law, is not the sole handiwork of authoritarian or despotic leaders. It has its origins in colonial and postcolonial state reconstruction, and aided in large measure by underlying values of social hierarchy and stratification existing in precolonial era. The process of modernization, through the introduction of bureaucratic administration and laws by the colonial powers, had a contradictory impact on the emerging colonial states. Elsewhere in the region, colonial offices became symbols of status and prestige, especially for precolonial elites, and also became a source for new breed of elites. The consequence of elite accommodation was the tendency to form 'clans' within the modernizing bureaucracy and to replicate the traditional conception of the bureaucracy as 'status and wealth-conferring'.[4] For people in the lower social strata however, colonial bureaucracy became a focal symbol of colonial powers' oppressive rule and also the preservation of the old hierarchical order.[5] Nationalist movements in the region had rejected the model of colonial bureaucracy but at the same time it also held appeal among the 'status-hungry, hierarchical Southeast Asia'.[6] The rapid bureaucratization in Southeast Asia in the 1870s would mark the beginning of a period of unrest and struggle for independence in the region.

The introduction of colonial laws was a means to rationalize relations between colonial authority, the European settlers and native inhabitants and would lean more towards the 'rule by law' than the rule of law. Colonial law was an essential component of colonial rule, acting not as a mechanism to constrain it, but a means to consolidate colonial rule and authority. With very few colonial personnel, the use of law was an extremely important tool which, for the first time, ushered a comprehensive use of a 'single' authoritative legal system that was superimposed on and regulated preexisting indigenous laws and traditions. In British colonies, law was imposed on the three main areas of stability and order, tax revenue and the flow of commerce. The use of law is a carefully laid out strategy which would promote stability rather than undermine colonial authority; colonial administration was cautious to create a fundamental

[4] Tony Day, *Fluid Iron: State Formation in Southeast Asia* (Honolulu: University of Hawaii Press, 2002), 198–200.

[5] Ibid., 213.

[6] Ibid., 189–91.

change in the colony's social and cultural foundations by adopting the policy of respecting indigenous customs and religions.[7]

The use of colonial laws – and the process of modernization – had its unintended consequences however. Laws and institutional arrangements either transformed existing social and political relations or created new ones, managed conflicts or gave rise to new problems, established the authority of state and its actors or encouraged challenges to authority. For instance, the residency system might have eroded the power of the Sultans but it also 'legitimized' their autonomy over matters of custom and religion that increasingly allowed them to foster the identification of Malay with Islam. This had the effect of awakening nationalism in the Malays and together with the perceived structural economic imbalance created during the colonial period, the privileging of the Malay race or '*bumiputera*' in terms of economic, educational and government service opportunities under the New Economic Policy (NEP) would be a salient component of the restructured social compact of postcolonial Malaysia.

5.2.1 The Rise of Authoritarian Regimes in ASEAN States

The re-emergence of authoritarian rule in postcolonial Southeast Asia in the late 1960s was driven by a confluence of factors that are both external and internal to the states. The evolution of distinctive institutional features of each Southeast Asian state can be explained by these influences. However by the 1970s, most regimes in the region, though professing adherence to constitutional democracy, had operated through an underlying state ideology that prioritizes 'communal goals' – the imperatives of unity and social order – over values of inclusive political participation and unfettered exercise of political rights. This is translated into a practice of formal democracy characterized by an ascendance or dominance of a single party and a strong executive virtually 'unrestrained' by law, and other state institutions backed by repressive security or military apparatus. The external factor is traced from the region's entanglement with the Cold War and attendant ideological alignment with the superpowers.[8] The formation of ASEAN in 1967 was in large part attributed to this phenomenon.

[7] John Schmidhauser, 'Legal Imperialism: Its Enduring Impact on Colonial and Post-Colonial Judicial Systems' (1992) 13(3) *International Political Science Review* 321–34, 323–4.

[8] See Malcolm H. Murfett (ed.), *Cold War Southeast Asia* (Singapore: Marshall Cavendish, 2012); Narayanan Ganesan, 'ASEAN's Relations with Major External Powers' (2000) 22(2) *Contemporary Southeast Asia* 258–78.

As an internal process, the rise of authoritarianism in the region can be traced back not from one factor but from the convergence of several elements. A recurrent theme in the literature is 'institutional continuity' which emphasizes the continuance of either or both traditional and colonial practices and structures.[9] The emerging state is seen as inheriting the bad features of precolonial and colonial values and institutions. For example, the weakness of the judicial institution in Indonesia has been traced from the inferior Indonesian side of the system, the *Laandrad*, which was mostly staffed with untrained personnel and local elites and operated through informal procedures and customs.[10] Thus it is observed that it was even easier to make a criminal conviction under the Indonesian side of court administration, which provided for simpler procedure and fewer protections against the authorities.[11] The British Residency system is also noted as the precursor of the strong executive in Malaysia where the State Council acting as the legislature was a mere rubber stamp, for it was the British Attorney General who drafted legislation which was approved by the Resident-General and Governor.[12] In the Philippines, the weak bureaucracy and low regard for the law can be traced to the 'rule by the friars', where Spanish clergy administered local government matters and were considered even more powerful than the Governor-Generals.[13]

The development of patrimonial elites and the powerful mobilizing role that nationalism, ethnicity and religion played in nation-state building had been – and continue to be so – influential in developing the strong state in the region. The persistence of elite domination and patrimonial rule – the patrimonial state – is a feature shared in common by most ASEAN states and regardless of the system of government adopted. This is characterized by the patterns of interpersonal relationship present in the politics and bureaucracies in Southeast Asia,[14] predominance of personal connections rather than rational–legal rule, values of particularism

[9] See Scott Fritzen, 'Public Administration' in Mark Beeson (ed.), *Contemporary Southeast Asia*, 2nd edn. (New York: Palgrave Macmillan, 2009), 74–89.

[10] Daniel S. Lev, 'Colonial Law and the Genesis of the Indonesian State' (1985) 40 *Indonesia* 57–74.

[11] Ibid., 59–61.

[12] Wu Min Aun, *An Introduction to the Malaysian Legal System* (Singapore: Heinemann Educational Books, 1975), 9–10.

[13] Hall, *A History of Southeast Asia*, 709–12.

[14] James Scott, 'Patron-Client Politics and Political Change in Southeast Asia' (1972) 66(1) *The American Political Science Review* 91–113; for discussion on kinship and personal networks, 'dyadic group', see Carl Lande, 'Networks and Groups in Southeast Asia: Some Observations on the Group Theory of Politics' (1973) 67(1) *The American Political Science Review* 103–27.

over universalism and the blurring of the line between private and public spheres of authority. In the economic sphere, a form of patronage capitalism known as 'crony capitalism' had emerged and cultivated a clique of business elites, usually from politically connected families, having a close relationship with state leaders.[15]

However, the formation of elites in Southeast Asia had varied. In Brunei Darussalam, the royal family continue to rule under an absolute monarchy. The Philippine elite developed from the landed families who expanded their power in politics and business, and subsequently the rise of business elites with close ties with the ruling elites.[16] The rise of bureaucratic elites is a feature shared by Thailand and Indonesia who played important roles in the transition from colonial to postcolonial rule.[17] There is a powerful military in many states in Southeast Asia that has exerted strong political influence, and at times power above that of the civilian authority at various stages in postcolonial state reconstruction. Military authority remains a feature of Thai and Myanmar politics. Party elites in Cambodia, Laos and Vietnam enjoy considerable power and privileges.[18] Conversely, Singapore is said to exhibit dominant features of 'corporatism', a state which is characterized as comprising an organic community but dominated by bureaucrats and technocrats acting for the state's interests rather than promoting a particular class interest.[19]

Nationalism or the project of nation-building had accompanied the rise of authoritarian rule. It has been observed that the more the governments became more authoritarian, the more they used nationalism to

[15] Tion Kwa, 'Different Shades of "Crony Capitalism": Not All Asian Values Are Alike' in Julian Weiss (ed.), *Tigers Roar: Asia's Recovery and Its Impact* (Armonk, New York: M.E. Sharpe, 2001), 84–7.

[16] See for example Edsel Beja, Jr., Ronald U. Mendoza, Victor S. Venida and David B. Yap, 'Inequality in Democracy: Insights from an Empirical Analysis of Political Dynasties in the 15th Philippine Congress' (Munich Personal RePEc Archive Paper No. 40104, Munich University, 15 July 2012), http://mpra.ub.uni-muenchen.de/40104/1/MPRA_paper_40104.pdf; Paul D. Hutchcroft, *Booty Capitalism: The Politics of Banking in the Philippines* (Ithaca: Cornell University Press, 1998), 13–31; Yuki Fukuoka, 'Demystifying "People Power": An Elite Interpretation of "Democratization" in Southeast Asia' in William Case (ed.), *Routledge Handbook of Southeast Asian Democratization* (London: Routledge, 2015), 85–101, 98.

[17] Daniel Lev, 'The Origins of the Indonesian Advocacy' in *Legal Evolution and Political Authority in Indonesia: Selected Essays* (The Hague: Kluwer Law International, 2000), 245 and 236.

[18] Martin Gainsborough, 'Elites vs Reform in Laos, Cambodia, and Vietnam' (2012) 23(2) *Journal of Democracy* 34–46, 39.

[19] David Brown, 'Ethnicity and Corporatism in Singapore' in *The State and Ethnic Politics in Southeast Asia* (London: Routledge, 1994), 67–75.

consolidate the regime instead of building the nation-state.[20] Elsewhere in Southeast Asia, newly formed governments embarked on the project of nationalism and construction of nationalist ideologies, which also became the rationale for distinct 'un-Western' processes of state-building. For instance, Singapore adopted a state ideology of 'survival'[21] as key to overcoming chronic poverty and underdevelopment in the midst of its economic and political expulsion from Malaysia in August 1965. This entailed promoting Singapore as an ideal foreign investments destination enjoying political stability, the absence of dissent and a pliant labour force.[22] Singapore's economic success and political stability have been flaunted as an alternative model of governance to developing countries which was anchored in its disdain of Western-style liberal democracy to a performance-based regime calling itself 'soft authoritarianism' or 'illiberal democracy' to others.[23]

The rule of law in Southeast Asia has necessarily followed a particular vision of a new polity and in responding to the homogenizing – often competing – forces of nation-state building. The issue of multiethnicity has been confronted by Southeast Asian states within the prism of varying nationalist conceptions; the state itself anchored its legitimacy in the identity of the nation. Where the idea of the nation did not immediately coincide with the notion of an 'imagined community' or the existence of shared community of interests such as language, ethnicity, culture or religion,[24] the project of state-building project became the means of creating the nation. This had impacted on claims of distinct values, norms and self-determination, matters that persist in the modern states and re-emerge in national discourse on central-regional/local relation or in the reappearance of conflicts among different ethnic or religious groups. As 'nation-statehood' became a contested process, it produced and built

[20] Nicolas Tarling, *Nationalism in Southeast Asia: 'If the People are with Us'* (Oxon: Routledge Curzon, 2004), 195–6.

[21] Melanie Chew, 'Human Rights in Singapore: Perceptions and Problems' (1994) 34(11) *Asian Survey* 939–41.

[22] See Harold Crouch, *Domestic Political Structures and Regional Economic Cooperation* (Singapore: Institute of Southeast Asian Studies, 1984), 14; Also Chan Heng Chee, *The Dynamics of One Party Dominance: The PAP at the Grass-roots* (Singapore: Singapore University Press, 1976), 205–6.

[23] Hussien Mutalib, 'Illiberal Democracy and the Future of Opposition in Singapore' (2000) 21(2) *Third World Quarterly* 313–38.

[24] See, for example, the seminal work by Benedict Anderson, *Imagined Communities: Reflections on the Origin and Spread of Nationalism*, revised edn. (London: Verso, 1991).

inequalities which are reproduced in state institutions and bureaucracy, including the rule of law.[25]

5.3 A Typology of Law Regimes in ASEAN States

The way the state and its apparatuses interact with society give us a glimpse or tendencies in which law has functioned to regulate or constrain the power of the state. As we have shown, the task of nation-state building became the salient function of and the key source of power for many states in ASEAN, perhaps excepting Brunei and Thailand whose monarchies have remained strong and the basis of the states' legitimacy or of sovereignty in itself. The nation-state building project has given the states the resources, ideology as well as the means to organize powerful military establishments to implement the state's task of maintaining order and stability.[26]

In the typology below, we take off from Mann's concept of state power through the functions it performs and the way it gains autonomy from the society's power.[27] The two variables are state power and civil society power. The former refers to state power gained through its state-building function and the way it deploys resources internal to it and that of society's to achieve this goal while civil society power refers to the extent general members of society are able to participate in their views of building the nation-state. The 'threats' to the integrity of the state in Southeast Asia which were addressed mainly through the process of territorialization, centralization and creation of national ideology have been perceived by states' elites as either external or internal, or both. External threats have come from either external powers' interference as in the Cold War, territorial disputes among ASEAN states or its neighbours including threats of use of force to resolve these disputes.

Internal threats have mostly come from the perception that politics – especially the divisive and violent ones – undermined the stability and integrity of the state and provided the justification for arbitrary or unconstrained state power. In recent times, internal threats have come from

[25] Sallie Westwood, 'Unequal Nations: Race, Citizen and the Politics of Recognition' in Mary Romero and Eric Margolis (eds.), *The Blackwell Companion to Social Inequalities* (Malden: Blackwell Publishing, 2005), 50–74, 51–6.

[26] See Michael Mann, 'The Autonomous Power of the State: Its Origins, Mechanisms and Results' (1984) 25(2) *European Journal of Sociology* 185–213.

[27] Ibid.

secessionist movements claiming their right to self-determination or autonomy arising from distinctive history and culture and state of marginalization from central authority. At the extreme are the emergence of 'terror' groups which use violence as means to undermine the state's territorial integrity and the centrality of the state. The capacity of society, including the marginalized groups, to participate in meaningful ways in state-building can be determined by how state and state elites have calibrated their position on civil society participation and inclusion. This can be triggered by external pressure, but mostly by internal dynamics that may include inter-elite rivalries and emergence of civil society groups.

In Figure 5.1, we build four 'ideal types' to which laws and institutional arrangements have tended to limit or enable state power in the region. These typologies also correspond to the various regime types in the region and reflect how law functions in each regime or the extent to which they are law regime. The main proposition is that state power and civil society power are locked in constant tension but can also be in the state of cooperation. A high level of capacity for civil society means that they may also have a capacity for cooperation – or opposition – with state building initiatives. A high level of state building function shows a high degree of state's assertiveness for centralization and thus the requirement for law's enabling force. A low civil society power intersecting with high state centralizing power can produce at least two scenarios. First, it can trigger rule

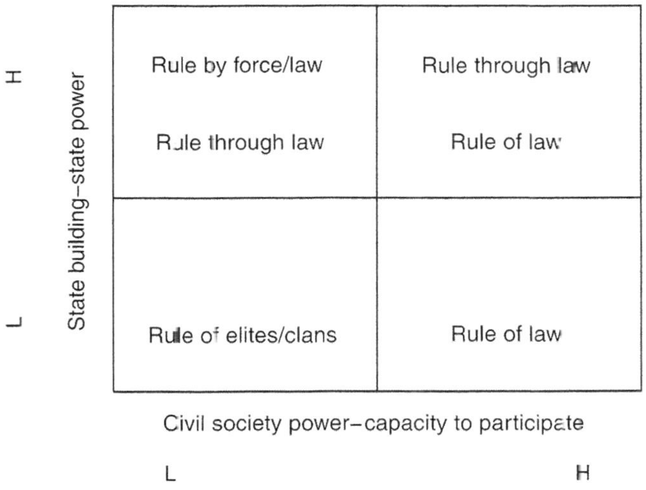

Figure 5.1 Typology of law regimes in Southeast Asia

by force as a means to subdue civil society's capacity to articulate alternative views or demand inclusion. Law is a means to enforce state authority and penetrate society, especially since the use of violence is not a sustainable means of ruling. Thus rule by force is often accompanied by use of arbitrary laws and since the regime is unconstrained by law or other social mechanisms and is unaccountable, the regime is often despotic. This type of regime was characteristic of authoritarian rule or dictatorships in Indonesia, the Philippines and Thailand before democratization in the 1980s, and of Myanmar until the democratization process began in the last few years.[28] This regime however may be genuinely motivated by strong economic redistributive goals and may tend to give the general population more economic freedom and opportunities; this regime however still exerts tight political control, and can still use force, over a generally weaker civil society. This is rule through law, as the regime can be more tolerant of alternative vision of economic development and has lower propensity to use force. This type tends to be characteristic of Singapore which has maintained one-party rule but more liberal economic freedom and accountability for its economic rule. To some extent, we can also argue that Vietnam and Laos, ruled through a vision of socialist ideology but embracing features of economic liberalism, are aspiring towards this law regime type. Both low level of state and civil society power look less of a law regime, which is likened to a period in the medieval era where particular families or clans or particular elites rule in often competing and alternating fashion.[29] In postcolonial Southeast Asia, this feature was demonstrated early on during postcolonial reconstruction where specific class or families vied for positions of state power.

The ideal type of 'rule of law', characterized by a constrained and accountable state, can only emerge in a situation where there is high civil society power, as shown in the figure. This can be realized in either high or low state power. In high state power, intersecting with high civil society power can result in either the ideal type of rule of law or the rule through law. It is possible to produce a rule of law type in this scenario where there is an authoritative neutral mechanism to mediate both high demands of state and civil society powers. In its absence, one force may exert over

[28] Morten Pedersen, *Understanding Myanmar's Democratic Opening* (3 April 2013) East Asia Forum, www.eastasiaforum.org/2013/04/03/understanding-myanmars-democratic-opening/

[29] See Mark S. Weiner, *The Rule of the Clan: What an Ancient Form of Social Organisation Reveals About the Future of Individual Freedom* (New York: Farrar, Straus and Giroux, 2013).

the other such as when the military takes over the civil government in Thailand or when civil society stages a 'people power revolution' in the Philippines and could result in deep polarization in society. In this latter scenario, law can either be used to legitimate authority and to regulate civil society behaviour in the political arena.

As history had shown, the ascendancy of civil society power in the power struggle with state and elites often resulted in constitutional arrangements promoting the rule of law. This is the low state power achieved immediately after democratization in Indonesia, the Philippines and Thailand in the 1980s but this has been a transient condition at best as when state elites reconsolidate their power or new state security challenges emerge that provides justification for the resurgence of a strong state. As shown in Thailand, there is a delicate balance between state and civil society powers that is 'necessary' to maintain; the emergence of a strong civil society coupled with the election of a popular civil ruler may upset the balance of power that is centred in the monarchy. As a space to which society's forces and values converge, most states in the region are 'insecure' and a high degree of insecurity has always propelled state elites, either out of altruism or self-interest, to bolster state's power over civil society. Sources, or perception, of insecurity to the states range from threats to territorial cohesion such as that of partition of Vietnam in the 1960s,[30] interethnic conflict that happened in postcolonial Indonesia,[31] challenges to central authority as the Philippines' communist insurgency or Muslim rebellion,[32] territorial disputes among ASEAN states[33] and, in recent years, the threats of radical Islam or forms of religious or cultural intolerance.[34]

Insecurity arising from economic underdevelopment however can trigger a range of responses from the state or state elites. As happened in the 1960s to 1970s, the developmental state model was accompanied by repressive rule as the state took the lead in steering the economy towards

[30] See Damodar SarDesai, *Vietnam: The Struggle for National Identity*, 2nd edn. (Boulder: Westview Press, 1992).

[31] See Jacques Bertrand, *Nationalism and Ethnic Conflict in Indonesia* (Cambridge: Cambridge University Press, 2004).

[32] See Mark Thompson, 'Off the Endangered List: Philippine Democratisation in Comparative Perspective' (1996) 28(2) *Comparative Politics* 179–205.

[33] See Lee Yong Leng, *The Razor's Edge: Boundaries and Boundary Dispute in Southeast Asia* (Singapore: Institute of Southeast Asian Studies, 1980).

[34] See Bernhard Platzdasch and Johan Saravanamuttu (eds.), *Religious Diversity in Muslim-Majority States in Southeast Asia: Areas of Toleration and Conflict* (Singapore: Institute of Southeast Asian Studies, 2014).

progress. With the exception of Singapore and to a certain extent Malaysia, this developmental paradigm did not deliver on its promise, benefitted only a few and caused massive human rights violations. This provided the impetus for civil society movements or activism in many countries in the region. As the Asian financial crisis ravaged the once 'robust' Southeast Asian liberal market economies, state elites had been overthrown or replaced by new elite players, or that a platform to renegotiate state–society relations was generated to craft a social compact in the form of new constitutions.[35] The process of constitutionalization brought about the salience of the rule of law – at least in theory, as a constraint to arbitrary power and the evil it brings, or as an authoritative arbiter of significant political disputes that provoke political instability and hamper economic development.

5.4 Constitutional Developments and Law Regime Types in ASEAN States

A strong push towards economic liberalism as the answer to economic – and political – insecurity helped in facilitating the emergence of a general consensus on the importance of some form of legal and institutional constraints to absolute rule. The rise of the urban middle class – consisting of loosely organized aggrupation of the educated, professional and business sector – became the countervailing social force and source of alternative models of governing.[36] Despite the wide diversity in the political and legal systems in the region, we can say that rule by force – though not completely eliminated – has increasingly been giving way to rule through law and in some countries the trend towards the rule of law. The salience of law as a function of governing provides a window of opportunity to move the political culture we described in the preceding sections towards peaceful and inclusive resolution of issues that affect the security of the state. The following discussion provides a brief discussion of constitutional developments in ASEAN states and to see how economic policies have evolved in these countries in relation to the changing law regimes.

[35] See Björn Dressel and Marco Bünte, 'Constitutional Politics in Southeast Asia: From Contestation to Constitutionalism?' (April 2014) 36(1) *Contemporary Southeast Asia: A Journal of International and Strategic Affairs* 1–22.

[36] See Takashi Shiraishi, 'The Third Wave: Southeast Asia and Middle-Class Formation in the Making of a Region' in Peter J. Katzenstein and Takashi Shiraishi (eds.), *Beyond Japan: The Dynamics of East Asian Regionalism* (Ithaca: Cornell University Press, 2006), 237–71.

5.4.1 Constitutional Democracy in Indonesia and the Philippines and Rapid Economic Growth

Both Indonesia and the Philippines are considered to belong to the fastest growing economies in the region, and in Asia in general at the moment.[37] This economic growth momentum has coincided with the political change that happened since post-authoritarian regimes. However, whether those changes directly correlate with economic performance of these two countries is an area that needs further empirical research. Constitutional democracy, based on separation of powers and multi-party democracy, has been enshrined in Indonesia and the Philippines after turbulent political upheavals in these countries. Arguably, these are the two countries in ASEAN which come closer to – or developing towards – the ideal 'rule of law' regime type. After more than 20 years of repressive authoritarian rule backed by a politically influential military, these two countries enshrined constitutional democracy in their constitutions with a strong emphasis on the rule of law as a bulwark against the resurgence of rule by force.

It was against the backdrop of abject marginalization of law (Guided Democracy under Sukarno and Pancasila Democracy under Suharto) and concentration of state powers in the hands of the President that the Indonesian *reformasi* or Reformation movement in Indonesia was anchored on and led towards democratization.[38] Democratization, human rights and constitutional change are the platform for the new Indonesian republic seeking to reestablish *negara hokum* and *trias politika* (separation of powers). From 19 October 1999 and until 2004, key amendments were introduced in the 1945 Indonesian Constitution that would put the country back towards democratic rule and to curb the military's strong influence and role in political affairs (*dwifungzi*).[39] The unbridled power of an authoritarian rule in the Philippines under former President Ferdinand

[37] Indonesia is the largest economy in ASEAN while the Philippines continues to perform robustly rivalling China's growth rate. See BBC News, *Indonesia Country Profile* (7 September 2015) www.bbc.com/news/world-asia-pacific-14921238; The Economist, *The Philippine Economy: Coming Up Jasmine* (23 August 2014) www.economist.com/news/finance-and-economics/21613336-once-laggard-economy-philippines-starting-catch-up-coming-up

[38] Edward Aspinall and Greg Fealy, *Local Power and Politics in Indonesia: Decentralisation and Democratisation* (Singapore: Institute of Southeast Asian Studies, 2003), 1–12.

[39] Marcus Mietzner, *Military Politics, Islam, and the State in Indonesia: From Turbulent Transition to Democratic Consolidation* (Singapore: Institute of Southeast Asian Studies, 2009), 195–250.

Marcos and its excesses precipitated mass demonstrations known as the EDSA People Power revolution in February 1986 that removed Marcos and his cronies from power. A consequence of this was the promulgation of a democratic 1987 Philippine Constitution which, similar to Indonesia's amended constitution, was a product of broad public deliberation and consultation.

The democratic constitutions in Indonesia and the Philippines are clearly a response to decades of authoritarian rule and therefore the framers saw the wisdom in limiting executive powers, strengthening checks and balances among the three key institutions of state power (the executive, legislature and the judiciary) and providing adequate legal protection for the enjoyment of individual rights. While the Indonesian Constitution has retained *Pancasila* Democracy, the principle of a unitary state based on belief in one God, humanity, unity, deliberation for representation and social justice for all Indonesians,[40] its significance remains that of Indonesia's historical symbol for its struggle for independence. A fundamental change in the constitution was that the Indonesian state is based on the rule of law and assured the supremacy of the law and of the constitution as the highest law of the land.[41] A limited presidency directly elected by the people, a robust lawmaking power of the legislature and guarantee for an independent judiciary are now key features of this parliamentary democracy. Conversely, the 1987 Philippine Constitution has also erected a strong constitutional barrier to the resurgence of authoritarian rule in the Philippines. A presidential form of government and with a president directly elected by the people and no lawmaking powers has been enshrined in the Constitution. A declaration of a state of emergency in exceptional circumstances is subject to parliamentary approval and also judicial review.[42] Judicial power has been enhanced in the new constitution that allows the Supreme Court to invalidate government acts and that of its institutions and test the legality of government decisions against the constitution.[43]

The emergence of relatively independent and activist review courts in the Philippines and Indonesia has assisted in the development of a rule of law regime and consolidation of democratic gains in these two countries.

[40] Constitution of the Republic of Indonesia (last amended 2002) [1945], preamble and art. 281(5).

[41] Ibid., art. 1(3).

[42] Constitution of the Republic of the Philippines [1987], art. 18.

[43] Ibid., art. 6, s. 23(1).

The Supreme Court of the Philippines contributed in political stabilization by providing authoritative decisions to political conflicts and popular change in governments. Aided by public support, the Philippine Supreme Court resisted attempts at democratic rollbacks such as moves to change the presidential term limits and imposition of emergency powers, and the protection of fundamental freedoms.[44] Similarly, the Indonesian Constitutional Court has emerged as a competent 'guardian of the Constitution', the most professional judicial institution, and at the forefront of democratic transition to usher Indonesia as the most democratic country in the region.[45]

Between the two countries, Indonesia experienced a relatively smooth transition to democratic rule except for a brief crisis in 2001 that led to the impeachment of President Abdurrahman Wahid.[46] Fierce inter-elite rivalry and political factionalism in the Philippines had resulted in several military coup attempts and extraconstitutional change of governments under the administration of Corazon Aquino in the late 1980s and during the terms of Presidents Joseph Estrada and Gloria Macapagal Arroyo between 2004 and 2010. Even the Supreme Court became embroiled in political partisanship that resulted in the successful impeachment of Chief Justice Renato Corona in 2011. In Indonesia, the moral integrity and innovative reasoning of the members of the Constitutional Court had weathered attempts to curb its powers in 2011 by the DPR, the supreme lawmaking body in the country, and generated respect by the political actors for its decisions.[47] Lower courts and many government bureaucracies however in these two countries are still generally seen as corrupt and inefficient.[48]

[44] See Imelda Deinla, 'Public Support and Judicial Empowerment of the Philippine Supreme Court' (2014) 36(1) *Contemporary Southeast Asia: A Journal of International and Strategic Affairs* 128–58.

[45] Simon Butt and Tim Lindsey, *The Constitution of Indonesia: A Contextual Analysis* (Oxford: Hart Publishing, 2012), 156–7; Marcus Mietzner, 'Political Conflict Resolution and Democratic Consolidation in Indonesia: The Role of the Constitutional Court' (2010) 10(3) *Journal of East Asia Studies* 397–419.

[46] To defend his position, President Wahid called on the Indonesian Armed Forces (TNI) to support him in the conflict with the DPR/MPR which approved his impeachment following allegations of massive corruption known as 'Bulogate' and 'Bruneigate'.

[47] Donald Horowitz, *Constitutional Change and Democracy in Indonesia* (Cambridge: Cambridge University Press, 2013), 243.

[48] On Indonesian lower courts, see Butt and Lindsey, *Constitution of Indonesia*; Surveys done by Makati Business Club consistently showed Philippine lower courts as among the lowest ranked government agencies in terms of efficiency and credibility.

5.4.2 Restrained Democracy in Singapore, Malaysia, Cambodia, Myanmar and Thailand

These four countries are discussed together as espousing a form of controlled democracy in the sense that political contestation and state powers are highly regulated or exercised by or through law or other forms of social control. In these five countries, the enabling power of the law is the defining character of their legal regimes. They all espouse constitutional democracy and subscribe to the principle of separation of powers and the institution of the judiciary. In one form or another, all of these countries provide for judicial review powers that can pass or rule on the constitutionality or legality of government actions. Myanmar, Thailand and Cambodia have separate constitutional courts or bodies that have powers to rule on the relationship among state institutions as well as of political disputes.

In Thailand, development towards the rule of law has stymied with two successive *coup d'ëtats* in 2006 and 2014 that rolled back constitutionalism following the institution of the democratic 1997 Constitution. Known as the 'people's constitution', the 1997 Constitution was meant to address the vicious cycle of *coup* by the military that is a constant feature of Thai politics since the overthrow of absolute monarchy in the 1932 rebellion.[49] This cycle is characterized by a succession of constitutions, revival of political parties, parliamentary elections, a honeymoon period and a crisis leading to another coup.[50] The establishment of the Constitutional Court and Administrative Court under the 1997 Constitution, the former to decide constitutional issues and conflicts or overlap of authorities of major constitutional institutions, and the second to adjudicate on disputes between ordinary citizens and public officials, was meant as a new social compact to promote transparency and accountability of the political system and the stability and effectiveness of government.[51] The Constitutional Court is generally well-regarded because of its well-reasoned decisions although some highly controversial decisions may not be regarded as independent

[49] Chaowana Traimas and Jochen Hoerth, 'Thailand: Another New Constitution as a Way Out of the Vicious Cycle?' in Clauspeter Hill and Jörg Menzel (eds.), *Constitutionalism in Southeast Asia* (Singapore: Konrad-Adenauer-Stiftung, 2008), 301–25.

[50] Muthiah Alagappa, 'Asian Civil-Military Relations: Key Developments, Explanations and Trajectories' in Muthiah Alagappa (ed.), *Coercion and Governance* (Stanford: Stanford University Press, 2001), 433–98, 461–2.

[51] See Thitinan Pongsudhirak, 'Thailand Since the Coup' (2008) 19(4) *Journal of Democracy* 140–53, 141.

given the political contexts of the cases.[52] However, the Constitutional Court was dissolved following the 2006 coup that removed the elected government of Thaksin Shinawatra, reestablished as a Constitutional Tribunal and reinstituted as a Constitutional Court in the 2007 Constitution.[53] There have been 20 charters or constitutions between 1932 and 2016 which reflects the supremacy of political forces that is reflected in the constitutional power arrangements.[54] A new Thai Constitution 2016 was approved in a plebiscite that is largely seen to entrench the role of the military and military-constituted National Council for Peace and Order in the government long after the 2014 coup led by General Prayuth Chan-ocha.[55]

Myanmar is undergoing remarkable transition to a new democratic regime after more than 40 years of absolute military rule from 1962 to 2011. The 2008 Constitution that ushered democratization enshrines the leading role that the *Tatmadaw* (the military) has in the new state and into the democratization process that is outlined in the democratic roadmap.[56] Prescribing a form of guided democracy, the Constitution itself states as one of the key objectives of the Burmese Union the 'flourishing of a genuine, disciplined multiparty democratic system'.[57] The military's role as protector of country and the Constitution is assured through the reserved seats at the National Legislative Assembly (Pyidaungsu Hluttaw),[58] reserved powers to take over and control the affairs of the state in a state of emergency[59] and exclusive authority to administer its own affairs.[60] The democratization process began in 2011 points to credible commitment by the military and key political actors towards full democratic transition, although the path is still uneven and requires a delicate balance among the

52 Andrew Harding and Peter Leyland, *The Constitutional System of Thailand: A Contextual Analysis* (Oxford: Hart Publishing, 2011), 159–72.

53 Thitinan Pongsudhirak, 'Thailand: Democratic Authoritarianism' in Daljit Singh and Chin Kin Wah (eds.), *Southeast Asian Affairs 2003* (Singapore: Institute of Southeast Asian Studies, 2003), 277–90, 277.

54 See Nidhi Eoseewong, 'The Thai Cultural Constitution' (2003) 3 *Kyoto Review of Southeast Asia*.

55 Al Jazeera, *Thailand Referendum: New Constitution Wins Approval* (8 August 2016), www.aljazeera.com/news/2016/08/thailand-referendum-vote-favor-constitution-160807120506423.html

56 Roadmap to Discipline-Flourishing Democracy was announced by military junta leader General Khin Nyunt on 30 August 2003.

57 Constitution of the Republic of the Union of Myanmar [2008], arts. 6(d) and 7.

58 Ibid., arts. 109 and 141.

59 Ibid., art. 40(b) and (c).

60 Ibid., art. 20(b).

various social forces.[61] A civilian-led government was returned to power after a landslide victory for the National League of Democracy (NLD) in November 2016 and allowed a *de facto* state leadership role for Aung San Suu Kyi as State Counsellor. The establishment of an independent and effective court system in Myanmar and the rule of law may need more time to develop and the imperatives of fostering a culture for law, given the long history of rule by force.[62]

Singapore and Malaysia are the most developed countries in ASEAN with per capita incomes comparable to the Western countries.[63] Having a common colonial historical tradition, Malaysia and Singapore have followed a similar path to statehood and in coping with the problems of state reconstruction. In the same vein, they have adopted a law regime that assures executive dominance of state power and where all other branches, the legislature and judiciary, consistently support and toe the line of the executive branch. The variation lies in the form but the results are almost the same. Malaysia, owing to its cultural roots, has instituted a federal constitutional monarchy, the *Yang di-Pertuan Agong*,[64] which when compared to their Thai contemporary has a purely ceremonial function. Both countries uphold the common-law British tradition of parliamentary supremacy. Malaysia has a bicameral legislature whose lower house, the *Dewan Rakyat*, elects the prime minister. Singapore has a unicameral assembly which is also responsible in electing the prime minister.

[61] Morten Pedersen, *The Real Threat to Democracy in Myanmar* (26 February 2013) The Fletcher Forum of World Affairs, www.fletcherforum.org/home/2016/8/24/the-real-threat-to-democracy-in-myanmar; Peter Chalk, *On the Path of Change: Political, Economic and Social Challenges for Myanmar* (Special Report, Australian Strategic Policy Institute, December 2013); Renaud Egreteau, 'Soldiers as Lawmakers?: Assessing the New Legislative Role of the Burmese Armed Forces (2010–15)' in Renaud Egreteau and Francois Robinne (eds.), *Metamorphosis: Studies in Social and Political Change in Myanmar* (Singapore: National University of Singapore Press, 2015), 15–42, 27.

[62] Melissa Crouch, 'The Judiciary in Myanmar: Beyond Reform?' (Research Paper No. 2016-10, University of New South Wales, 2016); Nick Cheesman, 'What Does the Rule of Law Have to Do With Democratization (in Myanmar)?' (2014) 22(2) *South East Asia Research* 213–32.

[63] See William Huff, *The Economic Growth of Singapore: Trade and Development in the Twentieth Century* (Cambridge: Cambridge University Press, 1994); Zubair Hasan, 'Fifty Years of Malaysian Economic Development: Policies and Achievements' (2007) 11(2) *Review of Islamic Economics* 101–18.

[64] The *Yang di Pertuan Agong* is, under the Malaysian Constitution, the supreme head of the federation of Malaysia, which following the Westminster model, exercised executive power only upon the advice of the Prime Minister. It is a position that is rotated every five years among the nine traditional rulers of the Malay states forming a Conference of Rulers.

Between the two countries, Singapore has a firmer and relatively peaceful hold on state power which is in part attributed to the development of a prosperous polity, a modern economy and political leadership less prone to corruption.[65] In large measure – and similar to that in Malaysia – it is also ascribed to tight control of activities of the opposition and civil society through laws and regulations on media and exercise of fundamental rights such as liberty, speech and assembly or association. These are reflected in Singapore's International Security Act (1960), Newspaper and Printing Presses Act (1974), Societies Act (1966) and other legislation that even preclude judicial review of acts or decisions made by the executive save only in regard to questions on procedural requirements.[66] Through these laws that enable the government to detain persons for indefinite length of time and the use of defamation suits that can bankrupt an individual through award of astronomical sums of money, the opposition has practically been neutered in the city-state.[67] The People's Action Party (PAP) in Singapore continues its one-party dominance since 1965; the last elections on 15 September 2015 allowed the party to widen its supermajority by winning 83 out of 89 seats.[68]

Unlike Singapore, Malaysia has not been insulated from the emergence of reform movement (*reformasi*) driven by a politically active middle class. While Malaysia had enjoyed a pliant citizenry under the iron hand of Mahathir Mohamad after the brutal suppression of the race riots in 1969, the 1988 *reformasi* continues to galvanize broader call for democratization and the linkup between civil society and opposition resulted in gradual erosion of the *Barisan National*, a coalition of parties led by the United Malays National Organization (UMNO), supermajority in parliament.[69] Issues of

[65] The Economist, *Lee Kuan Yew's Singapore* (22 May 2015), www.economist.com/blogs/graphicdetail/2015/03/lee-kuan-yews-singapore

[66] See for example the Employment Act (1996), s. 14(5); 'Administrative and Constitutional Law' (2003) *Singapore Academy of Law Annual Review 2003* 1–12.

[67] Leading opposition leaders like Chee Soon Juan and J. B. Jeyaretnam have been bankrupted. See The Economist, *Performance Legitimacy* (18 July 2015), www.economist.com/news/special-report/21657608-when-it-comes-elections-pap-leaves-little-possible-chance-performance. Recently, there has been tightening of internet control and prosecution of bloggers. See Austin Ramzy, *Singapore Court Wants Teenage Blogger Held for Psychiatric Review* (23 June 2015) New York Times, www.nytimes.com/2015/06/24/world/asia/singapore-court-wants-teenage-blogger-amos-yee-held-for-psychiatric-review.html?_r=0

[68] The Economist, *Singapore's Incumbent Power Wins a Striking Mandate* (12 September 2015), www.economist.com/news/asia/21664546-men-white-take-familiar-bow-singapores-incumbents-win-back-huge-majority

[69] In both the 2008 and 2013 elections, *Barisan National* lost its two-thirds hold on power and popular vote but retained its majority seat in parliament.

corruption, cronyism and nepotism that had been muted in the past have been exposed, such as those involving massive corruption in government-controlled financial institutions that suggest the participation of high-ranking government officials and Mahathir's family[70] and recently that of the massive corruption scandal involving Prime Minister Najib Razak.[71] Despite promises of current administration of Najib Razak to reform the dreaded Internal Security Law (1960), the government continues to use repressive measures to arrest opposition leaders and activists.[72] There has been targeted filing of seemingly innocuous nonpolitical crimes thrown at political leaders and critics that enabled authorities to lock people in jail and prevent them from running in elections.[73]

Both countries – Singapore and Malaysia – enjoy a relatively positive perception of the observance of the rule of law in respect to economic governance when compared to other ASEAN countries.[74] However, judiciaries in these countries also have a reputation for lack of independence in dealing with political cases, particularly adopting the technique of formal or strict legalism to sustain government bodies in cases involving the opposition or critics or those questioning the validity of official acts.[75]

[70] Tunku Abdul Aziz, 'Malaysia Incorporated: Ethics on Trial' (1999) 58(4) *Australian Journal of Public Administration* 19–25.

[71] Tom Wright and Simon Clark, *Investigators Believe Money Flowed to Malaysian Leader Najib's Accounts Amid 1MDB Probe* (2 July 2015) The Wall Street Journal, www.wsj.com/articles/SB10130211234592774869404581083700187014570

[72] ABC News, *Leading Human Rights Activist Among Dozens Arrested in Malaysia after May Day Protest* (2 May 2015), www.abc.net.au/news/2015-05-02/rights-activists-opposition-politicians-arrested-in-malaysia/6440154

[73] For example, the repeated filing of sodomy charges against Anwar Ibrahim is believed to be politically motivated. See Human Rights Watch, *World Report 2015: Malaysia: Events of 2014*, www.hrw.org/world-report/2015/country-chapters/malaysia; The Economist, *Malaysia's Dark Side* (14 February 2015), www.economist.com/news/asia/21643227-jailing-anwar-ibrahim-setback-whole-country-not-just-opposition-malaysias

[74] The World Bank has developed a benchmark on the rule of law based, in particular, on the quality of contract enforcement, the police, courts and the likelihood of crime and violence. See Daniel Kaufmann, Aart Kraay and Massimo Mastruzzi, 'Governance Matters VIII: Aggregate and Individual Governance Indicators 1996–2008' (Policy Research Working Paper No. 4978, The World Bank, June 2009). Singapore and Malaysia have garnered high percentile scores in rule of law and corruption index, with Singapore achieving one of the highest ranking of all countries polled.

[75] See Kelley Bryan, *Rule of Law in Singapore: Independence of the Judiciary and the Legal Profession in Singapore* (17 October 2007) Lawyers' Rights Watch Canada, www.lrwc.org/ws/wp-content/uploads/2012/03/LRWC.Rule_.of_.Law_.in_.Singapore.17.Oct_.07.pdf; Kanishka Jayasuriya, 'Introduction: A Framework for the Analysis of Legal Institutions in East Asia' in Kanishka Jayasuriya (ed.) *Law, Capitalism and Power in Asia: The Rule of Law and Legal Institutions* (London: Routledge, 1999), 1–27, 20.

In Malaysia, there have been very few cases where the judiciary decided against the state and its bureaucracy not on the basis of substance but on procedural infirmities which were also cured by enacting subsequent legislation or by amending the constitution.[76] Constitutional amendments in the two countries can also be easily done, requiring only a two-third vote in parliament to approve the changes, which is a reflection of the superiority of the party.[77]

Cambodia's 1993 Constitution is the outcome of political settlement, known as the Paris Peace Agreement 1993, which ended decades of civil war among various political forces.[78] It instituted a constitutional monarchy and the principle of separation of powers in a tripartite form of government with an executive, bicameral legislature (the Senate and National Assembly), and an independent judicial institution.[79] Having experienced episodes of horrific atrocities and with the participation of the United Nations and external powers in the peace settlement, the Constitution provided for a catalogue of fundamental rights and freedoms contained in Universal Declaration of Human rights and other international human rights instruments.[80] A Constitutional Council has also been provided that can decide electoral disputes, interpret constitutional provisions and determine the constitutionality of laws and of government acts. The Council can be accessed by the state officials such as the Prime Minister, the Senate and National Assembly. In theory, an individual can request the Supreme Court to bring a request for review before the Council but in practice, no such individual motion has reached the Council.[81]

The Cambodian judiciary is largely perceived to be weak and not independent.[82] Practically removed and supplanted by security networks during

76 Khoo Boo Teik, 'Between Law and Politics, The Malaysian judiciary since independence' in Jayasuriya (ed.), *Law, Capitalism and Power in Asia*, 208–10.

77 See Federal Constitution of Malaysia [1957], cl. 4A; Constitution of the Republic of Singapore [1965], art. 5.

78 Office of the High Commissioner for Human Rights, *Cambodia – 20 Years on from the Paris Peace Agreements* (21 October 2011), www.ohchr.org/EN/NewsEvents/Pages/Cambodia-20yearsonfromtheParisPeace.aspx

79 Constitution of the Kingdom of Cambodia [1993], art. 51.

80 Ibid., art. 31.

81 Ibid., art. 141; The Khmer Institute of Democracy, *The Constitutional Council*, www.khmerrough.com/pdf/CriticalThinking-Eng/Part2-CriticalThinking.pdf, 19.

82 Human Rights Watch, *World Report 2015: Cambodia: Events of 2014*, www.hrw.org/world-report/2015/country-chapters/Cambodia; Chandra Lekha Sriram, *Globalizing Justice for Mass Atrocities: A Revolution in Accountability* (London: Routledge, 2005), 92.

the dreaded Khmer Rouge regime (1975–9),[83] the judiciary continues to suffer from lack of credibility from the public owing to a combination of lack of resources, institutional weaknesses and external interference.[84] The courts are perceived to be biased towards party members belonging to the ruling party, the Cambodian People's Party (CPP), under Prime Minister Hun Sen, and used to persecute opposition members on trumped-up or unfair charges.[85] Courts are perceived to be as powerless in the political as in the economic, contributing to the perpetuation of impunity for political violence as are lack of capacity to provide remedy against corruption of government officials and abuses on land transactions or violation of labour rights.[86] The judiciary is perceived to be under-institutionalized and highly politicized and remains under tight control of the CPP which also appoints most judges and prosecutors.[87]

5.4.3 Constitutional Socialism in Vietnam and Laos and Absolute Monarchy in Brunei Darussalam

The grouping in this section among the countries of Vietnam, Laos and Brunei Darussalam (Brunei) is not meant to diminish the diversity among these countries but merely to show how they diverge in some measure from the declared 'constitutional democracy' in the rest of the countries in ASEAN already discussed above. In fact Brunei, owing to its enormous oil and gas reserves and small population, has one of the highest per capita incomes in the world.[88] Vietnam and Laos follow socialism as an ideology

[83] A socialist regime that removed all vestiges of Cambodia's past social fabric, separated families eradicated the educated class and forced people to move into rural areas under forced labour. See Ben Kiernan, *The Pol Pot Regime: Race, Power, and Genocide in Cambodia under the Khmer Rouge, 1975–79*, 3rd edn. (New Haven: Yale University Press, 2008).

[84] Subedi, Surya P., Report of the Special Rapporteur on the Situation of Human Rights in Cambodia, UN Doc A/HRC/27/70 (15 August 2014).

[85] See New York Times, *Cambodia's Subservient Judiciary* (6 June 2014), www.nytimes.com/2014/06/07/opinion/cambodias-subservient-judiciary.html?_r=0

[86] Kheang Un, 'The Judicial System and Democratisation in Post-Conflict Cambodia' in Joakim Öjendal and Mona Lilja (eds.), *Beyond Democracy in Cambodia: Political Reconstruction in a Post-Conflict Society* (Copenhagen: Nordic Institute of Asian Studies Press, 2009), 70–101.

[87] Sorpong Peou, 'Human Security in Post-Cold War Cambodia' in Brendan Howe (ed.), *Post-Conflict Development in East Asia* (New York: Routledge, 2016), 117–36, 128.

[88] OECD, 'Structural Policy Country Notes: Brunei Darussalam' in Organisation for Economic Co-operation and Development, *Economic Outlook for Southeast Asia, China and India: Enhancing Regional Ties* (Paris: OECD Publishing, 2016), http://dx.doi.org/10.1787/saeo-2014-en, 2.

underlying their political and legal orders, while Brunei also proclaims a form of state ideology called the MIB (Melayu Islam Beraja or Malay Muslim Monarchy) which emphasizes culture and monarchy functioning both as a code of conduct and as a way of life for the Bruneians.[89] Since 1962 when an armed uprising was suppressed with the assistance of the British forces, the Malay Islamic Sultanate of Brunei has been in perpetual or hypothetical state of emergency.[90] All of the three countries have also adopted liberal market economies, similar to their ASEAN counterparts.

A common feature of these three countries is the deliberate rejection of a plural and multiparty system. While elections of the Brunei Legislative Council, which was only reconstituted in 2004, is provided for in the 1959 Constitution of Brunei, no elections has taken place since 1962 when the Brunei People's Party (BPP) won 98 per cent of the seats in the Legislative Council. As a consequence, BPP was outlawed and so are other political parties but in the 1990s some parties have re-emerged and been given approval for registration.[91] Similarly both Vietnam and Laos privilege the communist party as the vanguard or leader of the state and society.[92] Vietnam's perspective is summed up in the phrase 'the party that rules and the state that manages'. The Lao Constitution declares the principle of 'democratic centralism'[93] while the Vietnamese Constitution emphasizes unity with delegation of powers and coordination among state organs and institutions.[94]

The privileging of the socialist party in Vietnam and Laos means that the party is in reality the repository of most political power that is translated into the power of state administration. In both Laos and Vietnam, the highest political organ is the National Party Congress, which elects the Central Committee, the Political Bureau (Politburo) and Party Secretary General. Formal political power is vested in these organs; senior state officials such as the President, Prime Minister and President of the National

89 Fatimah binti Hj Awg Chuchu and Mukul Saxena, 'Socio-Cultural Hierarchy in the Palace Language of Brunei Darussalam' (2009) 9 *Southeast Asia: A Multidisciplinary Journal* 42–51, 42.

90 Naimah Talib, 'A Resilient Monarchy: The Sultanate of Brunei and Regime Legitimacy in an Era of Democratic Nation-States' (2002) 4(2) *New Zealand Journal of Asian Studies* 134–47, 136.

91 There are at least three registered parties: Brunei National Solidarity Party, National Development Party and Brunei People's Awareness Party.

92 It is the Community Party of Vietnam for the SRV and Lao People's Revolutionary Party for Laos.

93 Constitution of the Lao People's Democratic Republic [2003], art. 5.

94 Constitution of the Socialist Republic of Vietnam [1992], art. 2.

Assembly are most often members of the Central Committee or the Politburo. An overwhelming majority of members of National Assembly in Laos and Vietnam come from the ruling communist party. In Laos, 128 out of 132 members are from LPRP; Vietnam's National Assembly is composed of 500 deputies where 458 come from the CPV while the rest come from non-CPV (Communist Party of Vietnam) organizations and independents.[95] All of the candidates undergo a vetting process conducted by the communist party. Conversely, the Sultan of Brunei possesses all state powers which are organized into five councils – the Privy Council, Council of Succession, Religious Council, Council of Ministers (the Cabinet with the Sultan as Prime Minister) and the Legislative Council, all answerable to the Sultan.

The lack of political openness in the three countries in this category reflects the absence or the weak voice of civil society. In Brunei, state control is done through such laws as the Internal Security Act (1982), Newspaper Act (1958), Defamation Act (2000) and Sedition Act (2005). The virtual lack of opposition can be partly attributed in good measure, like Singapore, to economic prosperity and generous social protection enjoyed even by those in the lowest social strata.[96] Vietnam and Laos are also highly intolerant regimes and impose tight controls on the exercise of fundamental rights and freedoms.[97] But unlike Vietnam and Laos, Brunei is very rarely cited for human rights violations or for incidents of atrocities.

While Brunei has not held elections, Laos and Vietnam hold elections regularly for their legislative bodies. While there is no perceived radical transformation of one-party rule in these countries, it is acknowledged that changes are taking place that impact on old patterns of political and economic power relations.[98] Allowing 'approved' independents or self-nominated candidates to run in the elections has been introduced in stark contrast to the total ban against nonparty members in the past. Business people, previously shunned by the old revolutionaries, could now be

[95] Results of the 22 May 2011 elections in Vietnam and results of the Laos National Assembly elections on 30 April 2011.

[96] Talib, 'A Resilient Monarchy'.

[97] See Human Rights Watch, *Laos: No Progress on Rights: Urgently End Disappearances, Systematic Suppression of Basic Freedoms* (10 June 2014), www.hrw.org/news/2014/06/10/laos-no-progress-rights; Human Rights Watch, *Vietnam: Tight Control of Critics, Democracy Advocates 2014: No Light at the End of the Tunnel for Activists* (29 January 2015), www.hrw.org/news/2015/01/29/vietnam-tight-control-critics-democracy-advocates-2014

[98] See, for example, Martin Gainsborough, *Vietnam: Rethinking the State* (Chiang Mai: Silkworm Books, 2010).

admitted into the party and vie for seats in the national assembly. In Vietnam, four prominent business people who head some of the country's biggest conglomerates have won seats in Congress.[99] The National Assembly in Vietnam has been observed as getting more assertive and critical of the government and is being regarded as 'the most independent in any Communist system, either contemporary or historically'.[100] As an institution that was largely perceived as a rubber stamp, Vietnam's Assembly has shown some rare forms of dissent from the party line such as halting the implementation of the high-speed national rail project and a rare show of call by a member of the Assembly for the resignation of Prime Minister Nguyen Tan Dung.[101] Similarly in Laos, the old military guards in the party are losing their predominance to a new generation of technocrats, many of them with doctorate degrees.[102]

The constitutional developments in these three countries, while policing state power and the status quo, have in certain ways worked to change the business of rule that allows a law-state or a law regime to take the place of unbridled arbitrary rule. Economic imperatives have encouraged these countries to adopt constitutional and law reforms. Brunei has long been part of the international trading system and is recognized, despite the sanctity of absolute monarchy, for its efficient and competent judicial system and personnel.[103] Prior to the introduction of the more expansive operation of the Shari'ah introducing criminal jurisdiction and harsher penalties in 2014 which had attracted international criticism,[104] Brunei

[99] John Ruwitch, *Party Wins Big in Vietnam, but with a Few Twists* (4 June 2011) Reuters, http://blogs.reuters.com/global/2011/06/04/party-wins-big-in-vietnam

[100] Remark by Zachary Abuza, Professor at the National War College in Washington cited in Bloomberg News, *Vietnam National Assembly May Get More Critical of Government After Start* (21 July 2011), www.bloomberg.com/news/2011-07-21/vietnam-national-assembly-may-get-more-critical-of-government-after-start.html

[101] BBC News, *Vietnam Prime Minister Nguyen Tan Dung Urged to Resign* (14 November 2012), www.bbc.co.uk/news/world-asia-20322830

[102] See Nick Freeman, 'Laos: Timid Transition' in John Funston (ed.), *Government and Politics in Southeast Asia* (Singapore: Institute of Southeast Asian Studies, 2001), 120–59, 146.

[103] Roger Kershaw, 'Brunei: Malay, Monarchical, Micro-State' in John Funston (ed.), Government and Politics in Southeast Asia (Singapore: Institute of Southeast Asian Studies, 2001), 1–35, 23–24.

[104] Andrew Buncombe, *International Outcry as Brunei Introduces Sharia Law and Takes Country Back to the Dark Ages* (30 April 2014) The Independent, www.independent.co.uk/news/world/asia/international-outcry-as-brunei-introduces-sharia-law-and-takes-country-back-to-the-dark-ages-9308088.html; Stuart Grudgings, *Brunei Adopts Sharia Law, Others in Region Consider It* (29 April 2014) Reuters, www.reuters.com/article/2014/04/29/us-brunei-sharia-idUSBREA3S15820140429

is known for a well-functioning common-law system it inherited from British colonial administration and for its professional and competent civil courts.[105] Corruption of state officials is dealt with although members of the ruling family are known to be treated with a slap on the wrist.[106] However, while the ruling family has immunity from domestic suits, it has allowed foreign entities to sue them in international tribunals.[107]

In the 1990s, the discourse on rule of law as part of the political reform agenda became prominent with the institution of economic reforms and ultimately the acceptance of the market economy, the so-called 'socialist-oriented market economy'. *Doi moi* or renovation was a period of reflection for the CPV as the leadership thought of realigning political reforms with economic reforms. Prior to *doi moi*, Vietnam's economy had suffered, which was directly attributed to the centrally planned, state enterprise-dominated economy as well as an arbitrary one-party rule. The reform was largely seen as a way to thwart increasing domestic opposition and to maintain the CPV in power.[108] This resulted in the framing of the 'socialist Rule of Law state' by government think tanks that became the basis for political renovation during the discussions in the seventh and eighth Congress of the CPV. Laos, conversely, adopted a constitution in 1991 which was amended on 28 May 2003. The state of Vietnam describes itself as a law-based state that is also subject to law. The 1992 Vietnam Constitution states that 'All organizations of the Party shall operate within the framework of the Constitution and the law' and that 'The State administers society by rule of law and constantly strengthens the socialist legislation.'[109] The principle of equality or that no one is above the law is further expressed in the provision that all state agencies, economic and social organizations, people's armed forces and citizens shall follow the Constitution and

[105] Elizabeth Ann Black, 'Brunei Darussalam: Ideology and Law in a Malay Sultanate' in Elizabeth Ann Black and Gary Bell (eds.), *Law and Legal Institutions of Asia: Traditions, Adaptations and Innovations* (Port Melbourne: Cambridge University Press, 2011), 299–339, 326–27.

[106] The Sultan and his family are known for their ostentatious lifestyle and extravagance. The 'suit' against Prince Jefri Bolkiah was merely settled amicably over the embezzlement of $20.7 billion during his terms as Chair of the Brunei Investment Agency. See Joseph Chinyong Liow, *Dictionary of the Modern Politics of Southeast Asia*, 4th edn. (New York: Routledge, 2015), 108–9.

[107] See Geoffrey Gunn, '"Trophy Capitalism", Jefrinomics, and Dynastic Travail in Brunei' (2008) 6(3) *Asia Pacific Journal*, http://apjjf.org/-Geoffrey-Gunn/2696/article.html

[108] Le Hong Hiep, 'Performance-based Legitimacy: The Case of the Communist Party of Vietnam and Doi Moi' (2012) 34(2) *Contemporary South East Asia* 145–72.

[109] SRV 1992 Constitution (as amended in 25 December 2001), arts. 4 and 12.

the law.[110] On one hand, the Laos Constitution of 2003 does not mention the phrase 'rule of law' but a new provision states that 'The State manages the society through the provisions of the Constitution and the laws. Party and State organizations, the Lao Front for National Construction, mass organizations, social organizations and all citizens must function within the bounds of the Constitution and the laws.'[111]

The general design of the socialist rule of law as reflected in the constitution is to state clearly the functions and authority between the party that leads and the state that manages and to define the delegation of powers to state organs. In this way, the aim is to depoliticize or minimize the politicization of state organs and the bureaucracy. In Vietnam's case, it means that the CRV has confined itself to policy role while direct management will be the responsibility of the state and its organs. As a consequence, more importance has been given to the Constitution and laws, and the authority and decisions of state organs such as the National Assembly, the Government and the People's Courts. Being bound by the Constitution and laws and having a clear delineation of jurisdiction, each state organ and their officials would, in theory, be performing within 'rules' and not by discretion. However, even from a theoretical perspective, the concentration of powers in the hands of the party and the primacy of the National Assembly, particularly in its role of general supervision of other state organs, means that discretion could be a vice as well as that of encroachment and overlapping of functions. The only mechanism that could guard against this vice is to rely on the strength of human discipline and self-restraint and whether there is an effective mechanism for internal self-criticism.

5.5 Conclusion

This chapter discussing 10 member countries in ASEAN – Indonesia, Philippines, Thailand, Singapore, Malaysia, Cambodia, Myanmar, Brunei, Vietnam and Laos – shows four broad processes or themes that have shaped the distinctive state systems and types of law regimes in each member state. These are the common experience of colonialism, postcolonial nation-state building, nationalism and the rise of the democratization movement. Globalization, though skimmed over through the discussion, underlies the growth of economic, social and political changes – and reforms – that are taking place in the region. The democracy movement

[110] Ibid., art. 12.
[111] Laos 2003 Constitution, art. 10.

itself is a product of this 'external' phenomenon and also of internal dynamics that force change even in unintended ways. It should also be added that countermovements, in the contemporary rise of Islamist radicalism and the continuance of insurgent ethnic and class struggles, continue to significantly define the state, how control of government is fought among contending elites and how these subsequently affect the relation between the state and the individual.

The confluence of these processes has determined the rule of law in the region – the manner it has shifted back and forth as an instrument of the state or as a limiting force. In this sense, this reflects the fluidity of law regimes in the states discussed, which depends on the interaction of these factors. We have shown however in the typology of law regimes that rule of law as a constraint on state power has more potential to develop under a climate of greater civil society cohesion and participation. Constraints on state power however can occur, not mainly because of law but through law, through a form of internal self-regulation and innovation as shown in controlled democracies or countries with different state ideologies or forms of government. Despite variation in political and legal systems in these 10 countries we can see that a 'rule of law' in its minimal conception as constraint to arbitrary rule can develop in 'imperfect liberal democracies' as in other forms of governments. In this imperfect state, the law regime provides a peaceful framework in resolving political conflicts that in the past escalated to violent and disruptive proportions; it also offers opportunity to depoliticize state institutions and bureaucracies and institute accountability mechanisms to bring relevant and effective services to the people. Conversely, rule by law can breed in seemingly democratic forms of government. As the following chapter demonstrates, this political differentiation or division becomes blurred in the economic field as countries even compete for greater liberalization.

To say that the region is static, or to lump all the states in one category, however, is to entirely miss the point. For each of the countries under study has undergone tremendous historical and political dynamism affecting not only the state but also the broader society and its people in a profound way. The peculiar social, economic and political conditions of each state has thus defined the manner by which the various functions of the rule of law are deployed to a lesser or greater degree. Thus, the story of the rule of law in Southeast Asia confirms that there is no 'one-size fits all' conception of the rule of law. These differences are not to deny that they share common characteristics which either inhibit or advance the rule of law.

The states in Southeast Asia have all changed which also brought back the necessity for the state to be governed under the rule of law and for the rule of law to transform state–society relations. These changes have ushered in or highlighted different aspects of the rule of law that can be points for learning and cooperation between the states. Constitutionalization is one of the major developments shared by Southeast Asian states that provide a general, albeit thin, basis of framework of governance. Democratization has also brought forth the development of constitutionalism in many countries that institutionalize the principle of separation of powers and respect for human rights. The creation of more independent institutions – to tackle elections, corruption and government efficiency, among others – has marked this new era. It is important to note the establishment of national human rights commissions in the countries of the Philippines, Thailand, Indonesia and Malaysia to promote and protect human rights.

Constitutional courts or courts that are vested with the power of judicial review over legislation and governments acts are also a recent development in these countries that has the potential to advance the rule of law. Judicial independence has also seen a revival, though still limited, in certain countries and shows that it can be a mechanism to provide stable and peaceful solutions to political conflicts. The 'semi-authoritarian' state of Singapore has also much to share on its rule of law practices in terms of operating an efficient bureaucracy and judiciary, particularly in dealing with economic matters and corruption. Malaysia had a relatively peaceful elections and its dominant party respected the results of its latest general elections, which is an important learning for states that experience widespread electoral violence. A caveat must be repeated, however, that individually, these changes or reforms do not operate in a vacuum.

All of the countries discussed share common challenges to nation-state building. The rule of law could serve as a framework for solving common problems at the regional level and this has been shown by the way certain territorial disputes between countries in the region have been effectively resolved. Bouts of internal turmoil and nationalism have occasionally given rise to 'tensions', but this does not diminish the value of the rule of law through its capacity to ensure stability, certainty and predictability of official actions, and also its ability to depoliticize politics. Socialization has now become an important process of building the rule of law and the experience of the CEE countries in the EU, with equally poor record of democracy and the rule of law in the past, could serve as guide to Southeast Asian states. In the following chapters, we discuss the opportunities and challenges in the 'new' ASEAN for the rule of law to function as a framework for regional governance and also as a common project for socialization among the member states.

6

ASEAN Community and Building the Law Regime in ASEAN

6.1 Introduction

The extent to which ASEAN Community building is accompanied by the institution of the 'rule of law' is the subject of this chapter. Apart from a heightened focus on economic cooperation, a defining feature of this new ASEAN, as enunciated in the ASEAN Charter, is a commitment to a 'rules-based' regime. The ASEAN Charter adopted during the 13th ASEAN Summit in 2007 as a foundational document for the ASEAN Community also declares adherence to the principles of the rule of law, good governance, democracy and human rights. There is a lot of ambiguity as to what is meant by this regime but what is clear is that ASEAN has shunned an EU-type legal system and has an aversion towards supranational organs.[1] But as discussed in previous chapters, ASEAN has clearly chosen an integration regime that combines domestic preferences with new ideas of regional integration and globalization. As such, the resulting legal architecture of the ASEAN Community has moved further than the ASEAN Way and is much more than the 'lowest common denominator' of legal regimes among member states.

The aim of the chapter is to show that ASEAN has started, albeit incrementally, the process of building its own legal regime and not as yet a rule of law regime. Regional integration and the imperatives of globalization have provided not only the demands for coherence, stability and effectiveness but also the incentive for the elites to try new methods of regional cooperation. Member states in ASEAN are not 'new' to this framework

[1] See, for example, Acharya, *Constructing a Security Community*, 264; Amitav Acharya, *Whose Ideas Matter? Agency and Power in Asian Regionalism* (Ithaca: Cornell University Press, 2009), 69–70; Termsak Chalermpalanupap, 'Institutional Reform: One Charter, Three Communities, Many Challenges' in Donald Emmerson (ed.), *Hard Choices. Security, Democracy, and Regionalism in Southeast Asia* (Singapore: Institute of Southeast Asian Studies, 2009), 91–134, 114; Laurence Henry, 'The ASEAN Way and Community Integration: Two Different Models of Regionalism' (2007) 13(6) *European Law Journal* 857–79.

of conducting multilateral relations as most of them are members of multilateral organizations that demand greater clarity and certainty in their entitlements and obligations. Whether ASEAN can complete this transformation to a rules-bound system is not a legal question but a political one. This chapter demonstrates that the narrow elite consensus and the lack of public participation have stymied political commitment for broader and deeper regional cooperation. These political barriers to ASEAN integration are responsible in limiting the scope and application of a rule-bound regime in ASEAN.

6.2 The ASEAN Charter and the Foundation of the Rule of Law in Regional Integration

The ASEAN Charter is, without doubt, a milestone for the region that has for more than 40 years operated through informal processes and non-binding commitments. Thus the ambitious aim for a legal regime is a gradual process that can be ascribed to both the variations in institutional capacity and legal culture in member states and in ASEAN and in how member states perceive the benefits of integration for their national interests. On the basis of the discussion on different law regimes in Southeast Asia, the ASEAN legal regime must also be seen in the light of its history, practices and the collective aims of member states in pursuing integration. Legal integration in ASEAN follows from the objectives of integration and not the other way around. A common misunderstanding in constructing the processes in ASEAN, particularly in regard to its legal developments, is to assign preconceived notions before its purposes. It is too simplistic however to dismiss it in a purely 'instrumentalist' manner, although it can be one of the observations that can be deduced from the circumstances.

The ASEAN Charter, as the fundamental instrument of ASEAN integration, lays down the basis for a law regime in ASEAN. The ASEAN leaders intended the Charter to 'serve as a legal and institutional framework, as well as an inspiration for ASEAN in the years ahead'.[2] At the outset, it must be stated that the institution of the Charter does not denote a process of 'constitutionalization', either in its national or in its international sense. This is not to say that there is no likelihood for constitutionalization in the years ahead; the process however can be uncertain and uneven. Even in the context of the EU, constitutionalization did not happen overnight

[2] ASEAN Charter 2007. See also Walter Woon, *The ASEAN Charter: A Commentary* (Singapore: National University of Singapore Press, 2016).

but was a dynamic process involving the interaction of supranational and national actors. If we consider however a very thin form of constitutionalization, then the ASEAN Charter may fall into this category which clearly creates expectations of and provides a stable and institutionalized framework of regional cooperation.[3]

The ASEAN Charter does not purport to usher a fundamental legal order that is deemed superior to state and other inter-state norms.[4] The establishment of the principle of supremacy which is the bulwark of the regional rule of law in the EU is clearly precluded in ASEAN. There is no mention in the ASEAN Charter or in other relevant ASEAN instrument that the Charter ought to be a superior law through which inconsistent domestic laws or acts could be declared invalid. The provision in the Charter that ASEAN is an 'intergovernmental' organization[5] also ensures that its institutions do not operate autonomously from the 'will' of member states.

Second, incidental to its intergovernmental character, there is no institutional arrangement for separation of powers, much less a provision for mechanisms of accountability of those who exercise regional authority. ASEAN authority is exercised exclusively by governments or executive officials.[6] Third, there is no legal institution that is vested with authority to determine conflict or inconsistency between norms that is capable of developing a form of ASEAN jurisprudence. Instead, conflicts among states are to be resolved on a case-by-case basis through *ad hoc* tribunals which are limited to cases of individuals who may want to have their investment disputes resolved with governments. Fourth, there is no autonomous regional body that is authorized to perform enforcement functions except by agreement or through voluntary action of member states.

While member states have committed to the rule of law as one of the fundamental principles in ASEAN, this has not as yet been embedded in the existing institutional and legal fabric of the organization. Our discussion in the previous chapter points to the convergence among

3 See Joseph Raz, 'On the Authority and Interpretation of Constitutions: Some Preliminaries' in Larry Alexander (ed.), *Constitutionalism: Philosophical Foundations* (New York: Cambridge University Press, 1998), 152–93, 153.

4 ASEAN Charter 2007, art. 2.2.

5 Ibid., art. 3.

6 See Imelda Deinla, *Giving the ASEAN Inter-Parliamentary Assembly a Voice in the ASEAN Community* (Stockholm: International Institute for Democracy and Electoral Assistance, 2013).

ASEAN states on the essence of rule of law as a constraint to arbitrary or unfettered exercise of power. The constitutional arrangements in ASEAN states, as the expression of power relations, demonstrate the necessity for a government bounded by 'law' and hence the requirement for the autonomy of law and institutions. In practice, many states, and at various episodes, have ruled through law which reflects the continuing tension between the enabling and constraining function of law. In ASEAN's context as an international organization, the rule of law refers to the necessity for rules and norms to check or to make accountable those who wield authority. Conversely, ASEAN needs to fulfil its functions of fostering greater cooperation, thus the imperative to constrain the exercise of 'sovereign prerogatives'. ASEAN's law regime is and remains subordinated to the will of the states and that enables states to resist or ignore their commitments and responsibilities, largely unchecked and thus inhibiting – rather than enabling – the processes of regional integration.

The commitment to the rule of law in ASEAN proceeds from a weak foundation. This necessarily flows from member states' decision to be an intergovernmental entity, their continued stress on respect for independence, sovereignty and non-interference as ASEAN's fundamental principles and observance of consultation and consensus as the main mechanism of reaching a decision.[7] But as pointed out by former Secretary General Rodolfo Severino, the defence of sovereignty in rejecting reforms is mistaken as all decisions are derived from the sovereign will of the states.[8] It follows therefore that apprehensions of member states towards supranational governance result from fear of losing control of regional institutions that may not serve their national interests.

The current power arrangement in ASEAN reflects the predominance of executive powers in member states without some form of controls or possibility of accountability except through their national constituents. The absence of a supranational organ and limited, *ad hoc* and informal participation by national parliaments and the public in deliberating regional decisions and policies meant that governments takes a firm hand in the process of integration. The heads of governments in member states, the ASEAN Summit, constitute not only the highest but also the sole

7 ASEAN Charter 2007, arts. 3.22(1), 20.1 and 23.

8 See Rodolfo C. Severino, 'From Political/Security Concerns to Regional Integration' in Ooi Kee Beng, Sanchita Basu Das, Terence Chong *et al.*, *The 3rd ASEAN Reader* (Singapore: Institute of Southeast Asian Studies, 2015), 17–22; Severino, *Southeast Asia in Search of an ASEAN Community*.

decision-making and lawmaking authority in ASEAN.[9] There is a limited form of delegation of this authority to the ASEAN Coordinating Council (ACC) of Foreign Ministers that is tasked with initiating policy or legislation. In practice, heads of governments make decisions through the ACC, formerly the ASEAN Foreign Ministers Meeting (AFMM) on less important and non-sensitive matters, except when there is no consensus reached and the subject is elevated to the Summit for discussion.[10] In most cases, the subject is simply dropped if there is no consensus. As we will discuss in the next chapter, informal rule-making on technical and non-sensitive matters takes place behind committees and working groups.

6.3 The Emergence of a Law Regime and Soft Regulation in ASEAN

In its nascent stages, a law regime is evolving the ASEAN Way and as is the possibility to develop a 'rule through law' regime. In this legal regime type, regional authority may be exercised through and regulated by regional institutions and other regulatory devices as functions, roles and responsibilities increase and are differentiated to manage the complexity of integration. This legal regime is a complex mix of formal but less rigid laws, decentralized policy-making and forms of soft mechanisms which seek to moderate or balance the exercise of sovereign discretion. As is the nature of most soft law regimes, the ASEAN legal regime is not a coherent or systematic system and is fragmented and uneven in the three pillars. Neither are these soft mechanisms bound to harden into hard legislation but they may be able to generate deepening institutionalization, legalization and harmonization. Or these soft mechanisms could be an end in themselves, depending on how member states perceive their individual and collective purposes. Informal external forms of regulation has also emerged, particularly with the emergence of transnational actors such as civil society and business groups engaged in advocacy and monitoring of government commitments.[11]

An important development in ASEAN governance that bodes well for the development of a legal regime has been the gradual opening up – on an informal, selective and controlled process – to private individuals and

[9] ASEAN Charter 2007, art. 7.2(b).

[10] Ibid., art. 20.4.

[11] See, for example, Kelly Gerard, *ASEAN's Engagement of Civil Society: Regulating Dissent* (New York: Palgrave Macmillan, 2014).

civil society groups. This started with the Track II initiative in engaging academics, elites and think tanks in reviewing the relevance of the organization and articulation of new frameworks for cooperation. The Eminent Persons Group (EPG) composed of respected former government officials and elites, and was first constituted during the Hanoi Summit in 1998, was particularly influential in advocating a broad-based support for and participation of the people in the region and with it the adoption of the theme, 'caring and sharing Community'. Significant inputs from this group went into the Vientiane Action Program (VAP) which prescribed the general blueprint for ASEAN integration and recommendation for the establishment of the ASEAN Charter. The recommendations of the EPG on the draft of the Charter, while not entirely adopted, gained considerable weight in according ASEAN with a more stable and predictable framework of cooperation, and espousing the principles of democracy, rule of law, good governance and human rights and conduct of consultations by ASEAN organs with non-state actors. The Charter now provides for accreditation of private entities and civil society groups wishing to engage with ASEAN organs[12] and rules and procedures relating to this engagement.[13]

The business sector was, and remains, a key driver for economic integration, contributing important policy recommendations on integration and institutional reforms. The McKinsey Consulting Report on ASEAN Competitiveness (McKinsey Report), which was based on interviews and surveys among businessmen, business groups and industries across the region, was commissioned by the ASEAN Economic Ministers (AEM) Meeting in 2001 to evaluate ASEAN countries' competitiveness and the feasibility of regional integration. The report highlighted three major concerns affecting economic integration which include subscale and fragmented markets, unnecessary costs due to different product standards and customs procedures and unpredictability of policy implementation of ASEAN member countries.[14] It noted domestic regulatory barriers that protect companies from competition, keeping small unproductive firms survive by tolerating evasion of taxes, labour standards and other product regulations, an unequal enforcement of regulations in many ASEAN countries that have curtailed efficiency and hindered competition among

[12] ASEAN Charter 2007, art. 16.

[13] For example, provision for civil society engagement is provided for in the Terms of Reference of the ASEAN Intergovernmental Commission on Human Rights (ToR AICHR).

[14] Adam Schwarz, Adam and Roland Villinger, 'Integrating Southeast Asia's Economies' (2004) 1 *McKinsey Quarterly* 37–47.

firms causing low productivity and low quality of product standards. The McKinsey Report recommended regional economic integration through a sector-based approach and elimination of barriers to intra-regional trade such as removing tariff and nontariff barriers and restrictions on cross-border investments transactions as well as the adoption of an ASEAN-wide competition policy.

While more robust institutional and legal reforms had been called in the proposals, an enhanced form of ASEAN Way, greater institutionalization and soft legalization has become the framework of reordering regional relations. ASEAN has a law regime underpinned by soft regulation which ties in with its preference for a building-blocks approach and a flexible and non-confrontational strategy towards integration. The concept of regulation presupposes that law is one among many mechanisms that seeks to influence behaviour towards a particular outcome.[15] Regulation can be identified as a 'sustained and focused attempt to alter the behavior of others according to defined standards'.[16] Regulation in the context of regulating an international entity has traditionally been associated with the concept of international law and generally associated with its less rigid and less binding nature and the weakness of international enforcement or coercive mechanism.

Regional integration has specific and highly desired outcomes, apart from high degree of interconnectedness, which necessitates compliance as a pivotal ingredient for its realization. Thus if one complies and the other member does not, this can result in the compliant member withdrawing its compliance as it will not only be disadvantaged by such non-conformance but may also result in loss or injury to itself. The aim is therefore to have all or most of its members comply than to lose the whole enterprise through the non-conformance of some members. An organization with varied membership and levels of intention for compliance has at least two options for compliance – to implement hard regulation characterized by punitive measures and binding coercion or to adopt soft regulation using flexible, persuasive and non-binding coercions. 'Non-binding coercions' refer to those mechanisms directed at eliciting compliance but are not necessarily judicially enforceable.[17] Soft methods are not non-coercive *per se* as they

[15] See, for example, John Braithwaite and Peter Drahos, *Global Business Regulation* (Cambridge: Cambridge University Press, 2000).

[16] Julia Black, 'Critical Reflections on Regulation' (2002) 27 *Australian Journal of Legal Philosophy* 1–35, 26.

[17] Zerilli, 'The Rule of Soft Law', 5–6.

can enjoin compliance through such methods as shaming, persuasion, pressure, self-interest, opportunity or fear that could be as effective as hard approaches.[18] Soft regulation in the context of regulating regional governance regimes entails a focused and sustained strategy to allow conformance to integration goals by member states and non-state actors who have an interest in this compliance.

How effective soft regulation is vis-à-vis desired outcomes can be measured by looking at the extent to which it may have involved standard setting, gathering of information and behavioural change.[19] Another test of regulation is whether regulation has been decentred, also called 'decentred regulation', which means broadly that the states are not the sole repository of authority or they do not play a role at all.[20] In many instances however, non-state actors may contribute in decision-making through informal institutions or mechanisms; in this case, state authorities may exercise control over these informal networks. Self-regulation is another concept that comes into play and whether it can apply, aside from non-state actors who voluntarily regulate themselves even in the absence of legislation,[21] to regulation of regional authority themselves, the member states, which are the ultimate repository of power. How regulation, specifically soft regulation, may gradually promote the development of the rule of law in the context of regional governance by constraining flexibility and discretion in complying with integration commitments and the possibility to self-regulate private actors will be evaluated in the following sections.

The following sections thus examine ASEAN's new architecture and how it structures regional authority and promotes standard setting and information gathering in the three pillars of the envisaged Community. We also look at whether there has been decentring of authority and modification of behaviour of member states and non-state actors in relation to the integration goals of a 'sharing and caring Community'. This section will focus mostly on the APSC and the ASCC as the AEC will be tackled separately in Chapter 7. It is in these two pillars where institution-building and legalization are lower compared to AEC and a much flexible, less structured approach to standard setting is being adopted.

[18] Ibid., 5.

[19] See Dimity Kingsford Smith, 'What is Regulation? A reply to Julia Black' (2002) 27 *Australian Journal of Legal Philosophy* 37–46, 42–3.

[20] Julia Black, 'Decentring Regulation: Understanding the Role of Regulation and Self-Regulation in a "Post-Regulatory" World' (2001) 54(1) *Current Legal Problems* 103–46.

[21] See Linda Senden, 'Soft Law, Self-Regulation and Co-regulation in European Law: Where Do They Meet? 2005 9(1) *Electronic Journal of Comparative Law* 1, www.ejcl.org/

Institutions are not merely expressions of power, of who constitute them and exercise authority. They are also expressions of rules, how authority is exercised and how rules are reinterpreted and made in the process.[22] This function is not limited to formal institutions but also holds true for informal institutions.[23] There were less motivations for formal and elaborate structures particularly in the first 10 years of ASEAN as it was mainly a venue for consultation and cooperation.[24] This is in addition to zealousness in holding on to 'sovereign prerogatives' and thus an aversion even to a central regional administrative body preferring loose, *ad hoc* and informal structures.[25] It was only in 1976 that the only common regional institution, the ASEAN Secretariat, was established to act as a central administrative and coordinating body.

6.4 ASEAN Institution-Building: Delegation, Coordination and Efficiency of Administration

Expansion, strengthening and innovation of institutions are the hallmarks of ASEAN Community building. ASEAN organs however are not in the nature of supranational institutions and are not intended to provide a regional authority with the competence to implement or enforce ASEAN agreements. The basic idea is that through commitments to the principles and purposes of regional cooperation, self-interest and mutual trust, member states will fulfil their roles and responsibilities. ASEAN institutions are aimed at facilitating voluntary compliance and in enhancing the efficiency through delegation and efficient coordination of intergovernmental initiatives through regular and consistent performance of functions or roles and the use of professional staff and experts. The expansion of structures and of personnel in ASEAN has occurred with the expansion of competence particularly of increasing interest in economic cooperation. The structures in Figures 6.1 and 6.2 show the first two stages of institutional development of ASEAN from an organization that relied on *ad hoc* and national structures to the institutionalization of ministerial meetings and the ASEAN

22 Hans-Joachim Lauth, 'Formal and Informal Institutions' in Jennifer Gandhi and Rubén Ruiz-Rufino, *Routledge Handbook of Comparative Political Institutions* (Oxon: Routledge, 2015), 56–69, 57.

23 Ibid., 57–8.

24 See Caballero-Anthony, *Regional Security in Southeast Asia*, 74.

25 See Marise Cremona, David Kleimann, Joris Larik, Rena Lee and Pascal Vennesson (eds.), *ASEAN's External Agreements: Law, Practice and the Quest for Collective Action* (Cambridge: Cambridge University Press, 2015), 261.

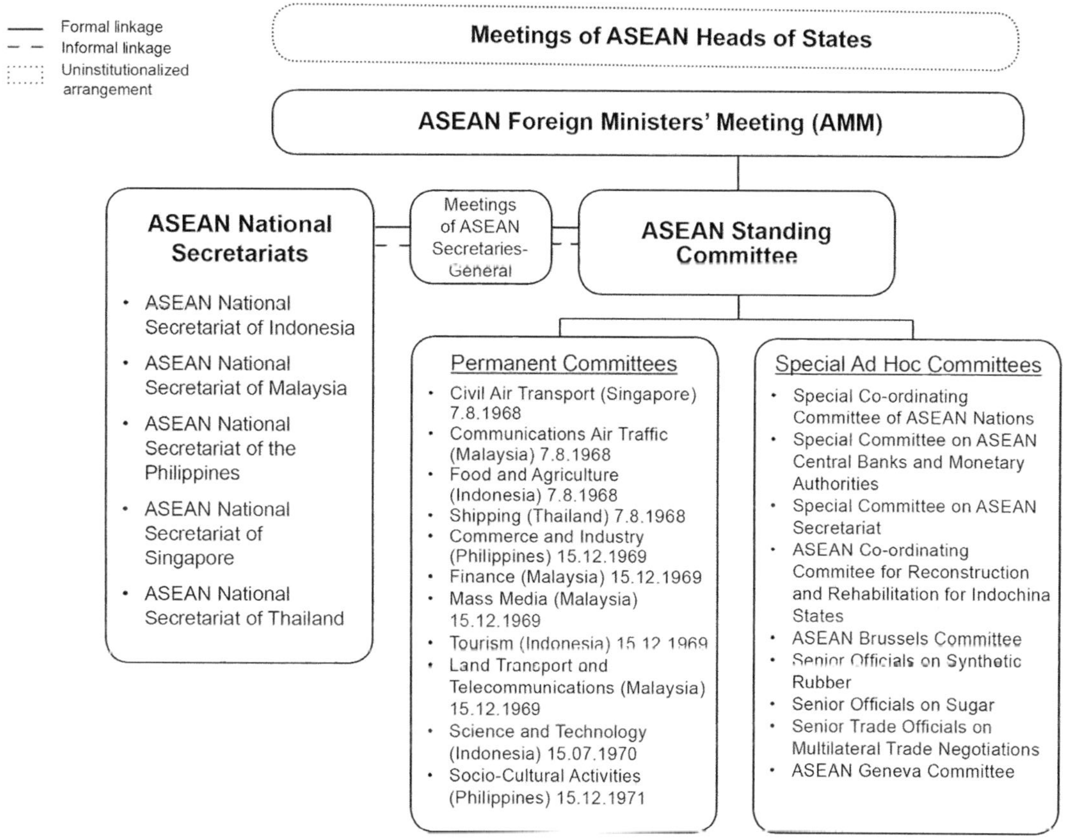

Figure 6.1 Organizational structure of ASEAN before 1976
Adapted from ASEAN Secretariat, *ASEAN Economic Co-operation: Transition & Transformation* (Singapore: Institute of Southeast Asian Studies, 1997), 22.

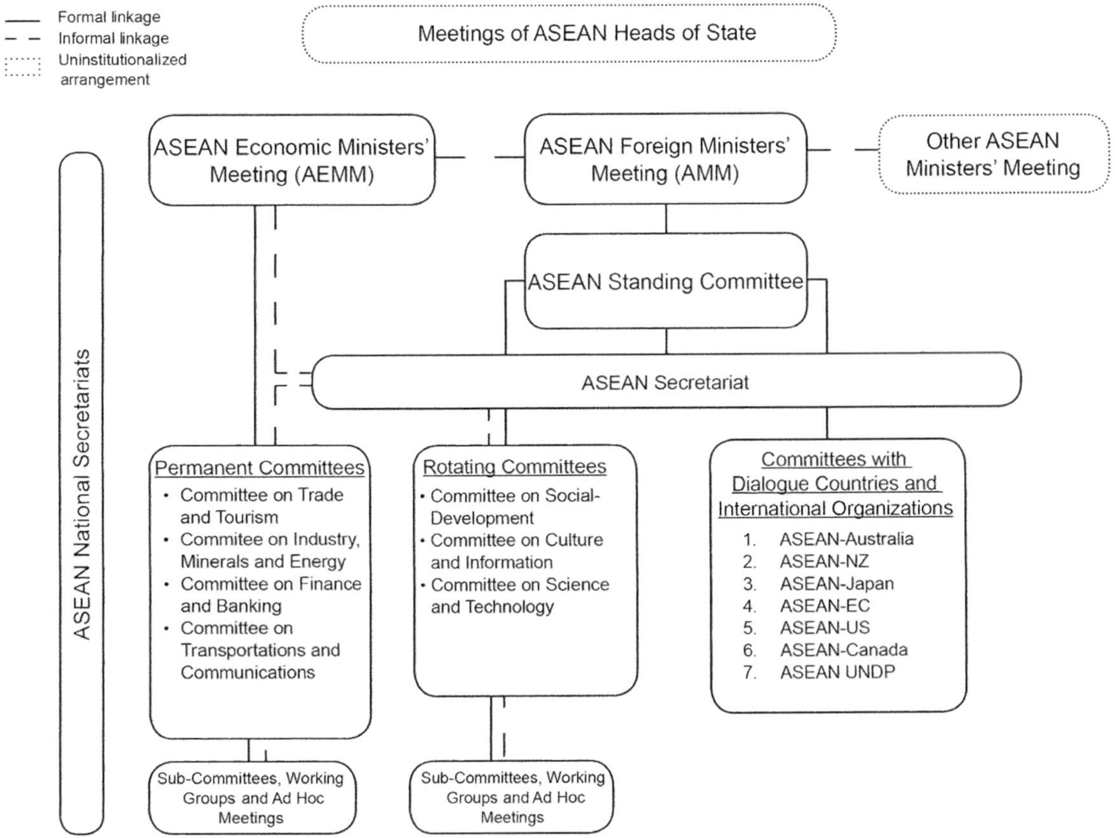

Figure 6.2 Organizational structure of ASEAN in 1983
Adapted from ASEAN Secretariat, *ASEAN Economic Co-operation*, 25.

Secretariat. In particular, the ASEAN Secretariat was strengthened in 1992 in line with the establishment of AFTA.

Delegation of regional authority, that is the ASEAN Summit as the primary repository of this power, is structured in the new three-pillar structure of the ASEAN Community. The ASEAN Community is comprised of the ASEAN Economic Community (AEC), ASEAN Political and Security Community (APSC) and ASEAN Socio-Cultural Community (ASCC) which is an innovation from the practice of holding ministerial and committee meetings. The ASEAN Community, with the ASEAN Summit or Meetings of the Head of States at the apex, is supported by ministerial bodies and senior officials from member states as well as by committees and working groups that involve private entities or individuals providing technical inputs. The pillared architecture in ASEAN rationalizes functional cooperation into three main sectors – economic, political and security and sociocultural. These organs still function through ministerial and committee meetings of more than 250 official meetings a year[26] but now are held in a more regular and coordinated fashion.

Coordination and cooperation and sometimes overlapping functional responsibility characterize the relationship of the organs of ASEAN under the Charter. In the EU, the constitutional system of checks and balances operates to maintain the integrity, independence and legitimacy of regional institutions even without a strict observance of separation of powers. The EU system permits nongovernment actors to work with government representatives as well as between independent supranational and intergovernmental institutions based on the practice of co-decision, cooperation and comitology.[27] However, these practices are to be based on adherence to the *acquis communitaire* or the body of laws which have developed in the course of community building in the EU.

The ASEAN Charter reiterates ASEAN's intergovernmental character and reaffirms the member states' aversion to supranational bodies.[28] All ASEAN organs are mandated to make decisions through the process of consultation and consensus.[29] A limited form of flexibility is however given in economic decision-making through the 'ASEAN – X' formula,

[26] As of 1 June 2015 official listed meetings in ASEAN at ASEAN, *Official Meetings 2015* www.asean.org/images/2015/June/Notional_Calendar/ASEAN%20Notional%20Calendar%2001062015.pdf

[27] See Craig and de Búrca, *EU Law*, 41–9, 105–6 and 144–7.

[28] ASEAN Charter 2007, art. 3.

[29] Ibid.

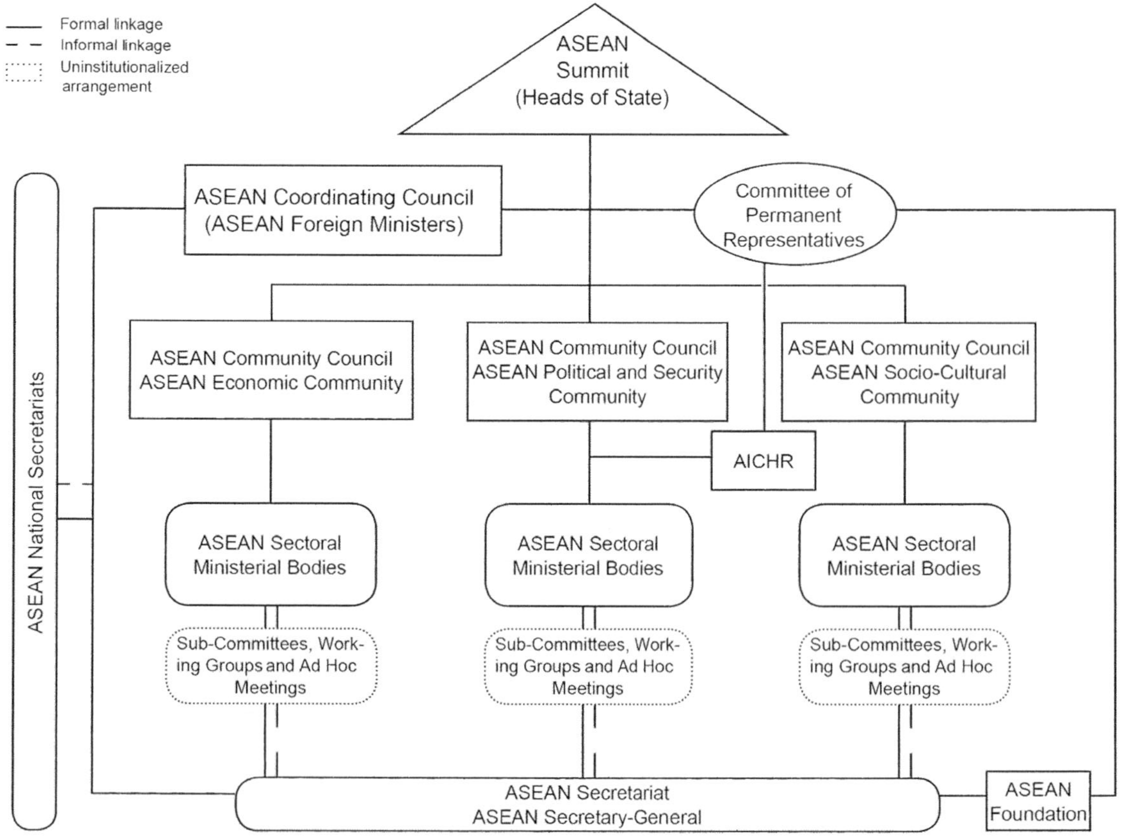

Figure 6.3 The ASEAN community

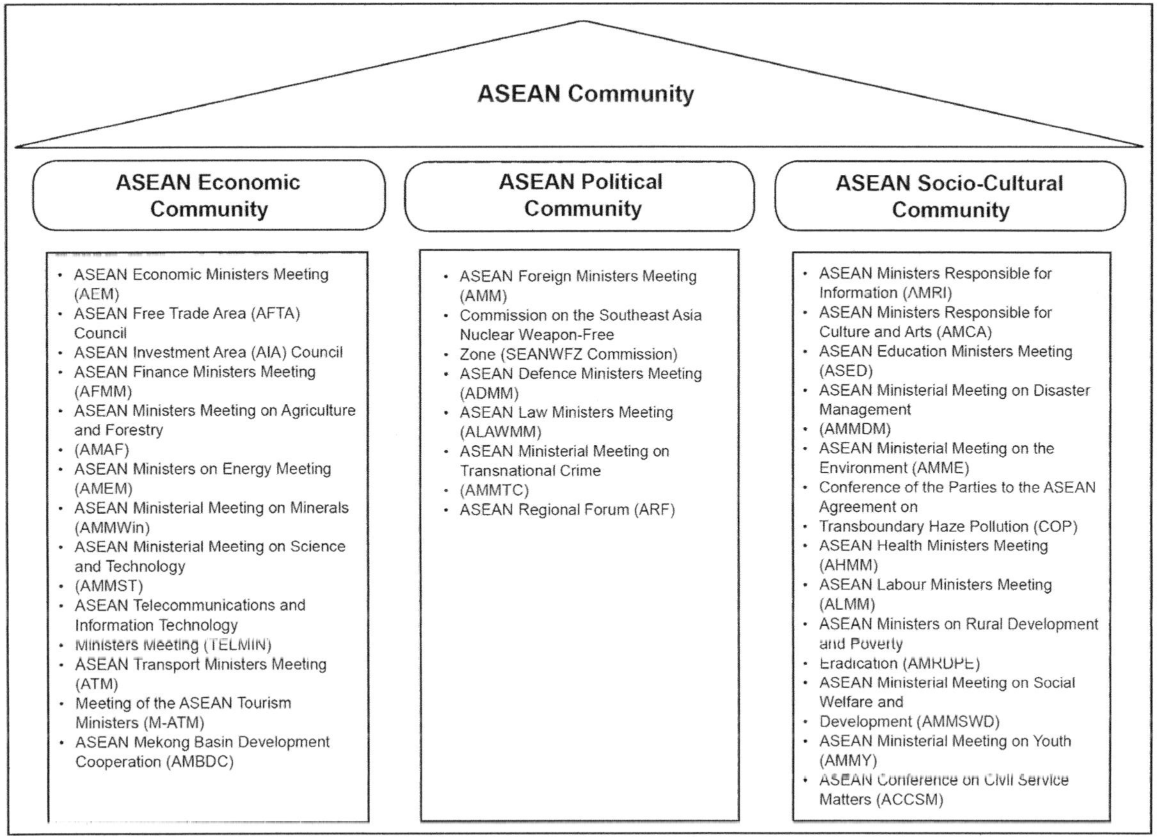

Figure 6.4 Pillar structure

Source: ASEAN Charter and ASEAN Community Blueprints.

whereby through the consent of all member states, some members perform or conduct aspects of economic integration ahead of the others, if all of the members are not in a position to perform the obligation as a group. The Charter institutionalizes the various regional organs and mechanisms that have been in existence in ASEAN on less regular, *ad hoc* or temporary basis. For example, an ASEAN National Secretariat (National Secretariat) which had been constituted on a temporary capacity in the past is established in each member country on a permanent basis. The National Secretariat serves as the national focal point and repository of all information regarding ASEAN at the national level and is responsible for coordinating the implementation of ASEAN decisions at the national level.[30] In addition, the ASEAN Foundation that already existed to promote ASEAN community-building is now institutionalized.[31] The Charter also added new mechanisms that will strengthen the capacity of existing organs of ASEAN. The Charter has certainly provided regularity, continuity and permanence of regional institutions that are hoped to undertake far-ranging programmes for ASEAN and its members.

6.4.1 Centralized 'Decentralization' of Functions

'Centralized delegation' or decentralization of function under close supervision from governments, rather than decentred authority, is the more appropriate term to describe the process of institution building in ASEAN. There are no non-state actors that are authorized to make 'decisions' but that does not mean that non-state actors do not at all play any role in decision-making. The new architecture enshrined in the ASEAN Charter is clear as to the primacy of intergovernmental powers as the sole repository of formal regional authority. Intergovernmental authority however has been decentralized as to enable room for policy initiatives and inputs from other national government departments or organs. With the ASEAN Community building, there is a trend away from regionalization merely as a 'foreign policy' matter but one that demands coordinated attention from government agencies directly involved in the planning and implementation of regional obligations and commitments. For example, some member states have started to nominate nongovernment leaders, such as from civil society and academia, to senior posts or portfolios in ASEAN organs.[32]

[30] Ibid.

[31] Ibid., art. 15.

[32] See, for example, the appointees to the AICHR from Indonesia Rafendi Djamin, the Executive Director of the Human Rights Working Group, from the Philippines, Ambassador

Like most other regional integration projects such as in SADC and MERCUSOR, ASEAN follows a hierarchical structure with the ASEAN Summit at the apex and all other organs at the bottom. The ASEAN Summit, comprised of the heads of state or government of member states, is the penultimate institution for decision-making, implementation and compliance and settlement of disputes in ASEAN. It has the ultimate control of all major areas of governance in ASEAN. The ASEAN Summit is the supreme policy-making body of ASEAN.[33] It is the sole authority to decide on a serious breach of the Charter or noncompliance by a member state.[34] Any unresolved disputes shall also be referred to the ASEAN Summit for decision.[35]

The ASEAN Summit is now to be held twice in a year and to be hosted by the member state holding the ASEAN Chairship.[36] The Country-in-Chair is headed by an ASEAN government head which is filled by rotation among the member states' leaders. Previously, the ASEAN Summit was held infrequently until its institutionalization at the Fourth ASEAN Summit in 1992 where member states agreed to hold a summit every 3 years and to hold informal ones in between. The present provision makes the Summit a twice-yearly event among member state leaders.[37] The institutionalization of the ASEAN Chair mechanism has been credited with dynamic agenda-setting since the 1990s that has pressed forward and mobilized initiatives for regional integration.[38] This has acted as a form of pressure on and opportunity for the member state to raise matters it deems important for its own national interests and enhance the prestige of its Chairship by claiming leadership in facilitating major agreements or decisions.

The ACC (Coordinating Council), composed of the ASEAN Foreign Ministers, acts as the policy/legislation initiator in the ASEAN Community and as the link or intermediary between the ASEAN Summit and the

Rosario Gonzales Manalo who lectures on international and Asian studies and Thailand's previous appointee, Dr Sirprapha Petcharamesree, http://humanrightsinasean.info/asean-intergovernmental-commission-human-rights/representatives.html

33 ASEAN Charter 2007, art. 7.2(a).

34 Ibid., arts. 20.4 and 27.1.

35 Ibid., art. 26.

36 Ibid., art. 7.3(a).

37 The 26th Summit in Malaysia in 2015 proposed the downsizing of the Summit to only one.

38 See Sanae Suzuki, 'Chairship System and Decision Making by Consensus in International Agreements: The Case of ASEAN' (Discussion Paper No. 471, Institute of Developing Economies, July 2014), https://ir.ide.go.jp/dspace/bitstream/2344/1376/1/ARRIDE_Discussion_No.471_suzuki.pdf

ASEAN Community Council (Community Councils) and all relevant bodies in implementing the agreements and decisions of the Summit.[39] It prepares the meetings of the ASEAN Summit and coordinates with the Community Councils to enhance policy coherence, efficiency and cooperation and the three Councils. It also considers the annual report of the Secretary-General on the work of ASEAN and of the functions and operations of the Secretariat. As its name implies, the work of the Coordinating Council is to coordinate the works of the main organs in ASEAN and loopback feedback onto the ASEAN Summit.

The ASEAN Community Councils comprise the ASEAN Political-Security Community Council, AEC Council and the ASCC corresponding to the three pillars of the ASEAN Community.[40] The Community Councils are, together with the ASEAN Sectoral Ministerial Bodies (Ministerial Body/Bodies), the main implementing organs in ASEAN. The Community Councils, whose members are designated by member states, are responsible for implementing the relevant decisions of the ASEAN Summit. Each of the ASEAN Community Councils shall have under its wing the relevant Ministerial Body which is in turn specifically tasked with implementing the agreements and decisions of the ASEAN Summit under its designated areas of responsibility and to submit reports and recommendations to their respective Community Councils.[41]

The three main organs discussed above are all staffed by government ministers or senior officials, that is, by the executives of member states. Institutional innovations have been put in place, however, to ensure efficiency and continuity in the area of implementation. Two institutions, given their limited mandate in the Charter, can assume some degree of independence and proactiveness in regional processes. First, the Committee of Permanent Representatives (Committee), composed of each country's Permanent Representative to ASEAN who will have a rank of Ambassador based in Jakarta, has been established.[42] Member states have all appointed their ambassadors to the ASEAN; most of them were appointed from the ranks of current or former diplomats and senior government officials.[43] This position has the capacity to provide institutional continuity in each

[39] ASEAN Charter 2007, arts. 8.1 and 8.2(a)–(f).

[40] Ibid., art. 9.1.

[41] Ibid., arts. 9.2 and 10.

[42] Ibid., art. 12.1.

[43] ASEAN, *List of Non-Ams' Ambassadors to ASEAN* (July 2015), www.asean.org/storage/images/2015/August/list_of_non_ams/Listofn-AMSAmbsasofJuly2015fortheWebsite_2.pdf

member's activities in ASEAN, being appointed on a permanent basis in contrast to the three previously mentioned organs which are staffed with ministerial or senior government ranks whose appointments could be withdrawn at any time by their governments or because of changes of governments.

But unlike the COREPER in the EU, the Committee does not perform any decision-making function nor does it have any precise or specific responsibility provided in the Charter in the three core areas of regional governance.[44] The Committee's function is vaguely defined as providing support or coordinating the work of other organs of ASEAN, with the exception of the ASEAN Summit.[45] The Charter does not say to which organ it is responsible to or where its findings or recommendations are to go although the Coordinating Council can delegate work to it.[46] In practice, the Committee's authority has started to overlap with the Secretary-General and issues have started to emerge on it assuming an oversight function over the Secretariat and its personnel.[47]

Under the ToR AICHR, the Committee is given a clearer function as an intermediary between the Commission and the AFMM on matters of human rights. It is delegated with the function of recommending to the AFMM the approval of the work plan and budget of the AICHR.[48] It can also consider and present to the AFMM a request for amendment of the ToR by a member state.[49] The Committee plays an influential role in the work and functioning of the newly constituted AICHR.

Another significant development has been the strengthening of the Secretary-General and the ASEAN Secretariat, which has been especially invested with an enhanced and independent status by the Charter. The Secretary-General is appointed for a fixed term of 5 years and selected

[44] The COREPER is a Committee attached to the Council of European Union staffed by senior national officials and whose function is to prepare the work of the latter in approving legislation.

[45] Art. 12(2d) of the ASEAN Charter 2007 provides, however, that the Committee is responsible for facilitating cooperation with external partners of ASEAN.

[46] ASEAN Charter 2007, art. 2(e).

[47] See Acharya, *Constructing a Security Community*, 239; Pitsuwan, Surin, 'ASEAN's Challenge: Some Reflections and Recommendations on Strengthening the ASEAN Secretariat' (Statement for H.E. Marty Natalegawa, Chair, ASEAN Coordinating Council, 12 December 2011).

[48] Terms of Reference of ASEAN Intergovernmental Commission on Human Rights, Phuket, 20 July 2009, in force 20 July 2009 (ToR AICHR), arts. 8.1–8.2.

[49] Ibid., 9.3.

on the basis of integrity, capability and professional experience.[50] The independence of the Secretary-General and the Secretariat is being guaranteed in the Charter by exhorting member states to refrain from influencing them in the discharge of their duties.[51] The institutional capacity of the ASEAN Secretariat is also being enhanced with the appointment of not just two but four Deputy Secretaries-General to the ASEAN Secretary-General. Two of the Deputy Secretaries-General will be appointed based on merit while the other two will be appointed from ASEAN nationals based on alphabetical rotation of member states.[52] As of 2010, there are about 300 ASEAN personnel with about 110 as technical staff; most of the staff are still however coming or seconded from the diplomatic corps or government service.[53] Three of its Deputy Secretaries-General are nominees from member states. It is also constrained by its limited budget of about $16 million a year, being equally contributed by its members.

One key innovation for the ASEAN Secretariat is the role it is entrusted with in facilitating and monitoring the progress in implementation of ASEAN agreements and decisions.[54] The Secretariat can initiate, advise, coordinate and implement ASEAN activities and also be responsible in monitoring the implementation of the AFTA, the backbone of economic integration in ASEAN. With the lack of a functioning enforcement mechanism, ASEAN has been authorized the use of the AEC Scorecard to track the implementation of AEC agreements; the Secretariat has been given this responsibility which it has initiated since 2008.[55] It is also given a central role in monitoring compliance with the findings, recommendations or decisions, resulting from an ASEAN dispute settlement mechanism also including the provision for good offices and mediation.[56] There is no indication that this role has been performed in an official capacity by the Secretary General. The Secretary-General is also given a prominent role

50 ASEAN Charter 2007, art. 11.1.

51 Ibid., art. 11.9.

52 Ibid., art. 11.6.

53 Asian Development Bank Institute, 'ASEAN Governing Mechanisms' in Ooi Kee Beng, Sanchita Basu Das, Terence Chong *et al.* (eds.), *The 3rd ASEAN Reader* (Singapore: Institute of Southeast Asian Studies, 2015).

54 ASEAN Charter 2007, art. 11.2(b); Protocol Amending the Agreement on the Establishment of the ASEAN Secretariat, Manila, 22 July 1992, in force 8 August 1992.

55 See ASEAN Secretariat, *ASEAN Economic Community Scorecard* (Jakarta: ASEAN Secretariat, 2010).

56 ASEAN Charter 2007, arts. 11 and 27.1.

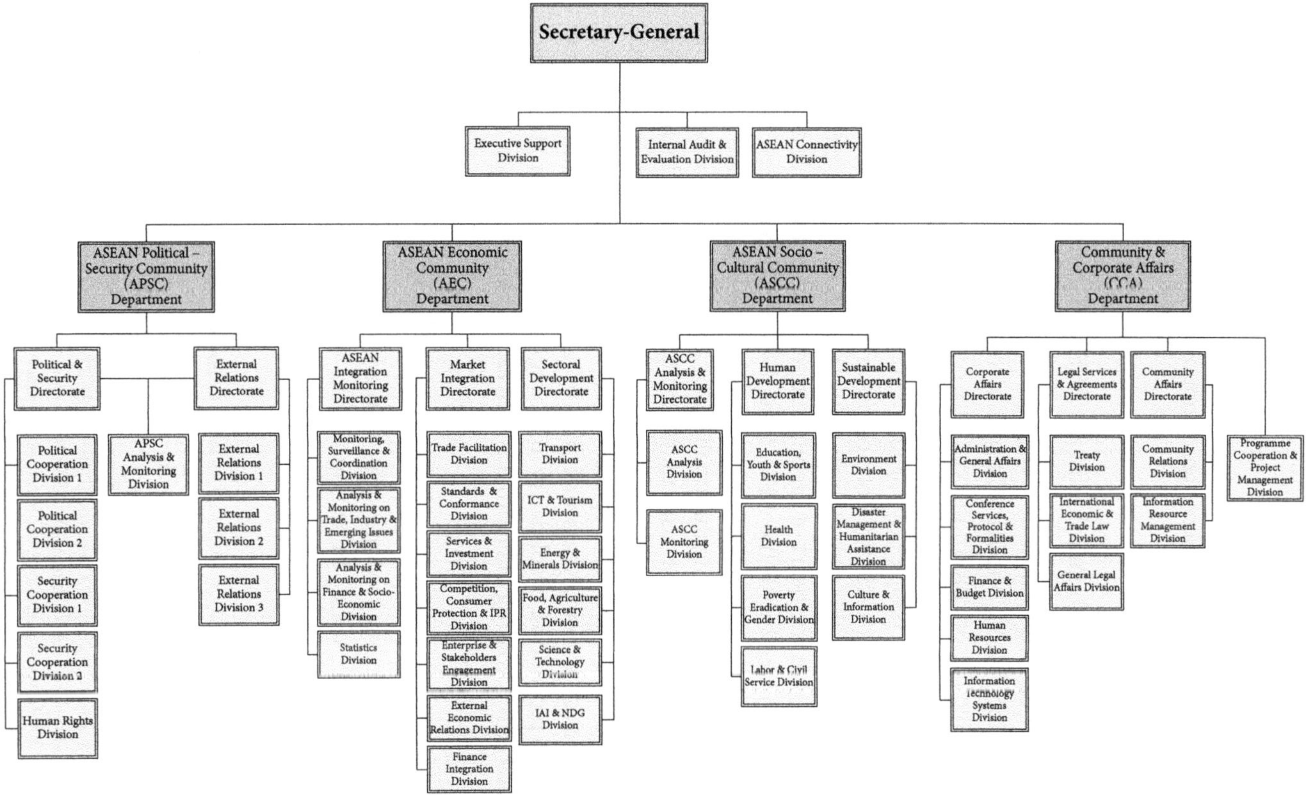

Figure 6.5 ASEAN Secretariat organizational structure, effective 1 January 2016

Source: ASEAN, *Organisational Structure* (January 2016), www.asean.org/asean/asean-structure/organisational-structure-2/

in the AICHR by bringing relevant issues to the Commission in relation to his role in monitoring the implementation of ASEAN agreements and in submitting an annual report on the work of ASEAN.[57] The Secretariat is also to provide necessary secretarial support to the AICHR to ensure its effective performance.[58]

6.5 Soft Regulation in the ASEAN Community

This section examines how soft regulation has been enshrined in the APSC and the ASCC. The APSC's role is the preservation of peace and security in the region and in its relations with the outside world,[59] while the ASCC seeks the promotion of solidarity and unity among the member states and their peoples by forging a common identity and building a caring and sharing society.[60] Both pillars employ political or soft means to accomplish their objectives which shows that these pillars, particularly the APSC, go into the heart of member states' vital political and security interests. Compared with the AEC, these two pillars represent the 'least developed' areas in ASEAN in terms of rules formation but are similarly undergoing a process of institutionalization and some form of norm promotion. Both pillars have also adopted their Blueprints which set out their respective objectives and measures.[61] Many of the covered areas have already seen the subject of cooperation, interaction or discussion among member states for many years such as on regional security, transnational crimes and promotion of solidarity in the region through inter-state activities such as the holding of biennial Southeast Asia Games since 1958.

6.5.1 Cooperation, not Integration, in the APSC and ASCC

Cooperation, not integration, is the byword to describe matters covered in the APSC and ASCC. In setting out the key objectives and nature of

57 ToR AICHR, art. 7.1.

58 Ibid., art. 7.2.

59 ASEAN Secretariat, *ASEAN Political-Security Community Blueprint* (Jakarta: ASEAN Secretariat, 2009) (APSC Blueprint), para. 2(8).

60 ASEAN Secretariat, *ASEAN Socio-Cultural Community Blueprint* (Jakarta: ASEAN Secretariat, 2009) (ASCC Blueprint), para. 1(4).

61 The APSC Blueprint and the ASCC Blueprint were both adopted at the 14th ASEAN Summit on 1 March 2009 in Cha-am, Thailand. ASEAN, *Chairman's Statement of the 14th ASEAN Summit, 'ASEAN Charter for ASEAN Peoples', Cha-am, 28 February–1 March 2009* (2 March 2009), www.asean.org/chairman-s-statement-of-the-14th-asean-summit-asean-charter-for-asean-peoples-cha-am-28-february-1-march-2009/, paras. 21 and 38.

the pillars, the framers made it clear in the language and mechanisms that 'cooperation' does not mean submission of sovereign prerogatives to declared regional norms. The key characteristics of APSC are as (1) a rules-based Community of shared values and norms, (2) cohesive, peaceful, stable and resilient region with shared responsibility for comprehensive security and (3) dynamic and outward-looking region in an increasingly integrated and interdependent world.[62] The APSC Blueprint clearly states that cooperation in these areas is 'cooperation in political development', which is not equivalent to or synonymous with 'political cooperation'. This is expressly stated in the declaration of its objectives and repeated throughout the text of the APSC Blueprint. Thus, the APSC states:

> The APSC shall promote political development in adherence to the principles of democracy, the rule of law and good governance, respect for and promotion and protection of human rights and fundamental freedoms as inscribed in the ASEAN Charter. It shall be a means by which ASEAN Member States can pursue closer interaction and cooperation to forge shared norms and create common mechanisms to achieve ASEAN goals and objectives in the political and security fields.[63]

The APSC is the vehicle for the promotion of a 'rules-based regime' and shared norms, including the rule of law. This is the pillar however that works mostly through the 'political' institutions of ASEAN and hardly any mechanism for compliance or monitoring of member state's commitments. Timelines for achieving the objectives, unlike the AEC and ASCC, are not generally indicated except the provision for the establishment of the ASEAN human rights mechanism, the AICHR which was inaugurated on 23 October 2009,[64] although defence ministers and law ministers have their own discussion forums.[65] The organs and activities under the APSC are mainly led by the ASEAN foreign ministry officials, particularly in setting the agenda and discussions. The human rights agenda, which had been placed at the forefront of ASEAN cooperation, had met resistance from some member states.[66]

62 APSC Blueprint, para. 2(10).

63 Ibid., para. 2(7).

64 ASEAN Intergovernmental Commission on Human Rights, *About* (2012) http://aichr.org/about/

65 These are the ASEAN Defence Ministers Meeting (ADMM) and the ASEAN Law Ministers Meeting (ALAWMM).

66 The CLMV countries were said to have put up strong opposition to the establishment of a human rights mechanism. See, for example, Gerald Clarke, 'The Evolving ASEAN Human Rights System: The ASEAN Human Rights Declaration of 2012' (2012) 11(1) *Northwestern*

For example, Myanmar's initial resistance was muted with assurances that the rights body would improve ASEAN's credibility. State officials had expressed concern that non-inclusion of human rights in the Charter 'will create a bad image' for ASEAN and could be interpreted to mean that it is not supportive of human rights.[67] 'The ASEAN charter presents us with a golden opportunity to make a bold and visionary political statement to the world. For others to take ASEAN seriously, we in the region must take ASEAN seriously,' says Singapore's Foreign Minister George Yeo.[68] However, it appears that the more persuasive approach to Myanmar's recalcitrance had been in reaching a consensus that the rights body is not envisaged as a mechanism that will impose punitive measures and embarrass governments. The Chair of the HLTF that drafted the ASEAN Charter remarked:

> In ASEAN, they work on consultation and consensus. If they can't work together what else they can do. That's it. There is no confrontation. ASEAN does not like confrontation. That's why they will never put phraseology that appears to divide the group, that appears to create confrontation in the group. They will not like that.[69]

'Cooperation in political development' denotes a more restrictive form of inter-state cooperation in the APSC. The areas of cooperation in this pillar are mostly couched in general terms and are meant for fostering mutual understanding, sharing and learning of best practices, confidence and trust building measures, education and academic exchanges. On the political aspect, matters for cooperation include understanding and appreciation of each member's political system and culture, free flow of information, rule of law and legal system, promotion of good governance, human rights and democracy, combating corruption and the promotion of peace and stability.[70]

Journal of International Human Rights 1–27, 8. John Arendshorst cites Myanmar in particular as having 'protested against the formation of a functional ASEAN human rights body' in 'The Dilemma of Non-interference: Myanmar, Human Rights, and the ASEAN Charter' (2009) 8 (1) *Northwestern Journal of International Human Rights* 102–21, 113.

[67] Agence France-Presse, *Image Worries Pushed ASEAN on Rights* (31 July 2007) Inquirer.net, http://archive.inquirer.net/view.php?db=1&story_id=79705

[68] Associated Press, *Myanmar Nixes 'Shame and Blame' Regional Rights* (2 August 2007) Inquirer.net, http://globalnation.inquirer.net/news/breakingnews/view_article.php?article_id=80237

[69] Rosario Manalo, HLTF Chair during preparatory meetings before the 12th ASEAN Summit in the Philippines quoted in Cynthia Balana, *Rights Violators To Be Treated 'ASEAN Way'* (1 August 2007) Inquirer.net, http://newsinfo.inquirer.net/breakingnews/nation

[70] APSC Blueprint, paras. A.1, A.1.1 and A.1.9.

Cooperation 'to strengthen rule of law, judicial systems and legal infrastructure' among member states is mandated through the process of socialization among law ministers, education through curriculum development and conduct of studies and cooperation with the private and academic sectors through the Track II initiative.[71] Legal harmonization, rather than judicialization, has been the strategy adopted to align disparate national laws with commitments in the ASEAN Charter and other agreements. Legal harmonization work has been taking place in *ad hoc* Working Groups in the AEC and in a small unit in the Secretariat, the Legal Services and Agreements Division (LSAD) established in 2008 with technical support and funding by the German Cooperation Agency (GIZ).

Another clear example of soft regulation in this pillar is the stipulated manner in which promotion and protection of human rights will be conducted by member states. As an intergovernmental organ, the AICHR is guided by ASEAN's overarching principles of independence, sovereignty and non-interference and the recognition that the primary responsibility to promote and protect human rights rests with each member state.[72] Its mandate falls within three broad themes – education and research, capacity building, advice and consultation.[73] This does not include any protection or supranational function.[74] Instead, it conducts its work through 'constructive and non-confrontational approach' to human rights protection and promotion and through 'evolutionary approach' to development of human rights norms and standards.[75]

The AICHR is also a highly 'regulated' organ, subjected not to one, but two oversight bodies. The AFMM serves as the highest authority overseeing the AICHR through its powers to delegate tasks and accept reports, to approve the work plan and budget of the Commission and to approve proposed amendments to the ToR of the AICHR.[76] The Committee of Permanent Representatives exerts immediate supervisory function over AICHR by giving its recommendations to the AFMM on the Commission's work plan and budget. As a semi-*ad hoc* organ in ASEAN, the AICHR has no permanent office and meets only twice a year to be held alternately at the ASEAN Secretariat and on the member state holding the Chair of

[71] Ibid., para. A.1.3.
[72] ToR AICHR, arts. 2.1–2.3.
[73] Ibid., art. 4.
[74] Clarke, 'The Evolving ASEAN Human Rights System', 12.
[75] ToR AICHR, arts. 2.4–2.5.
[76] Ibid., arts. 4.13–4.14, 8.1, 8.2 and 9.4.

ASEAN.[77] The ToR recommends that consultation with stakeholders be made in nominating AICHR members if required by the country's internal processes and that each member should act with impartiality. But practice shows that governments elect mostly senior government officials to this body, with the exception of Indonesia and Thailand which appointed a civil society leader and member of the academe, respectively. Members of ASEAN civil society have particularly decried the appointment of Malaysian representative, Tan Sri Muhammad Shafee Abdullah, and Chair of AICHR during Malaysia's Chairship in 2015, who is also the Special Prosecutor trying controversial cases against Malaysia's opposition and other cases with human rights implications.[78]

Lesser forms of delegation are seen in the APSC, compared to the ASCC, where many aspects of cooperation remain matters for decision at the highest political level. This is particularly salient in the area of defence and security cooperation where decision-making is arduously slow and protracted. Informal mechanisms however exist under the Track II mechanism that allows autonomous regional groups to exert pressure or influence and to act as mediator between intergovernmental institutions and civil society. The capacity of this network in influencing ASEAN decision-makers was evident in the adoption of the human rights agenda, in particular the establishment of the AICHR and the ASEAN Human Rights Declaration.[79] Cooperation in this area includes the shaping and sharing of regional norms to uphold peace, security and stability in the region, conflict settlement and pacific settlement of disputes, peacebuilding, humanitarian assistance, nontraditional forms of security cooperation and enhancing cooperation with external parties.[80]

ASEAN's handling of the South China Sea issue, which directly involves five ASEAN countries – Malaysia, Brunei Darussalam, the Philippines, Indonesia and Vietnam which have interlocking claims with each other and with China[81] – is a reflection of ASEAN's lack of mechanism for firm, speedy and effective processes for decision-making. ASEAN has been

[77] ToR AICHR, arts. 6.2–6.3.

[78] Malay Mail Online, *Malaysian Chairman's Legal Record Casts Doubt Over ASEAN Human Rights Commission* (30 March 2015), www.themalaymailonline.com/malaysia/article/malaysian-chairmans-legal-record-casts-doubt-over-asean-human-rights-commis

[79] Clarke, 'The Evolving ASEAN Human Rights System', 13.

[80] APSC Blueprint, paras. 6(A.2)–14(C).

[81] Ian James Storey, 'Creeping Assertiveness: China, the Philippines and the South China Sea Dispute' (1991) 21(1) *Contemporary Southeast Asia* 95–118, 96.

repeatedly criticized for adopting weak agreements such as the Declaration of Conduct of Parties in the South China Sea which merely smooth things for some time but failed to produce any tangible solution to the dispute. From a position of solidarity on the issue in the 1980s, the ASEAN is increasingly perceived as divided since the 1990s[82] which became more evident during the 21st Summit hosted by Cambodia.[83] This matter is seen as a 'litmus test' on ASEAN's centrality in facilitating a workable agreement amidst continuing escalation of tensions in the South China Sea and the long delay in the crafting of a Code of Conduct.[84] ASEAN's aspiration for a rules-based regime and in the shaping and sharing of regional norms is severely limited and constrained by its firm adherence to highly inflexible and demanding consensus decision-making processes.[85] This is just too high a bar to cross in order to tackle wicked problems of deep complexity.

There is greater scope for delegation of functions in specialized organs in the ASCC which is focused on the 'individual' or people component of the ASEAN Community, although this overlaps or is necessarily connected with the APSC. ASCC's agenda are on human development, social welfare and protection, social justice and rights, environmental sustainability and the building of an ASEAN identity. The ASCC Council and relevant ASEAN ministerial bodies are the principal organs directed to ensure implementation mainly through the process of mainstreaming the blueprint into each member states development plans, ratification of ASEAN Agreements and engagement with dialogue partners, the private sector and civil society.[86]

There are, however, significant areas in ASCC that are in the process of institutionalization. This development has coincided with member states' interests in dealing with inter-migration issues that have become critical agenda for negotiations among member states through bilateral or

[82] Gary Collinson and Christopher B. Roberts, 'The Role of ASEAN' in Lesek Buszynski and Christopher Roberts (eds.), *The South China Sea and Australia's Regional Security Environment* (Occasional Paper No. 5, National Security College, Canberra, 2013).

[83] Acharya, *Constructing a Security Community*, 131. The ASEAN Communique during the 29th ASEAN Summit in Laos omitted to mention the Permanent Court of Arbitration ruling on the South China Sea Arbitration of 12 July 2016 that ruled in favour of the Philippines.

[84] Declaration on the Conduct of Parties in the South China Sea, Phnom Penh, 4 November 2012.

[85] ASEAN Charter 2007, art. 20 provides that all organs abide by the process of consultation and consensus.

[86] ASCC Blueprint, para. 3.A.

multilateral agreements.[87] Migration within Southeast Asia is largely driven by disparities in economic development among member states in ASEAN and by the displacement of ethnic minorities as exemplified by Myanmar. The current trend at institutionalization is also influenced by member states' signing of international agreements or treaties and the push by civil society for member states to implement their commitments. Most notable are the initiatives establishing the ASEAN Commission on the Promotion and Protection of the Rights of Women and Children (ACWC) and the ASEAN Committee on the Implementation of the ASEAN Declaration on the Protection and Promotion of Rights of Migrant Workers, which are based on member states' commitments under international agreements and other voluntary commitments.[88]

In line with the transnational impact and security concerns on human trafficking, a landmark convention, the ASEAN Convention Against Trafficking of Persons, Especially Women and Children (ACTIP, 2015)[89], contains mandatory provisions for criminalization of various aspects of human trafficking and possible exercise of extraterritorial jurisdiction in prosecuting crimes.[90] These initiatives have also opened opportunities for participation of nongovernmental organizations, the academe and other members of civil society through the establishment of multisectoral working groups and the holding of consultation meetings.

Compared thus with the EU, many of the norms contained in the other two pillars have already been judicialized or are within the authority of independent institutions. Transposing these values to CEE countries had also required a mixed strategy of direct transplantation of laws and institutions through socialization. Or where soft methods are solely used in areas outside of the Union competence such as in social welfare, these were accompanied by clear guidelines and fully functioning institutions and the participation of parliaments and civil society. ASEAN's current approach therefore in these other pillars, particularly the APSC, still

[87] See, for example, Amarjit Kaur, 'International Labour Migration in Southeast Asia' (2007) 15 *Intersections: Gender, History and Culture in the Asian* Context, http://intersections.anu.edu.au/issue15/kaur.htm

[88] See Terms of Reference of ASEAN Commission on the Promotion and Protection of the Rights of Women and Children, Ch-Am, 22 October 2009; Statement on the Establishment of the ASEAN Committee on the Implementation of the Rights of Migrant Workers, Manila, 30 July 2007.

[89] ASEAN Convention Against Trafficking in Persons, Especially Women and Children, signed 21 November 2015, not yet in force.

[90] Ibid., art. 10.

manifests an aversion to broader non-state participation in regional affairs. One important element – and where ASEAN has shown little progress – is in providing for greater role of national parliamentarians or lawmakers in ASEAN Community building.

6.6 Reform or Status Quo in the ASEAN Dispute Resolution System

The provision for a comprehensive dispute settlement system has been hoped for as a mechanism to institute the rule of law in ASEAN integration. This follows the institutional trend in international relations where a mechanism for dispute settlement is designed to ensure the rule of law. For example, the WTO Dispute Settlement Body (DSB) has made substantial contribution to improving the compliance of member states' commitments.[91] The EU, conversely, through the European Court of Justice (ECJ), has secured the development of a huge body of regional law that is enforceable in member states. In ASEAN, compliance had been a matter of loose commitments by member states, and conflict adjudication is one of the most significant areas recommended for reform. According to the statement of the EPG on ASEAN Charter,

> ASEAN's problem is not one of lack of vision, ideas, or action plans. The problem is one of ensuring compliance and effective implementation. ASEAN must have a culture of commitment to honour and implement decisions, agreements and timelines.[92]

There has been significant progress in reforming ASEAN's dispute settlement system – at least on paper. Despite these reforms, ASEAN dispute resolution mechanisms remain largely unused. This only further confirms the role that soft regulation plays in implementation and enforcement of regional agreements, and to which the future of ASEAN integration mainly depends. The provision for various modes of dispute settlement mechanisms at all levels of economic and political disputes in the ASEAN Charter shows some promise of the institutionalization of conflict resolution in ASEAN.[93] There are now at least three modes of dispute resolution

[91] Yuka Fukunaga, 'Securing Compliance through the WTO Dispute Settlement System: Implementation of DSB Recommendations' (2006) 9(2) *Journal of International Economic Law* 383–426.

[92] ASEAN Secretariat, *Report of the Eminent Persons Group on the ASEAN Charter* (December 2006), www.asean.org/storage/images/archive/19247.pdf, 4.

[93] ASEAN Charter 2007, art. 22.2.

in ASEAN – through good offices, conciliation and mediation through the Chair of ASEAN or the Secretary-General,[94] through the ASEAN Summit, and an instrument-specific mode of dispute settlement. As already mentioned, the ASEAN Summit shall have the authority to decide on 'unresolved disputes' as well as to decide on issues of non-compliance by member states resulting from an ASEAN dispute settlement mechanism.

Article 24 of the Charter provides for an instrument-specific mode of dispute resolution in ASEAN. This provision brings a degree of clarity and specificity of avenues for conflict settlement, when compared to the uncertainty of informal channels in the past. Thus the rules, issues or conflicts relating to specific ASEAN instruments shall be settled through the mechanisms or procedures provided for in that instrument. For instance, the ASEAN Comprehensive Investment Agreement 2009 (ACIA), which superseded the 1987 Agreement for the Promotion and Protection of Investments, provides for two distinct mechanisms of dispute resolution.[95] One involves disputes between member states for which the ASEAN Protocol on Enhanced Dispute Settlement Mechanism (ASEAN Enhanced DSM, 2004)[96] is applicable and the other involves the investor and a member state. In the latter instance, an investor has the choice either to submit a claim before the domestic court or administrative tribunal of a disputing member state or to bring the claim before international or regional arbitral bodies.[97]

The drafting of the ACIA in 2007 is reported to have triggered investment treaty arbitrations against member countries.[98] As is the requirement of many arbitration proceedings on confidentiality, most cases are not publicly known however. As of 2014, eight ASEAN countries have been involved in arbitration either as respondent states or as investor's home states; of the 11 publicly known proceedings, 4 were ruled in favour of

94 Ibid., art. 23.

95 ASEAN Comprehensive Investment Agreement, Cha-Am, 26 February 2009, in force 29 March 2012.

96 ASEAN Protocol on Enhanced Dispute Settlement Mechanism, Vientiane, 29 November 2004, in force 29 November 2004.

97 ASEAN Comprehensive Investment Agreement, art. 33. These bodies could include the International Convention on the Settlement of Investment Disputes (ICSID), ICSID Additional Facility, the United Nations Commission on International Trade Law (UNCITRAL) and the Regional Centre for Arbitration in Kuala Lumpur.

98 Trinh Hai Yen, *International Litigation in Practice: The Interpretation of Investment Treaties* (Leiden: Brill Nijhoff, 2014), 186–200.

the sovereign on jurisdictional grounds and 2 were settled on confidential terms.[99] Only two of these known arbitrations involved the ASEAN investment agreement, where one case was dismissed for lack of jurisdiction[100] and the other resulted in settlement being embodied in the award.[101] Although arbitration decisions have no precedential value, the Tribunal's comments in Yaing Chi Oo case were taken on board in drafting the ACIA 2009 and thus require members to observe transparency in their investment requirements.[102]

Economic disputes between member states are now, as a rule, to be settled pursuant to the ASEAN Protocol on Enhanced DSM, unless a specific mechanism is provided for in a separate agreement. For issues that do not involve the interpretation or application of any ASEAN instrument, the mechanisms provided under the Treaty of Amity and Cooperation (TAC) shall be used. This would refer to highly sensitive political and security issues among member states or those that are likely to disturb the peace and harmony in the region. The creation of the High Council, which was stipulated in the TAC in 1976, has never been established. It was intended to function as a regional mechanism for good offices or a committee of mediation, inquiry or conciliation, and to recommend appropriate measures to prevent the deterioration of a dispute or situation.[103] The APSC Blueprint aims to strengthen cooperation under the TAC by convening a conference of High Contracting Parties to the TAC to review its implementing mechanisms.[104]

The ASEAN Enhanced DSM is perceived as the most radical attempt to date, to produce 'hard law' in ASEAN through dispute resolution and rule interpretation. It is patterned in most respects after the WTO Dispute Settlement Understanding and it is hoped it will address the criticisms of its earlier precursor, the 1996 Dispute Settlement Mechanism, for lacking specific complaint procedures and concrete mechanisms

[99] Ibid., 199–200, citing Cambodia, Indonesia, Myanmar, Malaysia, Philippines, Singapore, Thailand and Vietnam.

[100] *Yaung Chi Oo Trading Pte Ltd.* v. *Government of the Union of Myanmar*, ASEAN Case No ARB/01/1, Award, 31 March 2003, (2003) 42 ILM 540, involving AIA 1987.

[101] *Cemex Asia Holdings Ltd* v. *Republic of Indonesia*, ICSID Case No. ARB/04/3 (2007), Award of 23 February 2007.

[102] *Yaung Chi Oo Trading Pte Ltd.* v. *Government of the Union of Myanmar*, ASEAN Case No. ARB/01/1, IIC 278 (2003), (2003) 42 ILM 540, 31 March 2003, para. 58–9.

[103] Treaty of Amity and Cooperation in Southeast Asia, Bali, 24 February 1976, in force 21 June 1976, 1025 UNTS 316, arts. 13–17.

[104] APSC Blueprint, para. 7(A.2.2).

for compensation. Similar to the WTO DSB which is composed of an intergovernmental body, the Senior Economic Officers Meeting (SEOM) administers the ASEAN Enhanced DSM and provides for three stages or processes to settle disputes – advisory, consultative and adjudicatory stages.[105] The first two stages are informal and non-binding while adjudication takes place in the formal arbitration processes by convening the dispute settlement panels.

The findings and recommendation of ASEAN arbitration panel can be adopted with legal force by the SEOM whose decision can be appealed to the Appellate Body which shall be established by the AEM. ASEAN has likewise adopted the negative or reverse consensus practiced in the WTO DSB in the establishment of a panel and in adopting a panel or Appellate Body report. Thus, the SEOM shall adopt the panel report or report of the Appellate Body unless the SEOM decided by consensus not to adopt the report.[106] Enforcement mechanism in the ASEAN Enhanced DSM is generally seen as weak due to its poor enforcement procedures and serves a disincentive for the parties to submit to the mechanism.[107] Sanctions for non-compliance and the procedures for requesting suspension of concession are generally weak.

There is no clarity or specificity in resolving issues that may involve the interpretation or application of the Charter. All that the Charter states is that appropriate dispute settlement mechanisms, including arbitration, shall be provided.[108] There are a range of possibilities for such issues as affecting the relationships among the various ASEAN organs, between an ASEAN organ and member state and its agencies, between an ASEAN organ and an ASEAN citizen and issues of compatibility between the Charter and other ASEAN agreements or instruments to come under the purview of this mechanism. Although it has been specifically mentioned that ASEAN is an intergovernmental body, bestowing it with legal personality opens it to prospects of being subjected to suits from individuals or groups that may be affected by the operation of the Charter. Also, there is a possibility that the Charter

105 ASEAN Protocol on Enhanced Dispute Settlement, arts. 3, 5 and 12.

106 Ibid., arts. 9.1 and 12.13.

107 See Joshua Karton, 'Lessons from International Uniform Law' in Jean E. Kalicki and Anna Joubin-Bret (eds.), *Reshaping the Investor-State Dispute Settlement System: Journeys for the 21st Century* (Brill/Nijhoff, 2015), 48, 77.

108 ASEAN Charter 2007, art. 25.

and other ASEAN instruments may also be subject for adjudication or interpretation before domestic courts and administrative bodies.

None of these formal mechanisms have been used for settling disputes in ASEAN but ASEAN member states had used international tribunals like the International Court of Justice to settle disputes among themselves. In matters involving economic disputes, member countries have used the WTO DSB to bring complaints not only against non-members but also against each other. In 1995, the first case brought before the newly constituted DSB was a request for consultation by Singapore against Malaysia which was later settled.[109] On 7 February 2008, the Philippines made a request for consultation before the WTO DSB concerning Thailand's customs and tax measures on Philippine cigarettes.[110] These measures are considered to be non-tariff barriers which could have been resolved under ASEAN economic agreements or submitted before the ASEAN Enhanced DSM. These incidents serve to reinforce observations that ASEAN members are in general sensitive and reluctant to submit issues among themselves for adjudication and their preference is to resolve problems through bilateral negotiations or through international mechanisms.[111] Cultural factors have often been cited as an explanation for non-use of formal dispute mechanisms but it also points to lack of confidence in utilizing regional adjudication.

There are efforts to make the dispute mechanisms concrete and accessible to users such as the completion of the Special Service Agreement (SSA) for the establishment of the panels and Appellate Body, the ancillary ASEAN Administrative Guidelines for requesting the Establishment of the SSA, the ASEAN General Conditions Applicable to Panel and Appellate Body members under the SSA and the Working Procedures for the ASEAN Compliance Body.[112] It was reported in 2010 that an Instrument for Incorporation of the Rules for Reference of Unresolved Disputes to the ASEAN Charter on Dispute Settlement Mechanism was being drafted. A programme to encourage the use of the ASEAN DSM has been launched through the ASEAN-EU Program for Regional Integration and Support.

[109] Malaysia – Prohibition of Imports of Polyethylene and Polypropylene, WTO Doc WT/DS1/1 (10 January 1995) (Request for Consultation by Singapore).

[110] Thailand – Customs and Fiscal Measures on Cigarettes from the Philippines, WTO Doc WT/DS371/1,G/L/847,G/VAL/11 (7 February 2008) (Request for Consultation by Singapore).

[111] Muthiah Alagappa, 'Institutional Framework: Recommendations for Change' in *ASEAN Reader* (Institute of Southeast Asian Studies, 2004), 65–6.

[112] ASEAN Secretariat, *ASEAN Annual Report 2006–2007*, 20.

Provision for an entity in the ASEAN Secretariat responsible for delivering credible and independent legal advice and service is a modest step in building the legal capacity within ASEAN organs.[113]

Apart from its non-use, there is question about the capacity of ASEAN's dispute settlement mechanisms to resolve inter-state conflicts that challenges ASEAN centrality in the region and its avowed cohesiveness. One example was the perceived lack of diplomatic pressure on the Myanmar junta to open its doors to international humanitarian assistance after cyclone Nargis. Some observers believed that it was the United Nations' persistent efforts and the harsh condemnation from the world community that prompted the junta to finally open its borders, albeit on a limited scale.[114] Another incident involved the Thai–Cambodia military stand-off over the Preah Vihear temple that erupted in July 2008. The issue over the temple has long historical roots but was also triggered by domestic political instability in Thailand where the opposition sought to undermine the government led by Prime Minister Samak by criticizing its position in supporting Cambodia's bid to have the temple listed under the UNESCO world heritage list.[115] In the escalation of tension that followed, Cambodia had sought ASEAN to intervene and diffuse the crisis but the Thai government insisted that it should be resolved bilaterally.[116] ASEAN had to reject the request therefore and Cambodia sought the United Nations Security Council to ease the tension. While the crisis was diffused when the two countries mutually agreed to a voluntary troop withdrawal from the disputed border, the incident proved yet again the inadequacy of ASEAN's regional dispute mechanism framework to effectively and promptly respond to regional issues without the participation or intervention of third parties.

There are structural constraints that also underlie dispute settlement processes in ASEAN. Economic activities drive the imperatives to seek impartial and non-political mechanisms and this has been the trend in international dispute adjudication. As the EU experience demonstrates,

113 Jean-Claude Piris and Walter Woon, *Towards a Rules-Based Community: An ASEAN Legal Service*, 189–92.

114 *ASEAN's Shame* (5 June 2008) Philippine Daily Inquirer, http://opinion.inquirer.net/inquireropinion/editorial/view/20080605-140779/ASEANs-shame. In 1962, Thailand brought the issue of jurisdiction over the temple before the International Court of Justice.

115 Milton Osborne, *Preah Vihear: The Thai–Cambodia Temple Dispute* (8 February 2011) Open Democracy, www.opendemocracy.net/node/46044/pdf

116 Agence France-Presse, *ASEAN Ministers Confront Thai–Cambodia Crisis* (22 July 2008) Inquirer.net, www.services.inquirer.net/article_id=20080722-150068

the increase in the use of its dispute settlement mechanism has been triggered by increased demand for and assiduous use by the private sector of the judicial mechanism. The formal launching of the ASEAN Community in December 2015 could potentially spur greater economic activities, and the implementation of ACIA 2009 could give individuals the capacity to access both domestic and regional dispute mechanisms. These developments could potentially affect the dynamics of ASEAN dispute settlement mechanisms.

In the case of intra-member disputes however, the potential for the use of formal ASEAN dispute mechanisms remains doubtful. As discussed in Chapter 3, even member states in the EU have shown their hesitation to invoke formal proceedings against another member state and the procedure has been rarely used. In ASEAN, a culture of consensus and harmony prevails among state leaders. In the few instances where cases were brought for international adjudication, however, member states clearly did not feel averse to formal adjudication and this merely shows that such decisions do not depend as much on the consideration of the prevailing norm in ASEAN as their economic and strategic interests.

6.7 Conclusion

A law regime is certainly evolving in ASEAN – one that is incremental, fragmented and uneven along the three community pillars. The rationale for ASEAN Community which is focused on achieving economic integration underpins the processes of institution building and the soft regulatory regime that characterize this nascent law regime. There is an ambitious focus on the economics but more modest goals in the political field which show in the 'cooperative' rather than 'integrative' pursuits of the APSC and ASCC. These cooperative goals are reflected in the softer approach to community building in the two pillars although increasing common security concerns and the less contentious areas of women and children welfare, migration and human trafficking have encouraged member countries to adopt norms that are in consonance with international standards and firmer commitments. Gathering of information and standard setting have gained momentum in these areas although behavioural change may take some time. Centralized 'decentralization' rather than decentred regulation best describes the limited and, more often, informal role that the non-state sector participates in norm and standard making and in broader ASEAN processes.

Weak enforcement remains a crucial factor in developing a more stable and consistent law regime in ASEAN. Voluntary commitments and self-enforcement are the default mode in implementing regional agreements. Given the lack of interest and confidence in using the formal dispute resolution mechanisms, enforcement of agreements and the development of uniform laws and jurisprudence in ASEAN will be patchy and uncertain, particularly in the two pillars discussed. This may even cause serious problems in the future, like the exercise of extraterritorial jurisdiction in the ACTIP, where each member countries' judicial bodies make their own interpretation of legal provisions. In reality, there is no ASEAN body tasked with enforcement. The ASEAN Secretariat is a monitoring, not an enforcement, body. There is no systematic and persuasive non-binding coercion mechanism in ASEAN that may add some pressure to governments to honour their responsibilities in regional instruments. This weak provision for enforcement shows the unstable and uncertain path of the soft regulatory regime in ASEAN.

7

Soft Regulation and Informal Rule-Making in the ASEAN Economic Community

7.1 Introduction

The development of the ASEAN legal regime cannot be fully understood without discussing the ASEAN Economic Community (AEC) in particular. The AEC is the backbone of ASEAN integration and Community building. From a purely economic point of view, regional integration essentially involves the expansion of trade or of factors of production by removing distortions or impediments towards the free flow of trade. Both the EU and ASEAN and other regional integration projects considered in this book see economic development as the means to achieve broader political objectives of peace, security and stability whether at the domestic or regional level.

The EU's journey to the rule of law is one of progressive development, from negative integration to positive integration. Negative integration refers to the removal of trade barriers at the national level, which was accelerated with ECJ decisions invalidating national legislation and policies that hinder the free movement of goods, services and capital. Positive integration involves reconstructing economic systems of regulation through a process of developing common policies.[1] Through positive integration, the EU has devised innovative techniques of regulation that involves the use of soft laws, harmonization and forms of informal rule-making. This work is being performed by the European Commission, one of the main organs of the EU composed of independent members and technocrats, and of other Committees with autonomous rule-making powers. In fact it is claimed that the EU has the most vociferous use of soft laws and informal

[1] See, for example, Fritz W. Scharpf, 'Negative and Positive Integration in the Political Economy of European Welfare States' in Gary Marks, Fritz W. Scharpf, Philippe C. Schmitter and Wolfgang Streeck (eds.), *Governance in the European Union* (London: Sage Publications, 1996), 15–39, 16; Jan Tinbergen, *International Economic Integration*, 2nd revised edn. (Amsterdam: Elsevier, 1965).

rule-making, despite it having pioneered rule of law at the regional level through judicial review of Community and member states' actions.

In this chapter, we analyse how soft regulation is developing as an important mechanism for positive integration in the AEC. As already noted, there is noticeable absence of a judicial role in freeing interstate trade and commerce, except in cases involving the ASEAN Investment Agreement where there could be domestic legal remedy to individual persons or entities. A revitalized dispute resolution system in ASEAN has been provided for in the AEC that involves mostly quasi-judicial mechanisms that have remained untested due to their non-use. A key enquiry for this chapter is the extent to which soft regulation can drive economic integration and the prospect of developing an efficient regime for enforcement in the AEC. Another emerging aspect in ASEAN's soft regulatory regime is 'informal rule-making' in setting standards and producing legal harmonization in ASEAN members.

7.2 The ASEAN Economic Community and Progress of Regional Integration

Rule of law literature suggests that to foster the rule of law, what is essential is the stabilization of institutions and development of common policies that are legally enforceable.[2] But where there is wide divergence of interests among member states, unwillingness to loosen claims of sovereignty, or where flexibility is better suited to attain objectives, states have resorted to informal and less-restrictive tools of regulation. The diffusion of rules of international law or global rules has also contributed in influencing the way states interact, interpret and internalize their rules and norms of interaction. Thus, the advent of economic liberalism has pioneered a more open-ended, informal and plural legal system that affords more flexibility through the use of soft processes and mechanisms, or a combination of formal and informal processes, or hybrids.[3] These processes have put a limit to the erosion of state sovereignty brought about by deterritorialization of economic activities, creation of autonomous supranational institutions and international lawmaking bodies and increasing participation of non-state actors in rule-making. Informal mechanisms and processes which are prevalent in international trade and commerce and dispute

[2] See Michael J. Trebilcock and Mariana Mota Prado, *What Makes Poor Countries Poor?: Institutional Determinants of Development* (Cheltenham: Edward Elgar, 2011), 77–9.

[3] Twining, *Globalisation and Legal Theory*, 88–90.

resolution often use soft laws and mechanisms which are characterized by lesser degrees of precision, obligation and delegation of extensive powers. These include such instruments as memorandum of understanding, model laws, trade facilitation, harmonization and arbitral bodies. The features of soft regulatory regimes tie in with international organizations, such as ASEAN, which desire more control and flexibility.

'In-Law' or informal international lawmaking (also known as post-national rule-making or exercise of public authority) is the term that is being used to capture this open-ended and flexible system of international rulemaking.[4] It involves cross-border policy coordination and standard setting. It lies outside the state's constitutional system. Nor is it governed by international law, output is informal and non-legally binding but normative as it affects behaviour or that output is expected to be implemented at the domestic level. Processes could occur as loosely organized networks or groupings though they could also take place within a formal organization. Actors involved in rule-making are not traditional international law actors (such as heads of states, foreign ministries and embassies) but increasingly domestic public authorities and private actors.[5]

Assessing the effectiveness of ASEAN's soft regulatory regime may be premature considering that the AEC was only formally established in December 2015. Regional integration initiatives in ASEAN began in 1992 that culminated in the adoption of the AEC Blueprint at the 13th ASEAN Summit in 2007 that provided a comprehensive master plan towards the establishment of the AEC. We can say that regional integration began in earnest during this time as concrete measures with timelines and action leading towards an ASEAN free trade area started to be implemented. The establishment of a free trade area is a continuing agenda for the AEC. There is official recognition that AEC goals have been met on many fronts,[6] but delivery of tangible outcomes still need to be amply demonstrated. The post-AEC 2015 programme, in the form of newly signed AEC Blueprint 2025, aims at closing the gap between implementation and paper commitments.[7] In this chapter, it is demonstrated that the current soft and incomplete regulatory regime is lacking any persuasive coercive

[4] Joost Pauwelyn, 'Informal International Lawmaking: Framing the Concept and Research Questions' in Joost Pauwelyn, Ramses A. Wessel and Jan Wouters (eds.), *Informal International Lawmaking* (Oxford: Oxford University Press, 2012), 13–34.

[5] Ibid., 19–20.

[6] ASEAN Secretariat, *A Blueprint for Growth: ASEAN Economic Community 2015: Progress and Key Achievements* (Jakarta: ASEAN Secretariat, 2015), 5.

[7] ASEAN Economic Community Blueprint 2015, signed 15 December 2015 at Kuala Lumpur.

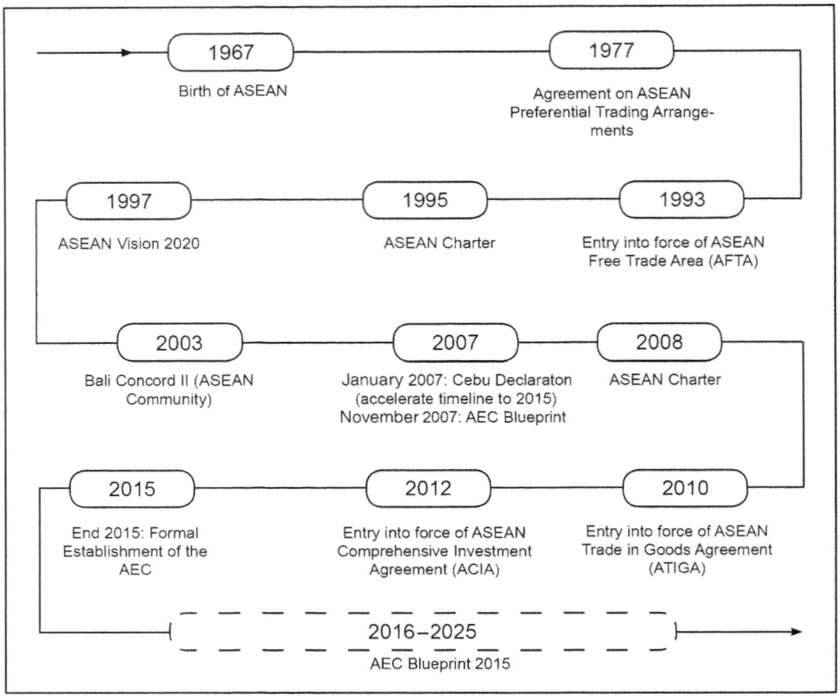

Figure 7.1 AEC milestones
Source: ASEAN Secretariat, *Blueprint for Growth*, 4.

mechanism, while having achieved modest gains, however stifles the effective functioning of the AEC and the realization of its far-reaching goals.

Figure 7.1 shows the timelines leading to the establishment of the AEC in 2015 and the recent adoption of the AEC Blueprint 2025. Figure 7.2 shows the four interrelated pillars comprising the AEC: (1) single market and production base, (2) competitive economic region, (3) region of equitable economic development and (4) region integrated into global economy. The AEC Blueprint 2008 specifies priority integration sectors and four timelines for implementation.[8]

[8] The 12 priority sectors are agro-based products, air transport, automotive products, e-ASEAN, electronics and electrical goods, fisheries, healthcare services, rubber-based goods, textiles and clothing, tourism, logistics services and wood-based products and has timelines of four implementation periods.

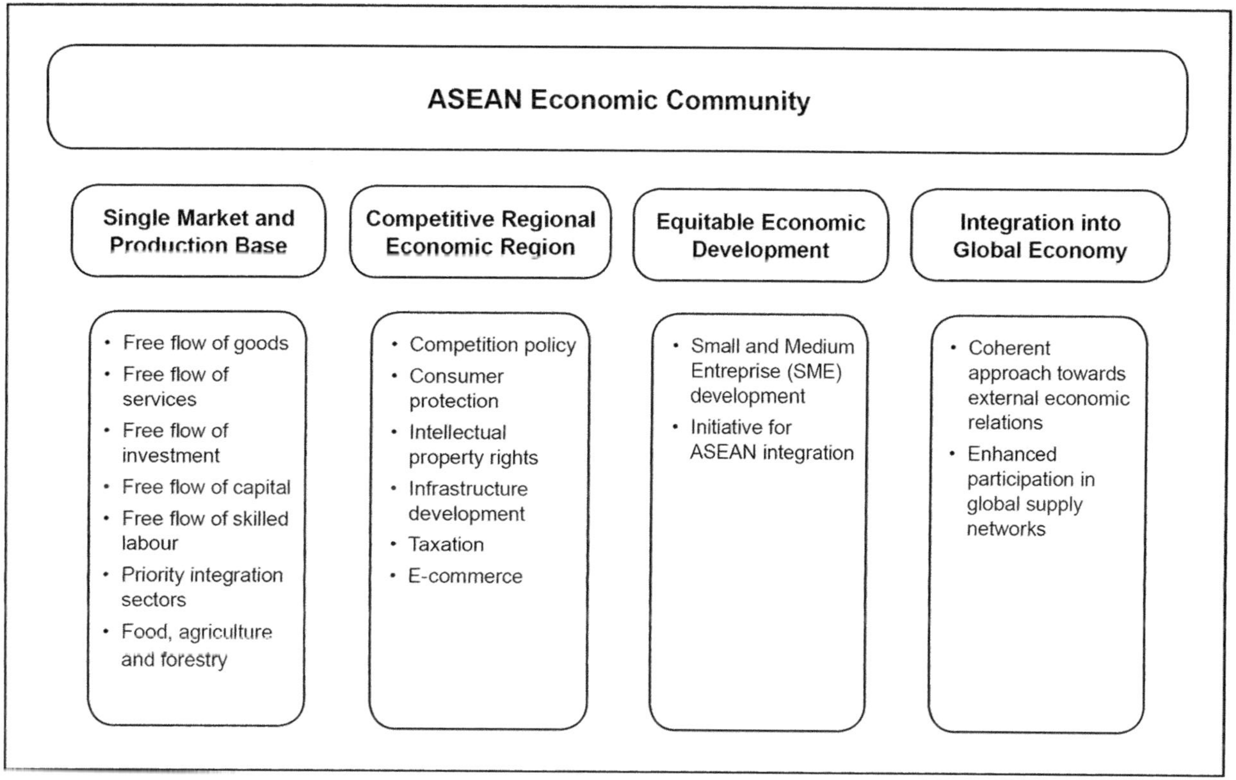

Figure 7.2 Four pillars of the AEC
Source: ASEAN Secretariat, *Blueprint for Growth*, 5.

Among the key achievements of regional integration claimed by ASEAN is the increase in intra-regional trade and investments and the elimination of tariff barriers. Intra-ASEAN trade constitutes ASEAN's largest trading partner with 24 per cent share of total ASEAN trade while intra-ASEAN foreign direct investment (FDI) is the second highest source of total FDI flows to ASEAN.[9] These figures are still small compared to intra-regional trade generated by EU-28, which is averaging more than 50 per cent in aggregate trade in goods, services and capital. EU has total trade share of over 62 per cent in merchandise flow in 2013 despite the onset of economic crisis.[10] ASEAN's intra-regional trade however is quite significant especially when compared against other vibrant regional groups such as MERCOSUR (over 15 per cent) and ECOWAS (less than 20 per cent).[11]

Intra-regional trade in ASEAN was clearly stimulated by the launch of the ASEAN preferential trade agreement in the late 1990s but became stagnant from 2010.[12] Intra-regional trade growth in ASEAN has been mostly driven by three of the larger economies – Singapore, Malaysia and Thailand[13] – which account for almost 70 per cent of total intra-ASEAN trade.[14] On the one hand, this points to the slower or weaker capacity of other member countries to contribute towards and benefit from trade liberalization. On the other hand, this shows the broader structural constraints to deeper regional trade liberalization. ASEAN member states have

[9] ASEAN Secretariat, *ASEAN Statistics Leaflet: Selected Key Indicators 2015* (Jakarta, ASEAN Secretariat, November 2015).

[10] See Eurostat, *Intra-EU Trade in Goods – Recent Trends* (7 April 2016) http://ec.europa.eu/eurostat/statistics-explained/index.php/Intra-EU_trade_in_goods_-_recent_trends

[11] See MERCOSUR intra-regional trade statistics International Trade and Integration Division, Economic Commission for Latin America and the Caribbean, 'MERCOSUR Intra-Regional Trade Statistics International Trade in Latin America and the Caribbean' (Trade Statistics Bulletin No. 19, United Nations ECLAC, 2015), www.cepal.org/sites/default/files/statistical_bulletin_n19.pdf; calculations of ECOWAS intra-regional trade in the period 1999–2009 in Wumi Olayiwola and Oluyomi Ola-David, 'Economic Integration, Trade Facilitation and Agricultural Export Performance in ECOWAS Member States' (Paper prepared for presentation at the Eighth African Economic Conference on 'Regional Integration in Africa', Johannesberg, October 2013).

[12] Organisation for Economic Co-operation and Development, *Economic Outlook for Southeast Asia, China and India: Enhancing Regional Ties* (Paris: OECD Publishing, 2016), 134. http://dx.doi.org/10.1787/saeo-2016-en

[13] Jörn Dosch, 'The ASEAN Economic Community: What Stands in the Way?' (AsiaPacific Issues No. 119, East West Center, September 2015), www.eastwestcenter.org/system/tdf/private/api119.pdf?file=1&type=node&id=35319, 4.

[14] Ibid., 4.

more competitive than complementary economies, producing a narrow range of similar primary products and labour-intensive manufactured goods for exports.[15] The wide diversity in economic development among member countries and large gap in the standard of living among the peoples in the region pose an even more difficult challenge in creating an integrated economy. Figure 7.3 shows the comparative GDP per capita income among ASEAN countries.

Substantial reduction of tariffs is also reported to be one of the ASEAN integration's successes.[16] In 2015, ASEAN reported to have virtually eliminated import duties among ASEAN-6 member countries, with 92.2 per cent of tariff lines at 0 per cent, while CMLV countries have achieved 90.86 per cent.[17] Tariff elimination does not translate to greater trade utilization nor does it automatically generate an open market.[18] This observation is bolstered by a recent survey that shows less than 10 per cent of intra-ASEAN trade uses the AFTA concessions.[19] Non-utilization of trade concessions is partly blamed on the difficulty complying with documentation (known as Form 'D') required to determine Rules of Origin (RoO) and also for the fact that 40 per cent regional value content (40 per cent VA rule) is hard to meet.[20] The elimination of non-tariff barriers (NTB), a central measure to trade liberalization, also remains a formidable challenge to ASEAN integration with their numbers increasing related to quotas and technical regulations.[21] One study has pointed to the difficulties in facilitating import clearances, licencing, testing, customs inspection and

15 Ibid., 5.

16 See, for example, Jayant Menon, *Moving Too Slowly Towards an ASEAN Economic Community* (14 October 2014) East Asia Forum, www.eastasiaforum.org/2014/10/14/moving-too-slowly-towards-an-asean-economic-community

17 ASEAN Secretariat, Blueprint for Growth, 10.

18 Ibid.

19 Hal Hill and Jayant Menon, 'ASEAN Commercial Policy: A Rare Case of Outward-Looking Regional Integration' (Working Paper on Regional Economic Integration No. 144, Asian Development Bank, November 2014), 8.

20 In The ERIA Survey on the use of FTAS in ASEAN, there is a high degree of lack of awareness of the existence of the process to obtain RoO. It is also argued that the local content requirement is hard to meet by ASEAN exporters as majority of export products consist of electronics and machinery which use high foreign content. Ikumo Isono and Yoshifumi Fukunaga, 'Utilisation of Free Trade Agreements by Service Industries in ASEAN' in Lili Yan Ing and Shujiro Urata (eds.), *The Use of FTAs in ASEAN: A Survey-Based Analysis* (Research Project Report, Economic Research Institute for ASEAN and East Asia, August 2015), 32; See also Dosch, 'The ASEAN Economic Community'.

21 Dosch, 'The ASEAN Economic Community', 3.

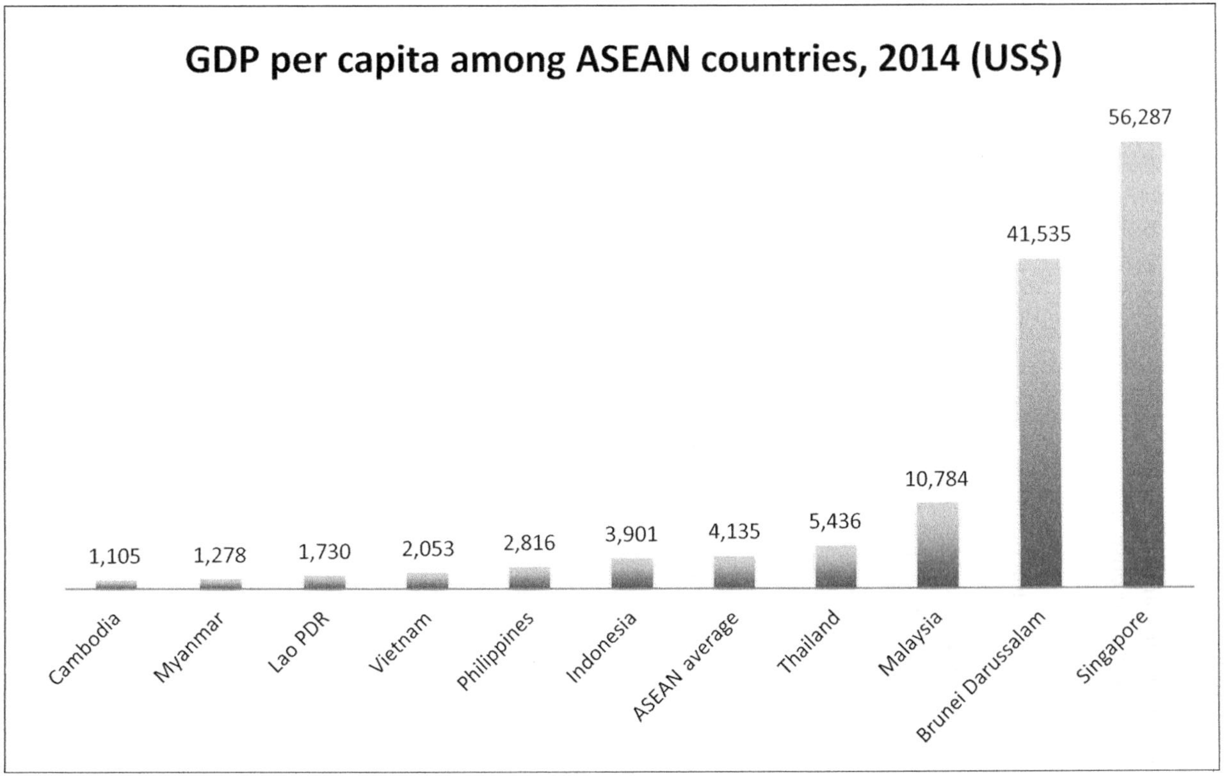

Figure 7.3 GDP per capita among ASEAN countries

Graph compiled with data from ASEAN Secretariat, 'Country Level Profile, 2014' in *ASEAN Statistics Leaflet: Selected Key Indicators 2015* (Jakarta: ASEAN Secretariat, November 2015).

work permits among the major concerns of business.[22] It is also noted that countries like Myanmar, Indonesia and the Philippines are applying the most NTBs while Cambodia and Thailand having the lowest NTB restriction among the members.[23] The increase in NTBs was also a trend in the early stages of the EU as a means to offset the loss associated with tariff reductions; this has necessitated a stronger regulatory regime to counter this creeping protectionism.[24] In ASEAN, NTBs have so far been free from any form of stringent measure but are mainly addressed through consultation with governments.[25]

Other aspects of economic integration have shown that slow or little progress is blamed on both sectoral sensitivities and a weak regulatory framework.[26] Domestic sensitivities are reflected in weak commitments for liberalizing trade in services and investments or that commitments often lag behind actual practice.[27] There is still as yet no comprehensive binding agreement on services liberalization. The ASEAN Framework Agreement on Services (AFAS) remains the key reference point for the services integration programme which contains eight packages of commitments from member states. While the ASEAN Comprehensive Investment Agreement entered into force on 29 March 2012, two countries – Thailand and Vietnam – have not ratified the agreement.

As movement of skilled persons is intertwined with trade in services, labour mobility in ASEAN has only been committed so far to a few professions – engineering, accounting, nursing, architecture, surveying, medical practitioners, dental practitioners and tourism professionals – which have been covered by mutual recognition arrangements (MRAs).[28]

22 Mitsuyo Ando and Ayako Obashi, 'The Pervasiveness of Non-Tariff Measures in ASEAN – Evidences from the Inventory Approach' in Mia Mikic with Martin Wermelinger (eds.), *Rising Non-Tariff Protectionism and Crisis Recovery: A Study by the Asia-Pacific Research and Training Network on Trade* (Bangkok: United Nations Publication, 2010), 27.

23 Ibid., 34.

24 E. Damsgaard Hansen, *European Economic History: From Mercantilism to Maastricht and Beyond* (Copenhagen: Copenhagen Business School Press, 2001), 432.

25 Stefano Inama and Edmund W. Sim, *The Foundation of the ASEAN Economic Community* (Cambridge: Cambridge University Press, 2015), 108.

26 Dosch, 'The ASEAN Economic Community', 7.

27 See Intal Ponciano S., Jr, Dionisius A. Norjoko, Yoshifumi Fukunaga, 'ASEAN Economic Community Scorecard' (Summary of ERIA Research Projects 2014–2015, Economic Research Institute for ASEAN and EAST Asia, April 2015), www.eria.org/Research-Summary-2014-15.pdf, 20; Philippa Dee, 'Does AFAS Have Bite? Comparing Commitments with Actual Practice' (2014) 35 *Journal of Asian Economics* 46–64.

28 ASEAN Secretariat and the World Bank, *ASEAN Services Integration Report: A Joint Report by the ASEAN Secretariat and the World Bank* (Jakarta: ASEAN Secretariat, 2015), 125.

Even with the signing of the MRAs, actual implementation remains slow and registration as a foreign professional is used more as an indicator of professional quality rather than to facilitate the movement of skilled persons.[29] Implementation also varies from country to country, with some countries reserving the practice of profession to their nationals and some having a more open regime.[30] For example, legal services liberalization, which is considered vital for trade liberalization and attracting FDI, remains a highly restrictive sector with only five member countries having signed on to ASEAN agreements.[31] The Philippines legal sector is considered to be highly protectionist despite its comprehensive and well-developed regulatory regime on the legal profession.[32]

7.3 The AEC Soft Regulatory Framework

It has been observed that contrary to the ambitious goals of the AEC, ASEAN is pursuing a shallow form of economic integration.[33] In this chapter, we observe that ASEAN has an incomplete soft regulatory regime that contributes to the slow and uneven pace of regional economic integration, and thus to a 'shallow' form of integration. It can also be said that this weak regulatory regime is a reflection of weak commitment towards deeper forms of economic integration. While the AEC is still in its infancy and has chosen an incremental bottom-up approach, creating a working regulatory regime is important if ASEAN wants to see significant progress in integration processes. A framework might be filled out over time. The EU shows a complete regulatory regime consisting of soft and hard rules,

[29] See Yoshifumi Fukunaga, 'Assessing the Progress of ASEAN MRAs on Professional Services' (ERIA Discussion Paper No. 2015-12, Economic Research Institute for ASEAN and East Asia Discussion Paper, March 2015), www.eria.org/ERIA-DP-2015-21.pdf

[30] Philippa Dee and Anne McNaughton, 'Promoting Domestic Reforms through Regionalism' (Working Paper No. 312, Asian Development Bank Institute, October 2011), www.adb.org/sites/default/files/publication/156167/adbi-wp312.pdf

[31] See Pasha L. Hsieh, 'ASEAN's Liberalization of Legal Services: The Singapore Case' (2013) 8(2) *Asian Journal of WTO and International Health Law and Policy* 475–97, 478.

[32] Ibid., 479.

[33] See Razeen Sally, 'ASEAN FTAs: State of Play and Outlook for ASEAN's Regional and Global Integration' in Sanchita Basu Das, Jayant Menon, Rodolfo Severino and Omkar Lal Shrestha (eds.), *The ASEAN Economic Community: A Work in Progress* (Singapore: Institute for Southeast Asian Studies, 2013), 320–81, 375; Jenina Joy Chavez, 'Regionalism Beyond an Elite Project: The Challenge of Building Responsive Sub Regional Economic Communities' in Melissa G. Curley and Nicholas Thomas (eds.), *Advancing East Asian Regionalism* (New York: Routledge, 2007)158–78, 171.

formal and informal processes and voluntary compliance and enforceable sanctions. But this took a long time to evolve.

Comparative studies on firm and industry regulation also show that compliance becomes effective when there is escalation of measures or sanctions[34] and that the compliance regime is, by and large, complete.[35] By a complete compliance regime, we simply mean the escalation of sanctions from soft informal measures towards one that is coercive and legally enforceable.[36] The compliance pyramid however does not have to move from the bottom up in order to work. The application can be flexible and recalibrated as needs arise.

At present, ASEAN's regulatory regime consists mainly of voluntary and flexible non-coercive measures and hardly any coercive measure for compliance. In Figure 7.4, the phases of AEC governance are divided into rule-making, implementation and enforcement. Rule-making is the process of creating, adopting and revising rules and norms in the conduct of trade and business among member countries and in resolving issues among the participants of regional trade. In AEC, rules and norm creation is the exclusive prerogative of member states through the ASEAN Summit as the supreme policy-making body in ASEAN. The AEM, AFTA Council and AIA Council are likewise vested with recommendatory powers but final decisions in the form of formal agreements rest with the Summit. We see however the increasing role of ASEAN Committees and *ad hoc* groups that provides significant inputs in policy formulation. The ASEAN Secretariat also plays an important role in formulating policies and rules through its function in providing studies and generating information. The ASEAN Secretariat's Statistics Division is responsible for collation, consolidation and dissemination of social and economic data and development of indicators used to assess the progress of integration goals.[37]

Compliance and enforcement are very similar in that they both aim for the implementation of member states' commitments and obligations

[34] Ian Ayres and John Braithwaite, *Responsive Regulation: Transcending the Deregulation Debate* (Oxford: Oxford University Press, 1992), 35–3; Valerie Braithwaite and John Braithwaite, 'An Evolving Compliance Model for Tax Enforcement' in Neal Shover and John Paul Wright (eds.), *Crimes of Privilege: Readings in White-Collar Crime* (New York: Oxford University Press, 2000), 405–19; Valerie Braithwaite and John Braithwaite, 'The Politics of Legalism: Rules versus Standards in Nursing-Home Regulation' (1995) 4 *Social and Legal Studies* 307–41.

[35] Ayres and Braithwaite, *Responsive Regulation*.

[36] Ibid.

[37] ASEAN, *About ASEANstats*, www.asean.org/storage/images/resources/Statistics/About%20ASEANstats.pdf

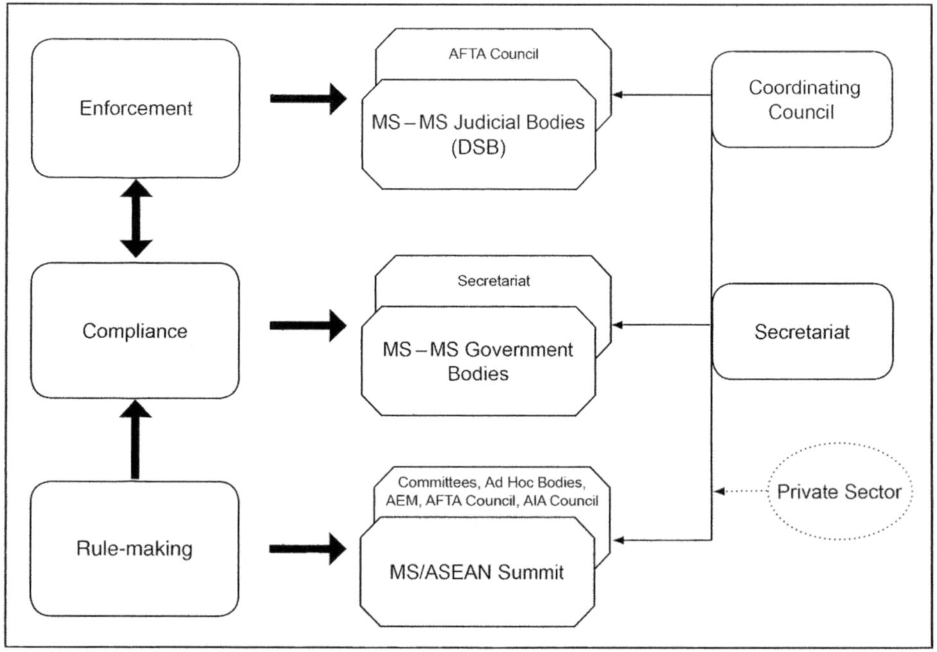

Figure 7.4 Phases of AEC governance

under the Charter and other regional agreements. In this book however, we refer compliance to member state's voluntary actions and initiatives, also akin to self-enforcement, while enforcement entails a degree of compulsion, through threats of legally enforceable sanctions. In this figure, we see that both aspects are exercised by, and left to the discretion of member states and a sparse regional mechanism to support these processes and mechanisms. Member states and national government bodies are the key mechanisms in rule-making and implementation of economic programmes of the AEC. The absence of an autonomous regional compliance and enforcement body is clearly an obvious flaw in AEC's governance framework. An overstretched ASEAN Secretariat is the main regional mechanism that is tasked with overseeing the range of these governance functions in the AEC (see Figure 7.5) through its role in providing secretariat functions to all three communities and the AFTA and AIA councils.

The ASEAN Secretariat is the key regional mechanism in facilitating compliance by member states. It must be stressed that enforcement, with the use of coercive enforceable measures, only exists on paper. The previous chapter discussed the unused ASEAN Enhanced DSM which provides for a WTO-like enforcement procedures. The AFTA Council, the main body responsible in overseeing the implementation of the ASEAN free trade area, is vested with authority to approve and provide recommendations on member states' notification to temporarily modify or suspend its tariff concessions.[38] The Council is composed of senior economic ministers of member countries, and are most often the same members of the ASEAN Economic Ministers' (AEM) Meeting. The ASEAN Secretariat provides informal and non-binding advice and consultation on business issues through its Legal Services and Agreements Division. A specific mechanism, the ASEAN Consultation to Solve Trade and Investment Issues (ACT) was established which is patterned after the EU SOLVIT, a mechanism private entities can access to resolve operational issues. These non-binding advisory mechanisms are intended to resolve issues in a quick and efficient manner, and are a way to avoid the escalation of 'formal disputes'. At present, there is no indication that these non-binding advisory mechanisms have been progressively used by the private sector. One reason cited

[38] ASEAN Trade in Goods Agreement, Cha-am, 26 February 2009, in force 17 May 2010, art. 23.

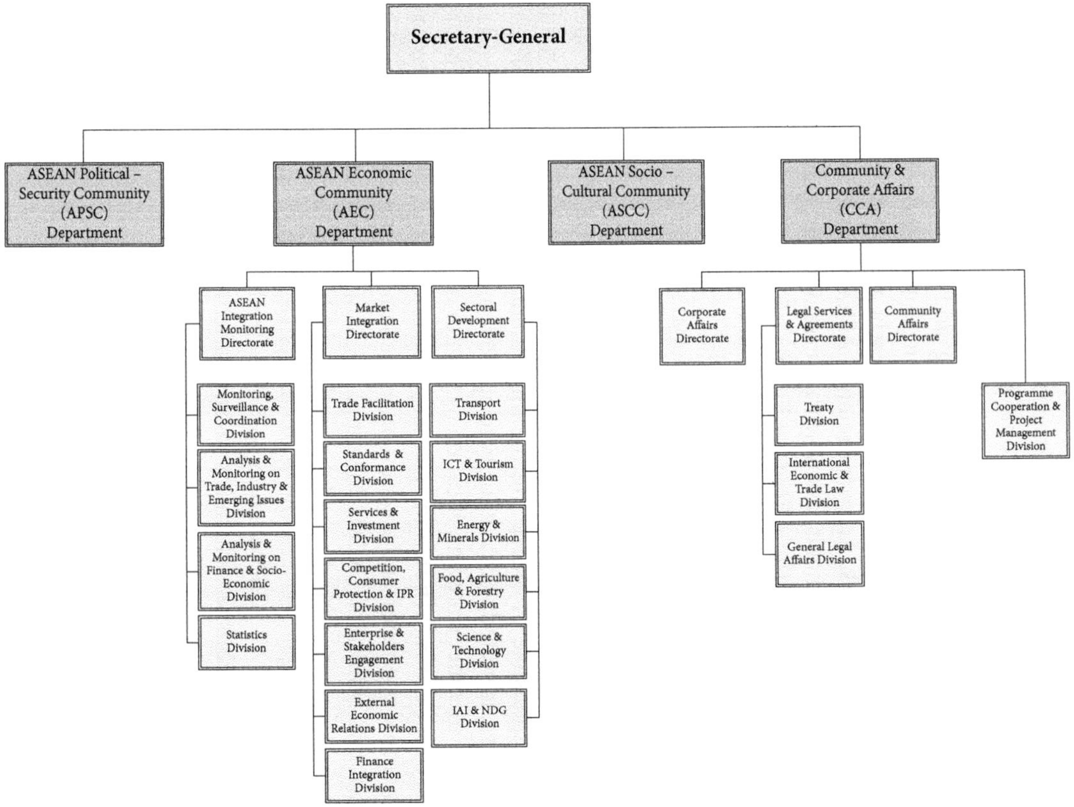

Figure 7.5 The AEC department of the ASEAN Secretariat

in the survey for the non-use of ASEAN trade concessions is the lack of awareness or knowledge of ASEAN processes and mechanisms.[39]

A key instrument for monitoring compliance being used by the ASEAN Secretariat is the ASEAN Scorecard which is a system devised to track the roadmap and measures outlined in the AEC Blueprint. Since the adoption of the mechanism in 2008, the ASEAN has issued three Scorecards in 2010, 2012 and 2015. The 2015 AEC Scorecard shows a full implementation rate for the two pillars, equitable economic development and global economic integration. The scores for single market and competitive region stood at 92.4 and 90.5 per cent, respectively.[40] ASEAN however acknowledges that there are at least 54 high priority measures that have not been implemented and where implementation can generate great impact on regional trade.[41] As a compliance monitoring measure, the Scorecard provides a checklist on whether countries have signed and ratified regional agreements and supportive activities to realize their commitments. It does not act as an impact assessment tool and does not therefore reflect the actual implementation of measures on the ground. There are also concerns how transparent the process is in coming out with the information as those involved are only governments nor is there any incentive provided for members complying with their commitments.[42] In essence, the Scorecard does not act as a peer-pressure mechanism, as the device – patterned after the EU Internal Market Scorecard – is known for.[43]

Conversely, private–public peer-pressure initiative happens in specific economic areas of mutual interest, and shows the necessity of a parallel process in the absence of a strong regional compliance regime. The ASEAN Governance Scorecard (AGS) is an initiative by the ASEAN Capital Markets Forum (ACMF) supported by the Asian Development Bank to benchmark governance standards and practices of ASEAN publicly listed companies (PLCs) in relation to regional and international standards and

[39] Marn-Heong Wong and Andre Wirjo, *Findings from 2013 ASEAN-BAC Survey on ASEAN Competitiveness* (Research Report, ASEAN Business Advisory Council, 2013).

[40] ASEAN Secretariat, *Blueprint for Growth*, 9.

[41] Ibid.

[42] See Sanchita Basu-Das, 'Assessing the Progress and Impediments Towards an ASEAN Economic Community' in Sanchita Basu-Das (ed.), *ASEAN Economic Community Scorecard: Performance and Perception* (Singapore: Institute of Southeast Asian Studies, 2013), 1–19.

[43] Ibid., 16; Jayant Menon and Anna Cassandra Melendez, 'Realizing an ASEAN Economic Community: Progress and Remaining Challenges' (Economics Working Paper Series, Working Paper No. 432, Asian Development Bank May 2015), www.adb.org/sites/default/files/publication/160067/ewp-432.pdf

best practices.[44] The AGS is meant to elevate the standards of corporate governance practices in the region towards an integrated capital market and in increasing their visibility to investors. Created in 2004 under the auspices of the ASEAN Finance Ministers, the ACMF's membership comes from public and private capital markets regulators. From a focus on harmonization of rules and regulations, ACMF shifted its track towards more strategic issues facing the region's capital markets.[45] The AGS adopts a rigorous methodology through a double process of assessment first by domestic ranking bodies (DRBs), followed by peer review and a discussion by the DRBs and reviewers.[46] Since its first launching in 2013, the number of PLCs assessed had increased from 35 to 529 and includes six member countries (Thailand, Malaysia, Singapore, Indonesia, Philippines and Vietnam).

In the absence of a regional judicial mechanism, legal enforcement depends on member state's national judicial and administrative procedures,[47] or by invoking commercial arbitration procedures under the ASEAN Enhanced DSM or other recognized arbitration bodies in the case of investment disputes.[48] Under current legal procedures, private individuals or entities are not authorized to bring suits on matters relating to ASEAN processes unless these fall into one of investor issues stated in the ACIA.[49]

Figure 7.6 summarizes the compliance and enforcement regime in the AEC. The pyramid shows not only the incomplete nature of the regulatory regime but also the excessive reliance on two highly non-coercive mechanisms: information gathering and monitoring and consultation. At present, the flow of regulation only moves between the first two bottom stages and does not deliver a threat of strong coercion for noncompliance. There is hardly any peer pressure being used as argued in the previous sections. While the three topmost mechanisms exist on paper, these

[44] James A. Nugent, 'Foreward' in Asian Development Bank, *ASEAN Corporate Governance Scorecard: Country Reports and Assessments 2013–2014* (Mandaluyong City, Philippines: ASEAN Development Bank, 2014), viii.

[45] *ASEAN Capital Markets Forum*, www.theacmf.org

[46] Asian Development Bank, *ASEAN Corporate Governance Scorecard*, 2–3.

[47] As is the case under Section B, arts. 28–41, Asian Comprehensive Investment Agreement 2009 for investment disputes.

[48] Apart from the ad hoc arbitration proceedings in the ASEAN Enhanced DSM, regional and international arbitration such as the International Centre for Settlement of Investment Disputes, New York Convention and UNCITRAL Arbitration Rules can be elected to handle arbitral disputes. See Section B, art. 28, Asian Comprehensive Investment Agreement 2009.

[49] Asian Comprehensive Investment Agreement 2009, arts. 4 and 19.

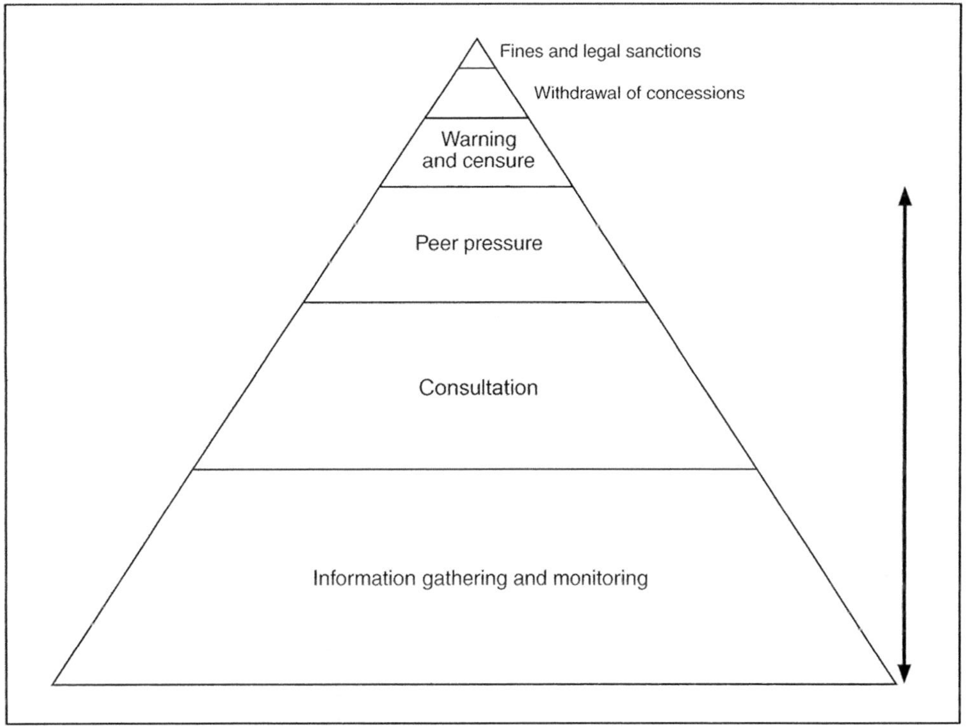

Figure 7.6 The AEC soft compliance and enforcement pyramid

instruments – warning and censure, withdrawal of concessions and use of fines and legal sanctions – do not exist nor are they being used in order to stimulate compliance. Unlike consultation, the first tier in the pyramid has increasingly been systematized with the use of Scorecard and statistical devices to provide a coherent and effective mechanism for gathering, collating and presenting information to the public.[50] The ASEAN Statistical system has been developed and increasingly improved with the development of indicators, benchmarking with international standards and transparency in the sources of information. The consultation procedures such as the provision of advisory services by the ASEAN Legal Services Department need to be systematized or that a separate legal unit for the AEC needs to be established given the scope and extent of AEC integration objectives. As argued previously, there is no real peer-pressure mechanism in AEC. The current system, such as the use of the Scorecard, can benefit from the AGS initiative on the use of peer review and grading system in order to improve voluntary compliance by member states.

7.4 Economic Integration through Trade Facilitation and the Role of Non-state Actors

Trade facilitation is an area that the AEC and its development partners have invested heavily in facilitating the free movement of goods and addressing some technical barriers to trade. As an area of positive integration, ASEAN countries are expected to implement trade facilitation measures. Regulating trade facilitation is important as it involves complex processes and interaction among multiple stakeholders from both the public and private sectors. Making trade facilitation more efficient, cost-effective and transparent is necessary in facilitating trade in goods but this also hinges on how it is implemented at the operational level. Trade facilitation refers to the simplification and harmonization of international trade procedures and involves activities, rules and formalities to assist the movement of goods including bank payments.[51] It is commonly used by institutions to improve the regulatory interface between government agencies and

[50] The ASEAN statistical regime provides various services and products that the public can use such as the interactive online ASEANstats, ASEAN Statistical Yearbook, etc. See ASEAN Secretariat, *ASEANStats: Building Knowledge in the ASEAN Community* (Jakarta: ASEAN Secretariat, October 2011), http://aseanstats.asean.org/

[51] A Grainger (2011) quoted in World Trade Organisation, *WTO Training Package: What is Trade Facilitation?* (Geneva: World Trade Organisation, 1998).

traders at national borders with a view to reducing cost, maximizing efficiency of international trade and enhancing competitiveness for foreign investments, while safeguarding legitimate regulatory objectives.[52]

Since 1996, there has been progressive development of trade facilitation measures in ASEAN that have accompanied the adoption of major economic instruments. The three areas of trade facilitation prioritized by AEC are the ASEAN Single Window (ASW) and ASEAN e-Customs, developing and harmonization of standards and technical regulations, and MRAs. Established in 2006, the ASW is a platform for single point of entry using national single windows where trade-related documents and information can be submitted to speed up customs clearance and reduce transaction costs.[53] The e-Customs complements the ASW and provides an online portal for submission of documents. Self-certification, now pilot tested in all member countries, authorizes certified exporters the freedom to declare their products having satisfied the ASEAN origin criteria and therefore the benefit of trade preferences. Apart from the MRAs for professional recognition, MRAs in three sectors were concluded: electrical equipment and electronics, cosmetics and medicinal products while those in prepared foodstuffs, automotive and building construction sectors are in progress.

In this section, we demonstrate that as a flagship programme in the AEC, effective regulation of trade facilitation can contribute towards clarity, certainty and transparency of economic rules. There is also opportunity to provide solutions to recurrent issues of corruption and arbitrariness associated with the exercise of public power. Strengthening of domestic institutions like the customs bureau, an agency that is perennially complained of as being highly corrupt, is seen as an outcome of improved trade facilitation.[54] Without a strong coercive enforcement regime, the success of trade facilitation measures is heavily dependent on voluntary compliance by member countries – by government bureaucracies working on the ground and the cooperation of industry sector. Within member countries, there should be inducements for governments to exercise strong domestic regulatory functions. Trade facilitation offers incentives for both the

[52] Andrew Grainger, 'Trade Facilitation: A Conceptual Review' (2011) 45(1) *Journal of World Trade* 39–62.

[53] Protocol to Establish and Implement the ASW, Siem Reap, in force 20 December 2006.

[54] Asian Development Bank, *Strengthening Institutional Knowledge and Capacity of Customs Administrations for Trade Facilitation within the Association of Southeast Asian Nations* (Technical Assistance Report, ASEAN Development Bank, August 2014), www.adb.org/sites/default/files/project-document/81936/46192-001-tar.pdf

government and private sectors to cooperate and work towards greater efficiency of the system.

Trade facilitation and harmonization is gradually reshaping the regulatory framework and practices in member states.[55] Although domestic regulatory reforms are slow, in general ASEAN member countries are predisposed to participate in trade facilitation measures. While in some countries there are strong domestic interests, including bureaucratic resistance, which put up barriers towards reforms, regional integration initiatives and fear of being left behind by other countries have provided the impetus to adopt programmes geared towards enhancing the movement of goods. For instance, the ASW initiative started with only three member countries – Thailand, Singapore and Malaysia – showing strong interest on the project. All ASEAN member countries have now signed in to the ASW and the Protocol on the Legal Framework to Implement the ASW on 15 September 2015.[56] Since December 2015, the live operation of the ASW has commenced with five members participation: Indonesia, Malaysia, Thailand, Vietnam and Singapore. Vietnam and Brunei Darussalam are expected to join the ASW by 2017; the remaining ASEAN members are in the process of completing their respective national single window infrastructure.

As an example of the ASEAN-X formula for decision-making, the ASW provides an illustration of how subtle forms of non-binding coercion can stimulate response and action from other parties. The benefits or gains from the programme also provide incentives for other countries to follow. This is also an example of multi-stakeholder support such as foreign funding and domestic and international industries pushing for greater efficiency and transparency in customs administration.[57]

The Philippines, known as a country with high business transaction costs and a highly corrupt customs bureaucracy, the Philippine Bureau of Customs (BOC), has made strides in reforming customs administration.[58] With strong political will and support of private industry groups, the BOC has become a priority agency for reform with a two-pronged objective of

[55] See, for example, ASEAN Secretariat and the World Bank, *ASEAN Services Integration Report*.

[56] ASEAN Single Window Portal, 'About ASEAN Single Window', *ASEAN Single Window: Trade Facilitation for the ASEAN Economic Community*, http://asw.asean.org/about-asw

[57] The United States and the European Union have provided financial and technical assistance to the programme, particularly to developing ASEAN countries in developing their NSWs.

[58] Myrna S. Austria, 'The Philippines and the AEC beyond 2015: Managing Domestic Challenges' (2015) 32(2) *Journal of Southeast Asian Economics* 220–38, 223.

increasing government revenues and providing a competitive business environment.[59] While revenue targets are still unmet in the last eight years, the BOC has steadily increased its customs collection year after year.[60] Perceived as the most corrupt among all government offices, corruption in the agency however has seen a declining trend since 2011.[61] Change management in leadership and bureaucratic reforms have also assisted the BOC in slowly addressing customs maladministration. The three other government offices – Office of the Ombudsman, Bureau of Internal Revenue and Commission on Audit – have increasingly shown their capacity in conducting corruption complaints, audit investigations and tax collection, respectively.[62] Significant legislation has also been passed, the Customs Modernization and Tariff Act (CMTA), aimed at instituting fair and transparent customs and tariff management and is expected to raise customs procedures in step with international best practices.[63] This legislation, which took more than five years to pass since the Philippines' ratification of the Revised Kyoto Protocol of the WTO in 2010,[64] finally supersedes the old Tariff and Customs Code (Republic Act No. 1937) which had been in force since 1 July 1957.[65] Customs reform in the Philippines has seen government and private initiatives and also energized civil society campaigns.[66] It has been observed that tariff facilitation in the Philippines has

[59] Contained in the Bureau of Customs Reform Project; see also Ron Mendoza, Fr Albert Alejo and Jess Lorenzo, *Bureau of Customs: A Few Good Men* (12 June 2014) Rappler, www.rappler.com/thought-leaders/60288-few-good-men-customs-bureau

[60] Michael Punongbayan, *BOC Revenue Shortfall Due to Unabated Smuggling – COA* (10 January 2016) The Philippine Star, www.philstar.com/headlines/2016/01/10/1540999/boc-revenue-shortfall-due-unabated-smuggling-coa

[61] *Corruption Complaints vs BOC Go Down* (8 March 2016) Inquirer.net, http://newsinfo.inquirer.net/771530/corruption-complaints-vs-boc-go-down

[62] Atty Simeon V. Marcelo, 'Investigating Corruption in the Philippines: A Former Tanodbayan's Experience' (Speech delivered at the 12th Regional Seminar of the ADB/OECD Anti-Corruption Initiative for Asia and the Pacific, Dili, Timor-Leste, 24–5 July 2013).

[63] Already approved by the Philippine Senate on 18 January 2016 and awaiting signing into law by the President.

[64] The Revised Kyoto Protocol entered into force on 3 February 2006 and promotes transparency, predictability and simplification of customs procedures as well as the maximum use of information technology for efficient flow of and regulatory controls on trade facilitation.

[65] Australian–New Zealand Chamber of Commerce (Philippines), *Business Groups Press for Passage of Customs Modernization Act* (23 September 2015), http://anzcham.com/business-groups-press-for-passage-of-customs-modernization-act/

[66] For example, Customs Watch and Philippine Customs Duties and Taxes do social media campaigns.

made progress and benefitted from initiatives for regional integration although significant gaps still need to be addressed.[67]

Informal rule-making, though less visible or prominent in greater ASEAN processes, is also a driving force behind AEC integration. Progress made on trade facilitation in the AEC has been made possible because of support and collaboration by non-state actors in regional processes and in implementation on the ground. Apart from the ASEAN Secretariat, Committees and Working Groups (WG) which are nested within sectoral ministerial meetings are the workhorses in the AEC. One such group that has been in the forefront of harmonization is the ASEAN Consultative Committee on Standards and Quality (ACCSQ). The ACCSQ was established as early as 1992 during the early stages of ASEAN economic cooperation to eliminate technical barriers to trade by eliminating the need for multiple or repetitive testing and certification. The ACCSQ is composed of three WGs and eight product WGs.[68] These WGs are headed by lead countries which are responsible in coordinating the work of the group and the implementation of standards in member countries. The ACCSQ is composed of bureau officials working with national standard bodies and working closely with international and regional organizations in drafting standards and regulations. Among these bodies are the International Organization for Standardization (ISO), International Electrotechnical Commission and International Trade Administration; regional industry associations like the ASEAN Federation of Textile Industries, ASEAN Automotive Federation, ASEAN Electronic Forum and ASEAN Cosmetics Association (ACA) also provide inputs to the WGs. Dialogue partners like Australia, New Zealand, Japan and the United States provide technical and financial support to the group. The collaboration between international, regional and domestic regulators in the ACCSQ have resulted in the development of MRAs, guidelines and other technical regulations or specifications for specific products. The work of the ACCSQ and its WG is similar to the work of the COREPER in the EU where their processes and deliberations involve mostly experts but limited public participation.

[67] See Melanie S Milo, 'The ASEAN Economic Community and the Philippines: Implementation, Outcomes, Impacts and Ways Forward' (Research Paper No. 2, Philippine Institute for Development Studies, 2013).

[68] The three WGs are on: MRAs, Accreditation and Conformity Assessment and Legal Metrology. Product WGs consist of Electrical and Electronic Equipment, Cosmetics, Pharmaceuticals, Prepared Foodstuffs, Automotives, Traditional Medicine and Health Supplements, Medical Devices and Rubber-Based products. See ASEAN, *ACCSQ Structure* (18 October 2012), www.asean.org/?static_post=accsq-structure

The work of the ACCSQ has generated impact on sectoral initiatives which shows the promise, and limits, of an incomplete and predominantly soft regulatory regime in ASEAN. The work of the WG on Cosmetics demonstrates the convergence of interests among diverse domestic and regional actors and the development of networks among industry groups that pushed for harmonization and the raising of quality and safety of cosmetics across the region. The work on cosmetics harmonization started with industry groups in the region which in 1997, through the ACA, formally requested the ASEAN Secretariat to facilitate the process of harmonization in cosmetics. The work of the ACA on WG Cosmetics is said to be one of the most concrete results of ASEAN economic integration.[69] It facilitated the convergence of technical regulations in the sector through the development of product mutual recognition arrangement[70] and the adoption by member countries of the ASEAN Harmonized Cosmetic Regulatory Scheme (2003) and the ASEAN Cosmetics Directive (ACD, 2003).[71] A directive is a term that is used in the EU that connotes a legally enforceable rule or regulation, a hard law. A directive needs however the process of transposition into national laws to be effective.

Considered a success story, the harmonized standards in cosmetics is one of the earliest harmonization arrangements in ASEAN and also the only sector which has so far adopted the formulation of a 'directive'.[72] The ASEAN harmonized cosmetics regime borrowed heavily from the 1976 EU Cosmetics Directive which provides more stringent regulatory framework than the US model.[73] The ACD facilitates regional trade by moving the focus away from prior government approval to post-marketing surveillance. The ASEAN Cosmetics Scheme states as its vision the creation of a single regulatory scheme.[74] It seeks to protect the health and safety of consumers by providing a list of negative or banned, restricted and

[69] Luke Nottage, *Cosmetics Regulation Under National and ASEAN Law* (1 June 2015) (University of Sydney; Japanese Law and the Asia Pacific), http://blogs.usyd.edu.au/japaneselaw/2015/06/cosmetics_regulation.html

[70] ASEAN Mutual Recognition Arrangement of Product Registration Approvals for Cosmetics, Schedule A: Agreement on the ASEAN Harmonized Cosmetic Regulatory Scheme, Phnom Penh, 2 September 2003, in force 1 January 2009.

[71] The ACD was reviewed and updated in 2015. See Janette P. Loreto-Garin, *Food and Drug Administration Circular No. 2015-009* (9 June 2015) www.fda.gov.ph/attachments/article/294902/FC2015-014%20-%20Reiteration%20of%20Grace%20Period%20Given%20to%20the%20Cosmetic%20Industry.pdf

[72] Luke Nottage, *Cosmetics Regulation*.

[73] The ASEAN Directive was updated in 2015.

[74] Agreement on the ASEAN Harmonized Cosmetic Regulatory Scheme, Phnom Penh, 2 September 2003, in force 1 January 2009, art. 1.

permitted products and ingredients and compliance by industry of claim guidelines and labelling requirements. The work on harmonization began in 2001 and was finalized in 2003 with the signing of the ASEAN Cosmetic Regulatory Regime. With the support of the ASEAN-EU Program for Regional Integration Support, member countries started the implementation of the ACD in their domestic jurisdictions in 2008 and by 2013 all members have implemented the directive.[75]

The ASEAN cosmetics regime is another illustration of 'lead' member countries providing the motivation for others to follow implementation of agreed commitments. In 2008, only Malaysia, Singapore and the Philippines started implementing the ACD but were followed less than two years later by Thailand, Cambodia, Laos, Myanmar and Vietnam. A regional regulatory body with a nondescript name, ASEAN Cosmetics Committee (ACC), was established to oversee the implementation of the ACD. Composed of regulators nominated by member countries, the ACC invites the cosmetics industry such as the ACA to attend its meetings. It is also assisted by the ASEAN Cosmetic Scientific Body, composed of regulators, industry representatives and the academe, in its role in reviewing ingredients lists and technical and safety issues.[76]

The speed with which the ACD was transposed into national legislations is also a considerable accomplishment for ASEAN. This is owed in particular measure to government bureaucracies which are tasked with responsibility of transposing the ACD into national legislation and in putting in place a notification system for cosmetics. In Singapore, which has enjoyed one-party dominance, legislative passage can be a smooth process while its highly regarded bureaucracy has the resources and technical capacity to put up the new scheme. Singapore's bureaucracy is well-placed to implement ASEAN integration measures with its decentralized authority given to particular ministries and statutory boards on specific ASEAN matters.[77] For instance, its Health Sciences Authority (HSA) was able to promptly put in place the mechanisms for the implementation of the ACD in time on 1 January 2008, the date committed for the start of implementation of the directive.[78]

[75] Indonesia was the last country to implement the ACD.

[76] ASEAN Cosmetic Directive, Schedule B: Agreement on the ASEAN Harmonized Cosmetic Regulatory Scheme, art. 10(3).

[77] See David Seth Jones, 'Governance and Meritocracy: A Study of Policy Implementation in Singapore' in Jon S.T. Quah (ed.), *The Role of the Public Bureaucracy in Policy Implementation in Five ASEAN Countries* (Cambridge: Cambridge University Press, 2016), 297–369, 341.

[78] See *Singapore Implements the ASEAN Cosmetic Directive* (17 December 2007), www.mirandah.com/pressroom/item/52-singapore-implements-the-asean-cosmetic-directive

Conversely, the Philippines legislative process is tedious and slow apart from the highly partisan nature of politics while its bureaucracy is better known for corruption than for their efficiency.[79] The Philippine Department of Health (DOH), a government agency that has consistently been rated as one of the best performing agencies in the country, had lobbied for the passage of the Food and Drug Administration Act 2009 (RA 9711)[80] which seeks to strengthen and rationalize the regulatory capacity of the agency. This legislation amended the 1963 Food, Drugs, and Cosmetics Act No. 3720 which was patterned after the US cosmetics regulatory model.[81] The Food and Drug Administration (FDA), the regulatory body created under RA 9711, had ensured the transposition and implementation of the directive. Under the FDA, the Center for Cosmetics Regulation and Research (CCRR) has been specifically constituted to regulate the manufacture, sale, trade, use and testing of cosmetics products including the conduct of research on cosmetic's safety, health and quality and formulation of standards.[82] With this authority, the CCRR has implemented the ACD directly without the need of a special legislation covering the directive. The FDA has also been active in surveillance of cosmetic products in the market and providing warnings to consumers on unlisted and dangerous products[83] while consumer groups like the EcoWaste Coalition has helped the agency track down products with hazardous materials.[84]

The ACD regime, however, is not without its shortcomings. The lack of an effective regional enforcement regime in the AEC meant an uneven process of transposing the ACD into national laws and regulations. Even those in the industry assail the lack of uniformity in the implementation in member states resulting in variations – and in some instances – an uneven

[79] Congress of the Philippines House of Representatives, *How a Bill Becomes a Law*, www.congress.gov.ph/legisinfo/?l=process; See Jon S.T. Quah, *Curbing Corruption in Asian Countries: An Impossible Dream?* (Bingley: Emerald Group Publishing, 2011), 112.

[80] Also known as Republic Act No. 9711, 18 August 2009.

[81] William H. Schmitt, 'An Overview of Worldwide Regulatory Programs' in Norman F. Estrin (ed.), *The Cosmetic Industry: Scientific and Regulatory Foundations* (New York: Marcel Dekker, 1984), 131–62, 147. Republic Act No. 3720, 22 June 1963 was amended in 1987 through Executive Order No. 175, 22 March 1987 known as the 'Foods, Drugs, Devices and Cosmetics Act'.

[82] Republic Act 9711 (2009), s. 5.

[83] See *Vendors Beware: Philippines to Seize Unauthorized Cosmetics* (19 December 2015), www.gcimagazine.com/business/management/regulation/FDA-of-Philippines-Warns-Consumers-About-Unauthorized-Cosmetics-361250361.html

[84] InterAkyson, *FDA bans Feyque and Other Mercury-Tainted Skin Whitening Creams Exposed by EcoWaste Coalition* (13 September 2014), http://interaksyon.com/article/95319/fda-bans-mercury-tainted-skin-whitening-creams-exposed-by-ecowaste-coalition

playing field for industry players.[85] They also cited that the ACD seems to advantage products or ingredients coming from the EU which are produced by big multinational cosmetics firms, and that work against the development of small and medium enterprises in ASEAN which struggle to meet higher standards required in the directive.[86] As demonstrated in the Philippines case, the lack of regional post-marketing surveillance mechanism in ASEAN also meant that ensuring the quality and safety of cosmetic products would depend on effective and proactive government bureaucracies and active consumer advocates.

7.5 Conclusion

In this chapter, we have shown the nature of AEC's regulatory regime that is based on an incomplete and predominantly soft system. This soft regulatory regime, which primarily consists of voluntary self-compliance and non-binding soft coercions, has certainly made inroads in facilitating positive integration in the AEC. Most of AEC's goals are highly dependent on how trade facilitation measures, as mechanisms for positive integration, can drive higher trade within member countries and with the world. Trade facilitation covers operational measures on the ground and has shown to have effected gradual changes in the regulatory environment in some ASEAN member countries as shown in the case of the Philippines. This bottom-up process in removing barriers to trade has helped in strengthening government institutions and building the confidence of the personnel to be proactive in implementing ASEAN programmes. This enables local bureaucracies to be in the loop of ASEAN and for ASEAN bodies to engage with them.

The role of the private sector and experts in the AEC committees and WG such as that in the ACCSQ and the WG on Cosmetics, though less evident, shows where the motor for ASEAN integration is coming from. Informal rule-making has become a key component in fuelling integration initiatives through advocacies, technical inputs and mobilizing public–private partnership in the implementation of agreed-upon rules and regulation.

85 Interview with some cosmetics industry players in the Philippines citing differences in implementing labelling requirements in Vietnam in Vincente Chua Reyes, Jr, 'Dysfunctional Bureaucracy, Corruption and Week Rule of Law: A Case Study of Policy Implementation in the Philippines' in Jon S. T. Quah (ed.), *The Role of the Public Bureaucracy in Policy Implementation in Five ASEAN Countries* (Cambridge: Cambridge University Press, 2016), 223–96, 271 and 275.

86 Ibid., 275.

This is apart from the critical function that a lean ASEAN Secretariat does in facilitating rule-making and compliance. Given the specific nature and requirements of industry groups and the extent of industry motivation for convergence, the current legal and regulatory framework can only deliver on specific areas and through an incremental approach. This strategy is also highly dependent on externalities and presupposes institutional capacity of member countries' bureaucracies where many of them have lower-level capacity. An effective regional regulatory scheme is essential to driving compliance at the domestic level and the addition of stronger forms of non-binding coercions, at the minimum, or the addition of some forms of binding coercions. An enhanced monitoring system and impact assessment mechanisms could help to ensure compliance, and uniformity of implementation. The current lack of effective monitoring mechanisms has resulted in the AEC's failure to objectively evaluate actual progress on the ground or the extent to which particular areas of trade have benefitted from or been affected by integration measures. A monitoring mechanism however is only a second best option for an autonomous regional enforcement mechanism which can deliver sustained, consistent and objective interpretation and application of regional measures.

As shown in the implementation of the AGS, an objective and credible peer-review mechanism stimulates healthy competition and improved voluntary compliance among industry groups. This example may serve as model for other ASEAN measures, as a form of an enhanced non-binding coercion and greater involvement of industry groups in ASEAN governance processes. However, should this happen, there should also be a concomitant increase in participation by the broader ASEAN public in deliberating and crafting regional policies and rules. As demonstrated in the case of the ASEAN cosmetics sector, elements of transparency and wider public participation are necessary for the ACD regime to gain further legitimacy and to ensure that regional standards and measures serve broader industry and consumer interests. The elements of fairness, transparency and participation are – and need to be – the basic requirements of any trade arrangements, whether they are based on the less rigid legal system. Accountability mechanisms, currently lacking in ASEAN processes, should be given attention to as greater economic interdependence among member states can generate not only gainers but also losers.

8

Conclusion: In Search of the Rule of Law in ASEAN

The overall theme in this work is how the processes of regional integration could promote the rule of law in ASEAN. Is the rule of law a salient component for the realization of the objectives of regional integration or is it, by itself, one of the goals through which regional integration may be achieved? The rule of law in regional integration has been mostly understood in the context of the EU and little has been written about other projects of regional integration that have proliferated since the 1980s. Investigating the rule of law in ASEAN has come at a time of its rapid institutional development – reflecting its responses to the changing economic and political landscape in the states in Southeast Asia, in the region as a whole and in the wider international community. The academe, scholars and observers have been divided on whether these developments could bring about real progress to regional cooperation and also to the promotion of democracy, the rule of law and human rights – values and principles that are still seen as 'weak' in member states.

There exists wide disagreement over what rule of law means in the context of states and this is further complicated by the phenomenon of regional integration. In situating the rule of law in the context of regional integration, this book has taken a view of the rule of law not from its conceptual meaning but from its functions. In certain ways, the approach is instrumentalist but a holistic and interdisciplinary approach has been adopted to show the motivations and interests among states in adopting a peculiar type of regional arrangement. The research project has shown that both internal (state) and external (globalization) processes have triggered the current drive for regional integration among states. Thus the development of the rule of law has to be considered from the legal, institutional and political processes in the state, region and international relations.

A corollary question that emerged from this book is whether a common framework of the rule of law as seen in the EU can be conceived in the context of regional integration given the diversity of rule of law practices in member states. ASEAN is one region where there is wide diversity in rule of law practices among its member states. This work finds that in the EU there is the possibility for regional integration to be a vehicle for transmitting rule of law in member states, given certain factors and conditions. Can ASEAN be in a similar position to generate a process for transmitting the ideas or values of the rule of law in its member states? Regional integration, situated within the broader context of regionalism, has been the outcome of coping with the challenges and opportunities of globalization and a regional avenue for promoting national interests and in fostering solidarity among countries. The rule of law is likewise situated in this environment.

This work has undertaken a search for the possible basis and function of the rule of law in ASEAN integration and has explored its future development. Instead of embarking on a polemical discussion on whether rule of law exists in ASEAN, this research has a more practical focus on the present – whether there is an evolving form of the rule of law in ASEAN integration. This work deems it more important to consider the significance of current developments in ASEAN, particularly from the 1990s onwards, as there is little disagreement about the highly informal and consensual framework of relations and the limited cooperative activities of member states before that period. But this is not to lose sight of the past practices, values and institutions through which current reforms have evolved. As such, this work started with examining the concept of the ASEAN Way, a catch-all phrase defining the mode of conduct and the norms and principles adhered to by member states since ASEAN's founding in 1967. The research then proceeded to investigate ASEAN's new legal and institutional framework and to determine whether this new framework has significantly departed from the ASEAN Way.

8.1 Key Issues of the Rule of Law in ASEAN Integration

There are four important issues that were looked into in examining the prospects of developing the rule of law in ASEAN integration. Does regional integration bring about conditions for the promotion of the rule of law? If so, what are the conditions through which the rule of law can develop in regional integration and is it possible to transfer features of the rule of law in the state to a regional setting? Is there such a particular form of the rule of law in regional integration or a model of a regional rule of law? What is the nature, as well as the prospects and limits, of the rule of law in ASEAN integration in its current legal and institutional arrangement?

This work has found – by looking at various projects of regional integration such as the EU, ASEAN, African Union and MERCOSUR – that regional integration can be a viable vehicle in promoting the rule of law in regional cooperation and in member states. The demands of deeper economic cooperation for a clear, stable and predictable legal regime require the institution of the rule of law, at least in its narrow and instrumentalist conception. Regional integration involves both economic and political cooperation, as part of the broader phenomenon of regionalism, but economic integration also requires a wider basis of support and legitimacy. The rule of law in regional integration assumes various functions – from providing stability, predictability and enforceability of rules, as a framework for inter-state relations and the functioning of regional organs, to imposing limits to member states' sovereign discretion, providing mechanisms for the accountability of regional authorities and providing protection to human rights.

The function of the rule of law in regional integration as a decisive constraint to state sovereignty is, however, distinctive of the EU. Increasingly, there is a trend towards the creation of more independent regional institutions that monitor the implementation of economic agreements or resolve disputes. There are also increasing avenues for stakeholder participation through either formal or informal process, legal or non-legal forums. ASEAN and other regional projects such as SADC and MERCOSUR are heading in this direction. In this sense, constraint to sovereignty is exercised through a range of regulatory mechanisms, rather than through a strictly legal process of accountability. ASEAN's focus on economic integration has drawn it towards the soft regulatory regime and informal rule-making that provides some form of checks on state discretion but not a limitation on its sovereign powers.

The conception of the rule of law is as highly contested in states as in projects of regional integration. The existence of greater plurality in national interests and the traditions of the rule of law in member countries makes it extremely difficult to forge a consensus of the type of rule of law in regional integration, particularly as a mechanism of constraint on state powers. The European Union represents an example by which it is possible for states to form a consensus on the rule of law, and in addition, the capacity to develop a state-like rule of law in regional integration that can be transferred to member states. This has been made possible by the development of a constitutional legal order based on the principle of supremacy, the adoption of a constitutional arrangement imbibing the principle of checks and balance, an independent judicial institution and access by individuals to regional mechanisms.

What have been the vital factors that promoted the rule of law in the EU? Through an exploration of the legal and institutional development in the Union, I have identified at least three key elements. The first factor is the common legal tradition of member states, particularly a common understanding and recognition by most member states of the function of the rule of law as a bulwark against arbitrary power. This has allowed member states to provide an initial commitment to the rule of law in the founding treaties. In particular, a regional judicial body independent from the states was instituted as the guardian of the rule of law.

In ASEAN, there is a wide variance in the rule of law traditions of member states and the development of rule of law practices that promote law as a symbol of state authority rather than as a constraint to its power. In the EU, the historical evolution of the rule of law as a bulwark against arbitrary power had grown internally – from the law's centralizing function in state formation to the peoples' struggle against tyrannical rule. Conversely, the rule of law in most ASEAN states has developed from a top-down approach. It has started with colonialism, which fostered a different conception of the rule of law, the institution of colonial rule, to the establishment of a strong centralizing state in the postcolonial era. This latter function still preoccupies most ASEAN states.

Second, a 'leadership' role provided by key member states in pushing for the establishment of the rule of law was evident in the EU. The political commitment to advance deeper cooperation encouraged those other member states still hesitant in forging the European project. Despite the initial recalcitrance of some states in recognizing the Community principles, 'obedience' to the decisions of the ECJ by a majority of the states made it possible for the uninterrupted development of a legal and constitutional foundation of the Union. A consensus on the necessity for the rule of law among member states has developed in the EU, with the new members acquiescing either by sheer commitment or by force of necessity. Hungary's controversial move to amend its constitution triggered a series of actions from the EU to protect 'shared values' of democracy and the rule of law – from outright criticisms from other EU leaders to a formal legal action brought by the European Commission.

At the current stage in ASEAN, a persuasive leadership role is yet to emerge precisely because its leading state, Indonesia, still faces many of internal political and security issues. Indonesia, or any other ASEAN state, does not possess effective 'moral suasion' given its own poor record on the rule of law. However, the relative stability that Indonesia has enjoyed since the fall of the Suharto regime has allowed it to renew its commitment to more strengthened regional cooperation, including initiatives to tackle human rights on the regional agenda and the strengthening of the ASEAN human rights mechanism.

Third, institutional strengthening was a defining feature in the development of the rule of law in the EU. The development of independent and credible supranational institutions enabled the continuous and progressive implementation of the treaties despite attempts of some member states in frustrating their terms. The ECJ, the intergovernmental organs and Parliament in the EU all performed to ensure the realization of the objectives of the treaties. In ASEAN, the member states need to support the capacity of the regional organs by giving them respect, independence and institutional support if building an ASEAN Community is to become a reality.

Moreover, the development of a form of substantive rule of law in the EU took place under a peculiar historical and political setting – as a means to end the war and bind German power, and the acceptance by member states of the rule of law as the framework of regional cooperation. Why it is possible for some countries to adopt a form of the rule of law, but not by others, reflects the sociopolitical basis of the rule of law, and thus the diversity of rule of law traditions. However, the experience of the EU in establishing its type of the rule of law to Central and Eastern European countries also presents the potential of regional integration as a mechanism for rule of law transmission. The function of the rule of law as arbiter of political differences and disputes, however, has shown its limits in the preeminence of the rule of politics in difficult domestic and regional issues such as those in Africa as in the unprecendented occurrence of Brexit.

Issues of compliance, sovereignty claims, democracy and legitimacy as well as the issue of coping with membership expansion and globalization are common challenges faced in lesser or greater measure by other projects of regional integration. The way the EU has coped with these problems makes it an inspiration for other regional projects. The EU cannot be a 'model', in the strict sense, to ASEAN because of their wide differences in legal, institutional, political and historical development. ASEAN needs to develop its own strategies which include the incorporation of the rule of law as a symbol of limit to state authority, in the member states' legal culture and political processes, and in the process of establishing the ASEAN Community. This is not an easy straightforward task.

Regional integration has provided an incentive and opportunity for ASEAN to develop the rule of law. The rule of law in ASEAN has been framed as a means to and one of the objectives of regional cooperation. The rule of law in ASEAN integration is essentially designed to provide a stable and coherent framework for interstate relations among member states and to achieve better implementation and compliance of member states of their economic commitments. As a limiting function on the sovereign capacities in regional relations, the rule of law in ASEAN does not show this potential, at least in the near future. In its current state, the rule of law in ASEAN integration can be characterized as state-controlled, limited, uneven, evolutionary and resting on a soft legal framework.

ASEAN has chosen a different path of regional integration and globalization has offered new techniques of the rule of law. The conception of the rule of law in ASEAN, however, has to be understood within the wider context of a new regionalism which opens up ASEAN to new challenges and opportunities in dealing with domestic and international challenges to nation-state building. While ASEAN and its member states have welcomed a deeper basis of regional cooperation, they have also sought to achieve this without departing radically from the classical tenets of sovereignty and non-intervention. As such, the legal framework of the revitalized ASEAN remains anchored in the 'ASEAN Way' although there are notable changes that can encourage the development of the rule of law.

8.2 Locating the Rule of Law in ASEAN Regional Integration

In locating the rule of law in ASEAN regional integration, this project sets out with four salient tasks. First, it looks at the particular condition of ASEAN regional integration by situating it within the broader context of globalization and regionalism. Second, this work enquires how the rule of law has developed in the context of globalization and its impact on rule of law practices in the nation state and in international relations. We have discussed in Chapters 2 and 6 how globalization acted as the crucial trigger to regional integration in ASEAN, which has been premised on closer economic cooperation. The discussion in Chapter 2 points to the seemingly contradictory influence of the processes of globalization on the rule of law – the way it is possible to either promote or inhibit the development of the rule of law. Moreover, Chapter 5 has outlined the rise of democracy movements in member states in ASEAN that have been in great part pushed by the emergence of the middle-class seeking greater economic and political participation and the accountability of state actors. In a certain measure, regional integration seeks to ameliorate the problem by creating or stimulating economic development and incremental political reforms without unsettling the power of entrenched elites.

In the context of globalization's influence on regional integration, we have seen that globalization has been a vehicle for the promotion of the rule of law as well as for generating new tools and institutions of the rule of law. Globalization has triggered new forms of rule of law mechanisms such as the use of soft laws, private and informal sources of rule-making or In-Law and nonjudicial forms of adjudication such as mediation and arbitration, in promoting the stability and predictability of transnational economic activities. The prominent role of non-state actors in global rule of law has been a point of vigorous debates among scholars as to whether it amounts to a weakening of the state. There is growing evidence, however, pointing to globalization's role in fostering the rule of law from liberalism's function of securing private property and contracts to the promotion of transparency, accountability and good governance at the national, regional and international levels. As we have shown, many aspects of the rule of law are brought to bear in regional integration. In the EU as in ASEAN, these new mechanisms of the rule of law are increasingly employed to achieve compliance with agreements and commitments. As shown in Chapter 7, the increasing use of soft law in ASEAN is the key mechanism for achieving the rule of law in economic integration in conjunction with greater institutionalization of intergovernmental cooperation.

The discussion in Chapters 2 and 6 has identified key economic and political factors that have driven a new regionalism in Southeast Asia in the 1990s. Of particular significance is the confluence of domestic, regional and international developments promoting the new regionalism – the end of the Cold War, the resolution of the Cambodian conflict in 1993, the Asian financial crisis in 1996, the democratization movement in some member states, September 11 and the rise of Islamist radicalism in the region. These developments in new regionalism ushered in critical developments in the region which seeks a broader basis of cooperation based on greater economic and political cooperation. There was also a re-examination by regional elites of the fundamental principles, values and institutions of ASEAN cooperation, and changing security perspectives in member states that encourage increased recognition for a comprehensive approach to national and regional security problems.

It is noted in the concluding part in Chapter 2 that regional integration remains an integral process of nation-state building in member states and thus suggests that respect for sovereignty and non-interference remains the overriding framework of regional integration. But ASEAN's fidelity to the principle of non-intervention has not been static and as mentioned in Chapter 5, member states have on several occasions violated or adverted to moderation of the principle in the form of 'flexible engagement' or 'enhanced interaction'. Chapter 6 points to the emergence of the concept of regional integration and the conception of the ASEAN Community 2015, and with it a much improved basis of economic and political cooperation requiring a more stable and coherent framework for interstate cooperation. In this sense, there is a loosening of the principle of non-intervention particularly in the economic sphere and also some step-by-step and incremental development at the political level.

Third, this book looks at the manner in which the rule of law is conceived in particular regional integration settings either as a means to achieve the goals of regional integration as one of its key principles or as an important objective to promote the rule of law in member states. We conclude that there is no particular model that could fit all regional integration arrangements. Even direct transplantation of mechanisms such as supranational courts produced variable results and unforeseen consequences as discussed on how supranationalism has fared in African integration. However, the discussion on the development of the rule of law in EU integration is useful as a point for comparison with and learning for ASEAN and other projects of regional integration in the developing world. The function of the rule of law in the EU suggests the possibility of a form of a state-like rule of law adopted in regional integration, in its modified form. The persistence of democracy deficit confirms the impossibility of developing perfect equality of the rule of law in the state and in regional integration. Recent events in the EU such as the Brexit, rejection of important reform treaties and divisions on refugee policy also underscore the limits of constitutionalism in the EU and the pressing challenges from member states themselves of their sovereign prerogatives and calls by their citizens for broader democratic participation. Thus the discussion in Chapter 3 also points to the way the nature of EU rule of law is shifting from a hard and well-ordered regime towards more flexibility, renationalization and decentralization that seek to incorporate domestic politics into the EU constitutional framework.

While EU and ASEAN have distinct political and economic environments as well as different rule of law traditions, there are areas of common interests that are points for learning. Some aspects of EU regional integration have found their way in other projects of regional integration such as the African Union, subregional groups in Africa such as SADC and ECOWAS and MERCOSUR. This is particularly seen in the establishment of supranational or independent institutions and development of regional integration law. In particular, SADC has adopted the EU process of regional judicial adjudication and preliminary reference procedure and is slowly building its own body of jurisprudence. As noted in Chapter 4, the SADC Tribunal's experience with Zimbabwe, however, points to the limits of judicial power in the absence of strong political will and capacity for judicial enforcement. The discussion on African integration also suggests that the establishment of rule of law institutions competes with other equally pressing priorities of dealing with conflict and political settlement.

ASEAN has shied away from the use of supranational institutions and judicial means of dispute resolution but there are other rule of law mechanisms that can be explored to suit the conditions of ASEAN and without undermining its sovereignty claims. In fact, our discussion in Chapter 3 shows the steadfast position of member states in both the old and newer member states in the EU in claiming and exercising their sovereign authority vis-à-vis Union authority. There are various rule of law techniques that have been employed in the EU to balance the interests of member states which could be useful in a highly plural community like ASEAN.

The concept of variable or differentiated integration could be used in a variety of sectors of cooperation allowing some member states to advance in their chosen areas for deeper cooperation. As discussed in Chapter 7, flexible mechanism for integration can be a pathway for sectoral integration that is dependent on leading member states and industry participation. The use of hard and legally binding rules could also be explored in ASEAN using the technique of the principle of subsidiarity as a way to temper the rigid application of laws, especially when flexibility for implementation is desired. EU's mixed use of the *acquis communitaire*, soft law and socialization in transposing the rule of law to new members with 'weaker' rule of law traditions is an example for other projects of regional integration with substantial differences. However, it must be pointed out that this was also achieved by imposing compliance with the Accession criteria and strong economic incentives.

Another point for learning is the way soft law is being employed to achieve the demands of member states for flexibility, to encourage voluntary action and compliance by member states in the absence of Union authority or where wide differences exist among member states and to accommodate demands for greater deliberation and participation by stakeholders and civil society. The use of independent experts and committees in drafting proposals and implementation guidelines has been effective in the EU. Even demands for accountability can be achieved through the process of co-decision and cooperation. National parliaments in member states can be accommodated in this process. This is by no means an exhaustive and definitive investigation but it is a general exploration of how the EU is still a relevant and viable model of regional integration. As discussed in Chapter 7, soft regulation, informal rule-making and non-binding coercions have generated inroads in trade facilitation measures in the AEC and are influencing governance and regulatory framework in member states. These achievements are however incremental and limited in many respects. This could be an interesting area for further research as ASEAN continues to implement programmes outlined in the Blueprints for the three pillars.

Fourth, this book enquires into the attitudes to and the function of the rule of law in ASEAN's legal and institutional framework. Regional integration in ASEAN has been conceived of as a state-centred programme. Following this, the promotion of the rule of law is treated as a political programme for cooperation by member states, to be promoted mainly through the creation and socialization of norms among state agencies and officials. As such, the rule of law practices of member states reflect the proclivity of individual member states to support a type of rule of law based on thin constitutionalism to provide a more coherent and stable framework for intergovernmental relations and an instrumentalist conception that facilitates economic integration. As a form of constraint or mechanism of accountability, the 'rule of law' in ASEAN is as yet to be developed, although there is some progress in instituting a 'rule through law' regime type through the soft regulatory framework that enables and facilitates, rather than constrains, intergovernmental actions. While this system provides the vehicle for voluntary compliance and self-restraint by member states, this has not adequately delivered on efficiency, coherence of legal rules and system of accountability.

As mentioned in Chapter 5, there is divergence but also convergence of rule of law practices in member states that makes it difficult to establish a rule of law regime in ASEAN based on constraint to sovereign or institutional powers. Despite democratization and the development of constitutionalism in some member states, a common pattern among them is the predominance of executive powers over other state institutions, the legislative and judiciary. However, there is growing consensus among member states, regardless of their forms of government, of the necessity to adhere to and rule through law at both the national and regional levels. Domestic political changes – and the imperatives in tackling issues of economic growth and redistribution – have driven legal and institutional reforms in Southeast Asia that aim to manage or curb excessive government powers through the institution of the principles of separation of powers or checks and balance, the creation of independent institutions, the strengthening of legal and judicial institutions and increasing the space for civil society advocacy. The extent of reforms and actual practices has remained varied in member states however. The expansion of the middle class translated into well-informed and committed civil society encourages further political and institutional reforms, and at least the development of a rule through law regime types. In Chapter 7, it was demonstrated that committed programmes and mechanisms for decision-making and enforcement in the AEC have gradually affected lawmaking, policies and governance in particular member states like the Philippines.

8.3 Challenges and Prospects of the Rule of Law in ASEAN

The constraints in building the rule of law in ASEAN, whether in its thin or thick senses, are rooted in its structural and legal and institutional foundation. We have identified four main issues constraining the development of the rule of law. First, the economic basis of regional integration rests on a reaction to globalization that is narrowly focused on attracting foreign investments and not so much on deepening intra-regional trade. Regional economic cooperation strategy remains locked on tariff removals and is yet to launch a dynamic economic programme aimed at deepening intra-regional trade by removing or lessening non-tariff barriers, facilitating integration in the services sector and the movement of people. In the EU, the removal of non-tariff barriers to trade was the main source of Community institution-building and of case laws establishing the foundation for legal integration. With a narrow basis of integration, ASEAN economic integration yields limited activities and thus there is less need or incentive to establish clear rules and institutions. As a response mechanism to economic challenges, regional integration generates institutions through which economic measures could function. Having a limited basis of cooperation means that there is fewer incentive and opportunity for rule creation and strengthening regional institutions.

The second constraint is that a critical flaw of the rule of law in ASEAN is its weak institutions. To raise the prestige of its institutions should be an indispensable component of ASEAN Community-building. This would entail investing regional organs with respect and independence, allowing these mechanisms the capacity to generate credible actions and decisions and supporting their institutional continuity. This task is constrained by at least two main factors. One is the lukewarm attitude by member states towards establishing independent institutions and provision for at least some form of institutional accountability. At present, there is basically a form of intergovernmental system guided by the principle of cooperation and coordination.

Despite the enhancement of its functions, the ASEAN Secretariat remains a small bureaucracy in the context of its multifarious support functions to the three Community pillars. It still lacks independent authority over other ASEAN organs, particularly in relation to implementing regional commitments. Second, the current soft legal and regulatory framework has limited impact on broader and deeper integration, including that in the economic community. The lack of coercive sanctions or at least a credible and effective monitoring mechanism provides an incentive for member states to be complacent with or renege on their commitments. The current soft system also has the tendency to reinforce the weakness of institutions in the absence of efforts to strengthen these institutions. For instance, with the built-in flexibility afforded to member states in their agreements, and absence of specific punitive sanctions for nonperformance of obligations, there is very little incentive to use the enhanced dispute settlement mechanism.

The third constraint on the development of the rule of law is the historical basis in the establishment of a type of law regime in member states that does not impose restraint on state power and is expressed mainly through the executive. Despite constitutional reforms in Southeast Asian states, the idea of separation of powers either exists only on paper or is rendered meaningless by weak institutional and sociocultural practices. This means that the state, represented by the executive, is still the prime mover in international relations in Southeast Asia or the pivotal source of regional norm or law creation.

Strong sovereignty claims have always come from 'strong' states while those states having instituted constitutional reforms and formal democracy tend to be supportive in moderating the principle of non-intervention in ASEAN. These latter states have been more receptive to broader participation by non-state actors and civil society groups in the regional processes and to the idea of independent regional mechanisms. There is now a diversity of views among member states on non-intervention but such differences are not strong enough to overcome the dominance of the traditional view still espoused by most member states. This is compounded by the absence of a strong leadership position by a member state in ASEAN which could espouse bold and decisive reforms. As such, consensus and flexibility remain the mode of conduct among member states.

Fourth is the predominance of the 'extralegal' norm in ASEAN, the 'ASEAN Way' and the persistence of attitude among state leaders and officials that it is 'the way' and the identity of the association. This inhibits the development of clear, stable and predictable rules – although there are now increasing efforts at providing agreements with more precise language in the economic field. As discussed, discretion still predominates in the implementation even of economic agreements. Also, the existence of these 'cultural' norms discourages member states from actively using formal regional institutions as shown in continued reticence to use formal regional mechanisms for dispute settlement. To raise the integrity of ASEAN demands that regional institutions are respected and used and that they work in managing regional relations and activities. The fact that individuals and non-state actors are given restricted access to regional formal mechanisms also inhibits the creation of more responsive, effective and relevant regional institutions. Investors and the business sector are the groups that have been given special status in terms of access to dispute settlement and informal rule-making. They have become an important driver towards the development of a rules-based regime in ASEAN economic integration.

There is no doubt, however, that ASEAN integration brought opportunities for developing the rule of law through the introduction of principles, rules and institutions and the opportunity for enhanced interaction with non-state actors. Economic, social and political conditions have determined the nature and form of the rule of law. But laws, institutions and agents have comprised the change-agents of the rule of law and in these factors come the potential for transformation. A phenomenon of gradual spillover is taking place in ASEAN whereby demands for deeper economic cooperation triggers the necessity for legal and institutional changes. This spillover is however distinctive of ASEAN given its own unique political and economic foundation.

The ASEAN Charter is an intergovernmental agreement but it also outlines commitment to the principles of democracy, the rule of law, human rights and good governance which are applicable to the states as well as to the peoples in the region. The various economic agreements and declarations signed by governments are intergovernmental in character but these are matters that affect the lives of the people. These instruments, including the Charter, can be pushed for implementation and advocacy in national agencies and institutions but they can likewise be tested in domestic jurisdictions. The fact that the Charter went through the process of ratification by the peoples' representatives in member countries has made it 'jusiticiable' in countries permitting the judicial review of government acts and agreements. Parliaments in member countries are now in a better position and can be urged to demand parliamentary oversight of executive actions in ASEAN. Increasing the assertiveness of a growing number of legislators in member countries in democratizing states could start the process of constructive engagement with ASEAN.

The use of soft law has its own advantages and this project has given an outline as to how soft law techniques can be explored within AEC's limited institutional framework. The point is that there is plenty of room to explore the use of soft law by regional and domestic personnel and also by non-state actors wishing to engage with ASEAN. Repetitive practices of soft law could also result in crystallizing it to hard law, and socialization among state officials and agencies has been a useful process for adopting habits of the rule of law. The process for voluntary adoption of rules through harmonization and standard setting provides encouragement to member states for voluntary compliance through its non-intrusive process.

The soft regulatory regime and informal rule-making, through the participation of private actors, regulators and domestic bureaucrats, have become the fuel for initiatives to deepen integration in ASEAN. The committees and working groups in the ASEAN Economic Community as well as public–private sector cooperation at the regional and national levels have provided the space for non-state actors to participate in norm creation and assist in compliance and enforcement in member states. In the absence of a centralized regional enforcement body, a decentralized mechanism for self-compliance and enforcement has started to develop in specific areas of economic cooperation. Trade facilitation, as a strategy for positive integration, has tended to generate initiatives from domestic agencies to improve trade efficiency and governance.

A key challenge in ASEAN, however, is how to expand the function of the rule of law in regional integration, as a mechanism for accountability and inclusive participation. Even at its minimum conception, rule of law – or rule through law – demands the basic idea of fairness. As shown in the discussion on harmonized cosmetics regime, achieving consistency, uniformity and stability of rules requires that broader public participation in rule-making is needed to guarantee that wider public interest is served. Accessible accountability mechanism is needed to ensure that those adversely affected by integration measures have avenues to seek redress or to demand that rules and institutions are changed to make them fair. After all, if there is anything that ASEAN Community – and economic integration – should strive for is a fair and level playing field and opportunity – not only for a narrow sector of ASEAN elites but also for all ASEAN peoples.

BIBLIOGRAPHY

Books

Acharya, Amitav, *Constructing a Security Community in Southeast Asia: ASEAN and the Problem of Regional Order*, 3rd edn. (Oxon: Routledge, 2014).

The Quest for Identity (Singapore: Oxford University Press, 2000).

Whose Ideas Matter? Agency and Power in Asian Regionalism (Ithaca: Cornell University Press, 2009).

Adejumobi, Said and Adebayo Olukoshi (eds.), *The African Union and New Strategies for Development in Africa* (New York: Cambria Press, 2008).

Alagappa, Muthiah, 'Asian Civil-Military Relations: Key Developments, Explanations and Trajectories' in Muthiah Alagappa (ed.), *Coercion and Governance* (Stanford: Stanford University Press, 2001), pp. 433–98.

Alagappa, Muthiah, 'Institutional Framework: Recommendations for Change' in Sharon Siddique and Sree Kumar (eds.), *The 2nd ASEAN Reader* (Singapore: Institute of Southeast Asian Studies, 2003), pp. 22–7.

Alston, Philip, Mara Bustelo and James Heenan (eds.), *The EU and Human Rights* (Oxford: Oxford University Press, 1999).

Alter, Karen, *Establishing the Supremacy of the European Law: The Making of an International Rule of Law in Europe* (Oxford: Oxford University Press, 2001).

Anderson, Benedict, *Imagined Communities: Reflections on the Origin and Spread of Nationalism*, revised edn. (London: Verso, 1991).

Antolik, Michael, *ASEAN and the Diplomacy of Accommodation* (New York: M.E. Sharpe, 1990).

Asian Development Bank Institute, 'ASEAN Governing Mechanisms' in Ooi Kee Beng, Sanchita Basu Das, Terence Chong *et al.* (eds.), *The 3rd ASEAN Reader* (Singapore: Institute of Southeast Asian Studies, 2015), pp. 184–8.

Aspinall, Edward and Greg Fealy, *Local Power and Politics in Indonesia: Decentralisation and Democratisation* (Singapore: Institute of Southeast Asian Studies, 2003).

Ayres, Ian and John Braithwaite, *Responsive Regulation: Transcending the Deregulation Debate* (Oxford: Oxford University Press, 1992).

Bannister, Judith, Gabrielle Appleby, Anna Olijnyk and Joanna Howe, *Government Accountability: Australian Administrative Law* (Port Melbourne: Cambridge University Press, 2015).

Barr, Michael D., *Cultural Politics and Asian Values: The Tepid War* (New York: Routledge, 2002).

Basu Das, Sanchita, 'Assessing the Progress and Impediments Towards an ASEAN Economic Community' in Sanchita Basu-Das (ed.), *ASEAN Economic Community Scorecard: Performance and Perception* (Singapore: Institute of Southeast Asian Studies, 2013), pp. 1–19.

Beckman, Robert, Leonardo Bernard, Hao Duy Phan, Tan Hsien-Li and Ranyta Yusran, *Promoting Compliance: The Role of Dispute Settlement and Monitoring Mechanisms in ASEAN Instruments* (Cambridge: Cambridge University Press, 2016).

Bertrand, Jacques, *Nationalism and Ethnic Conflict in Indonesia* (Cambridge: Cambridge University Press, 2004).

Besson, Samantha, 'Sovereignty in Conflict' in Colin Warbrick and Stephen Tierney (eds.), *Towards an International Legal Community* (London: British Institute of International and Comparative Law, 2006), pp. 131–90.

Black, Elizabeth Ann, 'Brunei Darussalam: Ideology and Law in a Malay Sultanate' in Elizabeth Ann Black and Gary Bell (eds.), *Law and Legal Institutions of Asia: Traditions, Adaptations and Innovations* (Port Melbourne: Cambridge University Press, 2011), pp. 299–339.

Braithwaite, John and Peter Drahos, *Global Business Regulation* (Cambridge: Cambridge University Press, 2000).

Braithwaite, Valerie and John Braithwaite, 'An Evolving Compliance Model for Tax Enforcement' in Neal Shover and John Paul Wright (eds.), *Crimes of Privilege: Readings in White-Collar Crime* (New York: Oxford University Press, 2000), pp. 405–19.

Brown, David, *The State and Ethnic Politics in Southeast Asia* (London: Routledge, 1994).

Brownlie, Ian, *Principles of Public International Law*, 7th edn. (Oxford: Oxford University Press, 2008).

de Búrca, Gráinne, 'The Institutional Development of the EU: A Constitutional Analysis' in Paul Craig and Gráinne de Búrca (eds.), *The Evolution of EU Law* (Oxford: Oxford University Press, 1999), pp. 55–81.

Butt, Simon and Tim Lindsey, *The Constitution of Indonesia: A Contextual Analysis* (Oxford: Hart Publishing, 2012).

Caballero-Anthony, Mely, *Regional Security in Southeast Asia: Beyond the ASEAN Way* (Singapore: Institute of Southeast Asian Studies, 2005).

Capie, Davie and Paul Evans, 'The ASEAN Way' in Sharon Siddique and Sree Kumar (eds.), *The 2nd ASEAN Reader* (Singapore: Institute of Southeast Asian Studies, 2003), pp. 45–51.

Cason, Jeffrey W., *The Political Economy of Integration: The Experience of Mercosur* (New York: Routledge, 2011).

Chalermpalanupap, Termsak, 'Institutional Reform: One Charter, Three Communities, Many Challenges' in Donald Emmerson (ed.), *Hard Choices:*

Security, Democracy, and Regionalism in Southeast Asia (Singapore: Institute of Southeast Asian Studies, 2009), pp. 91–134.

Chavez, Jenina Joy, 'Regionalism Beyond an Elite Project: The Challenge of Building Responsive Sub Regional Economic Communities' in Melissa G. Curley and Nicholas Thomas (eds.), *Advancing East Asian Regionalism* (New York: Routledge, 2007), pp. 158–78.

Chesterman, Simon, *From Community to Compliance?: The Evolution of Monitoring Obligations in ASEAN* (Cambridge: Cambridge University Press, 2015).

Chryssochoou, Dimitris, 'Democracy and the European Polity' in Michelle Cini (ed.), *European Union Politics*, 2nd edn. (Oxford: Oxford University Press, 2007), pp. 359–74.

Chua Reyes, Vincente, Jr, 'Dysfunctional Bureaucracy, Corruption and Week Rule of Law: A Case Study of Policy Implementation in the Philippines' in Jon S.T. Quah (ed.), *The Role of the Public Bureaucracy in Policy Implementation in Five ASEAN Countries* (Cambridge: Cambridge University Press, 2016), pp. 233–96.

Cichowski, Rachel, *The European Court and Civil Society: Litigation, Mobilization and Governance* (Cambridge: Cambridge University Press, 2007).

Cini, Michelle and Nievez Pérez-Solórzano Borragan, *European Union Politics*, 4th edn. (Oxford: Oxford University Press, 2013).

Closa, Carlos and Lorenzo Casini, Comparative Regional Integration: Governance and Legal Models (Cambridge: Cambridge University Press, 2016).

Coleman, William and Geoffrey Underhill, 'Introduction: Domestic Politics, Regional Economic Co-operation, and Global Economic Integration' in *Regionalism and Global Economic Integration: Asia, Europe and the Americas* (London: Routledge, 1998), pp. 1–16.

Collins, Alan, *Security and Southeast Asia: Domestic, Regional, and Global Issues* (Singapore: Institute of Southeast Asian Studies, 2003).

Cordenillo, Raul and Kristen Sample (eds.), *Rule of Law and Constitution Building: The Role of Regional Organisations* (Stockholm: International Institute for Democracy and Electoral Assistance, 2014).

Craig, Paul and Gráinne de Búrca, *EU Law: Text, Cases, and Materials*, 3rd edn. (Oxford: Oxford University Press, 2003).

Cremona, Marise, David Kleimann, Joris Larik, Rena Lee and Pascal Vennesson (eds.), *ASEAN's External Agreements: Law, Practice and the Quest for Collective Action* (Cambridge: Cambridge University Press, 2015).

Crouch, Harold, *Domestic Political Structures and Regional Economic Cooperation* (Singapore: Institute of Southeast Asian Studies, 1984).

Cutler, Claire, Virginia Haufler and Tony Porter (eds.), *Private Authority and International Affairs* (Albany: State University of New York Press, 1999).

Czarnota, Adam, 'Barbarians Ante Portas or the Post-Communist Rule of Law in Post-Democratic European Union' in Wojciech Sadurski, Adam Czarnota and

Martin Krygier (eds.), *Spreading Democracy and the Rule of Law?: The Impact of EU Enlargement for the Rule of Law, Democracy and Constitutionalism in Post-Communist Legal Orders* (Dordrecht: Springer: 2006), pp. 283–97.

Davidson, Paul J., *ASEAN: The Evolving Legal Framework for Economic Cooperation* (Singapore: Times Academic Press, 2002).

Day, Tony, *Fluid Iron: State Formation in Southeast Asia* (Honolulu: University of Hawaii Press, 2002).

Dehousse, Renaud, *The European Court of Justice* (London: Palgrave Macmillan, 1998).

Deinla, Imelda, *Giving the ASEAN Inter-Parliamentary Assembly a Voice in the ASEAN Community* (Stockholm: International Institute for Democracy and Electoral Assistance, 2013).

Devlin, Robert and Antoni Estevadeordal, 'Regional Integration, Trade and Development' in Robert Devlin and Antoni Estevadeordal (eds.), *Bridges for Development: Policies and Institutions for Trade and Development* (Washington: Inter-American Development Bank, 2003), pp. 3–17.

Dosch, Jörn, 'The Post-Cold War Development of Regionalism in East Asia' in Fu-Kuo Liu and Philippe Régnier (eds.), *Regionalism in East Asia: Paradigm Shifting?* (New York: Routledge Curzon, 2003), pp. 30–51.

Dworkin, Ronald, *A Matter of Principle* (Oxford: Clarendon Press, 1990).

Law's Empire (Cambridge: Harvard University Press, 1986).

Edgeworth, Brendan, *Law, Modernity, Postmodernity: Legal Change in the Contracting State* (London: Ashgate Dartmouth, 2003).

Egreteau, Renaud, 'Soldiers as Lawmakers?: Assessing the New Legislative Role of the Burmese Armed Forces (2010–15)' in Renaud Egreteau and Francois Robinne (eds.), *Metamorphosis: Studies in Social and Political Change in Myanmar* (Singapore: National University of Singapore Press, 2015), pp. 15–42.

Ferguson, Gerry and Douglas M. Johnston (eds.), *Asia-Pacific Legal Development* (Vancouver: University of British Columbia Press, 2011).

Freeman, Nick J., 'Laos: Timid Transition' in John Funston (ed.), *Government and Politics in Southeast Asia* (Singapore: Institute of Southeast Asian Studies, 2001), pp. 120–59.

Friedman, Jonathan (ed.), *Globalization, the State and Violence* (Walnut Creek: AltaMira Press, 2003).

Fritzen, Scott A., 'Public Administration' in Mark Beeson (ed.), *Contemporary Southeast Asia*, 2nd edn. (New York: Palgrave Macmillan, 2009), pp. 74–89.

Frost, Ellen L., *Asia's New Regionalism* (Boulder: Lynne Rienner Publishers, 2008).

Fukuoka, Yuki, 'Demystifying "People Power": An Elite Interpretation of "Democratization" in Southeast Asia' in William Case (ed.), *Routledge Handbook of Southeast Asian Democratization* (London: Routledge, 2015), pp. 85–101.

Fuller, Lon, *The Morality of Law*, revised edn. (New Haven: Yale University Press, 1969).

Gainsborough, Martin, *Vietnam: Rethinking the State* (Chiang Mai: Silkworm Books, 2010).

Gaja, Giorgio, Peter Hay and Ronald Rotunda, 'Instruments for Legal Integration in the European Community – A Review' in Mauro Cappelletti, Monica Seccombe and Joseph Weiler (eds.), *Integration Through Law: Europe and the American Federal Experience* (Berlin: Walter de Gruyter, 1986), pp. 113–60.

Geertz, Clifford, *Negara: The Theatre State in Nineteenth-Century Bali* (Princeton: Princeton University Press, 1981).

Gerard, Kelly, *ASEAN's Engagement of Civil Society: Regulating Dissent* (New York: Palgrave Macmillan, 2014).

Gillingham, John, 'A German Solution to Europe's Problems? The Early History of the European Communities, 1950–1965' in *European Integration, 1950–2003: Superstate or New Market Economy?* (Cambridge: Cambridge University Press, 2003), pp. 3–80.

Glencross, Andrew, 'Federalism, Confederalism and Sovereignty Claims: Understanding the Democracy Game in the EU' in Rebecca Adler-Nissen and Thomas Gammeltoft-Hansen (eds.), *Sovereignty Games: Instrumentalizing State Sovereignty in Europe and Beyond* (New York: Palgrave Macmillan, 2008), pp. 105–26.

Haacke, Jürgen, *ASEAN's Diplomatic and Security Culture: Origins, Development and Prospects* (London: Routledge Curzon, 2005).

Haas, Ernest B., *Beyond the Nation State: Functionalism and International Organization* (Stanford: Stanford University Press, 1964).

Hall, Daniel George Edward, *A History of Southeast Asia*, 4th edn. (New York: St Martin's Press, 1986).

Hansen, E. Damsgaard, *European Economic History: From Mercantilism to Maastricht and Beyond* (Copenhagen: Copenhagen Business School Press, 2001).

Harding, Andrew and Peter Leyland, *The Constitutional System of Thailand: A Contextual Analysis* (Oxford: Hart Publishing, 2011).

Harlow, Carol, 'Access to Justice as Human Right: The European Convention and the European Union' in Philip Alston, Mara Bustelo and James Heenan (eds.), *The European Union and Human Rights* (Oxford: Oxford University Press, 1999), pp. 187–214.

Harris, David, *Civil War and Democracy in West Africa: Conflict Resolution, Elections and Justice in Sierra Leone and Liberia* (London: I.B. Tauris, 2011).

Held, David, Anthony McGrew, David Goldblatt and Jonathan Perraton, *Global Transformations: Politics, Economics and Culture* (Stanford: Stanford University Press, 1999).

Heng Chee, Chan, *The Dynamics of One Party Dominance: The PAP at the Grass-Roots* (Singapore: Singapore University Press, 1976).

Horowitz, Donald L., *Constitutional Change and Democracy in Indonesia* (Cambridge: Cambridge University Press, 2013).

Hsu, Locknie, 'Towards an ASEAN Charter: Some Thoughts from the Legal Perspective' in Rodolfo C. Severino (ed.), *Framing the ASEAN Charter: An ISEAS Perspective* (Singapore: Institute of Southeast Asian Studies, 2005), pp. 45–52.

Huff, William, The Economic Growth of Singapore: Trade and Development in the Twentieth Century (Cambridge: Cambridge University Press, 1994).

Hutchcroft, Paul D., *Booty Capitalism: The Politics of Banking in the Philippines* (Ithaca: Cornell University Press, 1998).

Inama, Stefano and Edmund W. Sim, *Rules of Origin in ASEAN: A Way Forward* (Cambridge: Cambridge University Press, 2015a).

The Foundation of the ASEAN Economic Community: An Institutional and Legal Profile (Cambridge: Cambridge University Press, 2015b).

Jayasuriya, Kanishka (ed.) *Law, Capitalism and Power in Asia: The Rule of Law and Legal Institutions* (London: Routledge, 1999).

Jones, David Seth, 'Governance and Meritocracy: A Study of Policy Implementation in Singapore' in Jon S.T. Quah (ed.), *The Role of the Public Bureaucracy in Policy Implementation in Five ASEAN Countries* (Cambridge: Cambridge University Press, 2016), pp. 297–369.

Karton, Joshua, 'Lessons from International Uniform Law' in Jean E. Kalicki and Anna Joubin-Bret (eds.), *Reshaping the Investor–State Dispute Settlement System: Journeys for the 21st Century* (Leiden: Brill Nijhoff, 2015), pp. 48–90.

Keating, Michael, 'Plurinational Democracy and the European Order' in Sonja Riekmann, Monika Mokre and Michael Latzer (eds.), *The State of Europe, Transformation of Statehood from a European Perspective* (Frankfurt: Campus Verlag, 2004), pp. 196–216.

Keohane, Robert O., *After Hegemony: Cooperation and Discord in the World Political Economy* (Princeton: Princeton University Press, 1986).

Kershaw, Roger, 'Brunei: Malay, Monarchical, Micro-State' in John Funston (ed.), *Government and Politics in Southeast Asia* (Singapore: Institute of Southeast Asian Studies, 2001), pp. 1–35.

Kiernan, Ben, *The Pol Pot Regime: Race, Power, and Genocide in Cambodia under the Khmer Rouge, 1975–79*, 3rd edn. (New Haven: Yale University Press, 2008).

Koentjaraningrat, Raden Mas (ed.), *Villages in Indonesia* (Ithaca: Cornell University Press, 1967).

Koh, Kheng-Lian and Nicholas Robinson, *ASEAN Environmental Legal Integration: Sustainable Goals?* (Cambridge: Cambridge University Press, 2016).

Krygier, Martin, 'Rule of Law' in Michel Rosenfeld and András Sajó (eds.), *The Oxford Handbook of Comparative Constitutional Law* (Oxford: Oxford University Press, 2012), pp. 233–49.

Krygier, Martin, 'The Rule of Law: Legality, Teleology, Sociology' in Gianluigi Palombella and Neil Walker (eds.), *Relocating the Rule of Law* (Oxford: Hart Publishing, 2009), pp. 45–69.

Kwa, Tion, 'Different Shades of "Crony Capitalism": Not All Asian Values Are Alike' in Julian Weiss (ed.), *Tigers Roar: Asia's Recovery and Its Impact* (Armonk, New York: M.E. Sharpe, 2001), pp. 84–7.

Lauth, Hans-Joachim, 'Formal and Informal Institutions' in Jennifer Gandhi and Rubén Ruiz-Rufino (eds.), *Routledge Handbook of Comparative Political Institutions* (Oxon: Routledge, 2015), pp. 56–69.

Leng, Lee Yong, *The Razor's Edge: Boundaries and Boundary Dispute in Southeast Asia* (Singapore: Institute of Southeast Asian Studies, 1980).

Lev, Daniel S., *Legal Evolution and Political Authority in Indonesia: Selected Essays* (The Hague: Kluwer Law International, 2000).

Liow, Joseph Chinyong, *Dictionary of the Modern Politics of Southeast Asia*, 4th edn. (New York: Routledge, 2015).

MacCormick, Neil, *Questioning Sovereignty: Law, State and Nation in the European Commonwealth* (Oxford: Oxford University Press, 1998).

Magen, Amichai and Leonardo Morlino (eds.), *International Actors, Democratizations and the Rule of Law: Anchoring Democracy?* (New York: Routledge, 2009).

Majone, Giandomenico, *Dilemmas of European Integration: The Ambiguities and Pitfalls of Integration by Stealth* (Oxford: Oxford University Press, 2005).

Maravall, José María and Adam Przeworski (eds.), *Democracy and the Rule of Law* (Cambridge: Cambridge University Press, 2003).

Marks, Gary, Francois Nielsen, Leonard Ray and Jane Salk, 'Competencies, Cracks, and Conflicts: Regional Mobilization in the European Union' in Gary Marks, Fritz W. Scharpf, Philippe C. Schmitter and Wolfgang Streeck (eds.), *Governance in the European Union* (London: Sage, 1996), pp. 40–63.

Marks, Gary and Liesbet Hooghe, 'Contrasting Visions of Multi-Level Governance' in Ian Bache and Matthew Flinders (eds.), *Multi-Level Governance* (Oxford: Oxford University Press, 2004), pp. 15–30.

Mietzner, Marcus, *Military Politics, Islam, and the State in Indonesia: From Turbulent Transition to Democratic Consolidation* (Singapore: Institute of Southeast Asian Studies, 2009).

Min Aun, Wu, *An Introduction to the Malaysian Legal System* (Singapore: Heinemann Educational Books, 1975).

Mittelman, James H., 'The Dynamics of Globalization' in James H. Mittelman (ed.), *Globalization: Critical Reflections* (Boulder: Lynne Rienner, 1996), pp. 1–19.

Muchie, Mammo, Phindile Lukhele-Olorunju and Oghenerobor Akpor (eds.), *The African Union Ten Years After: Solving African Problems with Pan-Africanisms and the African Renaissance* (Pretoria: Africa Institute of South Africa, 2013).

Murfett, Malcolm H. (ed.), *Cold War Southeast Asia* (Singapore: Marshall Cavendish, 2012).

Murray, Rachel, *Human Rights in Africa: From the OAU to the African Union* (Cambridge: Cambridge University Press, 2004).

Murray, Rachel and Debra Long, *The Implementation of the Findings of the African Commission on Human and Peoples' Rights* (Cambridge: Cambridge University Press, 2015).

Organisation for Economic Co-operation and Development, *Economic Outlook for Southeast Asia, China and India: Enhancing Regional Ties* (Paris: OECD Publishing, 2014).

Economic Outlook for Southeast Asia, China and India: Enhancing Regional Ties (Paris: OECD Publishing, 2016) http://dx.doi.org/10.1787/saeo-2014-en

Palmujoki, Eero, *Regionalism and Globalism in Southeast Asia* (New York: Palgrave, 2001).

Pauwelyn, Joost, Ramses A. Wessel and Jan Wouters (eds.), *Informal International Lawmaking* (Oxford: Oxford University Press, 2012).

Peerenboom, Randall, *Asian Discourses of Rule of Law: Theories and Implementation of Rule of Law in Twelve Asian Countries, France and the U.S.* (London: Routledge Curzon, 2004).

Peou, Sorpong, 'Human Security in Post-Cold War Cambodia' in Brendan Howe (ed.), *Post-Conflict Development in East Asia* (New York: Routledge, 2016), pp. 117–36.

Pescatore, Pierre, *The Law of Integration: Emergence of a New Phenomenon in International Relations based on the Experience of the European Communities* (Leiden: A.W. Sijthoff, 1974).

Piris, Jean-Claude and Walter Woon, *Towards a Rules-based Community: An ASEAN Legal Service* (Cambridge: Cambridge University Press, 2015).

Platzdasch, Bernhard and Johan Saravanamuttu (eds.), *Religious Diversity in Muslim-Majority States in Southeast Asia: Areas of Toleration and Conflict* (Singapore: Institute of Southeast Asian Studies, 2014).

Poggi, Gianfranco, *The State: Its Nature Development and Prospects* (Stanford: Stanford University Press, 1990).

Pollack, Mark, *The Engines of Integration: Delegation, Agency, and Agency Setting in the European Union* (Oxford: Oxford University Press, 2003).

Pongsudhirak, Thitinan, 'Thailand: Democratic Authoritarianism' in Daljit Singh and Chin Kin Wah (eds.), *Southeast Asian Affairs 2003* (Singapore: Institute of Southeast Asian Studies, 2003), pp. 277–90.

Pomfret, Richard, 'Blocs: The Threat to the System and Asian Reactions' in Bijit Bora and Christopher Findlay (eds.), *Regional Integration and the Asia-Pacific* (Melbourne: Oxford University Press, 1996), pp. 13–24.

Quah, Jon S.T., *Curbing Corruption in Asian Countries: An Impossible Dream?* (Bingley: Emerald Group Publishing, 2011).

(ed.), *The Role of the Public Bureaucracy in Policy Implementation in Five ASEAN Countries* (Cambridge: Cambridge University Press, 2016).

Quisumbing, Purificacion V., 'Problems and Prospects of ASEAN Law: Towards a Framework for Regional Dispute Settlement' in R.P. Anand and Purificacion

V. Quisumbing (eds.), *ASEAN: Identity, Development and Culture* (Manila: University of the Philippines Law Center and East–West Center Culture Learning Institute, 1981), pp. 300–18.

Rajah, Jothie, *Authoritarian Rule of Law: Legislation, Discourse and Legitimacy in Singapore* (Cambridge: Cambridge University Press, 2012).

Raquiza, Antoinette R., *State Structure, Policy Formation, and Economic Development in Southeast Asia: The Political Economy of Thailand and the Philippines* (New York: Routledge, 2012).

Rasmussen, Hjalte, *On the Law and Policy of the European Court of Justice* (The Hague: Martinus Nijhoff, 1998).

On Law and Policy in the European Court of Justice: A Comparative Study in Judicial Policymaking (Dordrecht: Martinus Nijhoff, 1986).

Rawls, John, *A Theory of Justice* (Cambridge, MA: Harvard University Press, 1971).

Raz, Joseph, 'On the Authority and Interpretation of Constitutions: Some Preliminaries' in Larry Alexander (ed.), *Constitutionalism: Philosophical Foundations* (New York: Cambridge University Press, 1998), pp. 152–93.

Raz, Joseph, *The Authority of Law: Essays on Law and Morality* (Oxford: Clarendon Press, 1979).

Razeen, Sally, 'ASEAN FTAs: State of Play and Outlook for ASEAN's Regional and Global Integration' in Sanchita Basu Das, Jayant Menon, Rodolfo Severino and Omkar Lal Shrestha (eds.), *The ASEAN Economic Community: A Work in Progress* (Singapore: Institute for Southeast Asian Studies, 2013), pp. 320–81.

Rivera, Salvador, *Latin American Unification: A History of Political and Economic Integration Efforts* (Jefferson: McFarland, 2014).

Rodan, Garry and Caroline Hughes, *The Politics of Accountability in Southeast Asia: The Dominance of Moral Ideologies* (Oxford: Oxford University Press, 2014).

SarDesai, Damodar, *Vietnam: The Struggle for National Identity*, 2nd edn. (Boulder: Westview Press, 1992).

Sassen, Saskia, *Globalization and its Discontents* (New York: The New Press, 1998).

Scharpf, Fritz W., 'Negative and Positive Integration in the Political Economy of European Welfare States' in Gary Marks, Fritz W. Scharpf, Philippe C. Schmitter and Wolfgang Streeck (eds.), *Governance in the European Union* (London: Sage Publications, 1996), pp. 15–39.

Schmidt, Vivien Ann, *Democracy in Europe: The EU and National Polities* (Oxford: Oxford University Press, 2006).

Schmitt, William H. and Emalee G. Murphy, 'An Overview of Worldwide Regulatory Programs' in Norman F. Estrin (ed.), *The Cosmetic Industry: Scientific and Regulatory Foundations* (New York: Marcel Dekker, 1984), pp. 131–62.

Sen, Amartya, *Development as Freedom* (New York: Alfred Knopf, 1999).

Severino, Rodolfo C., 'From Political/Security Concerns to Regional Integration' in Ooi Kee Beng, Sanchita Basu Das, Terence Chong *et al.* (eds.), *The 3rd ASEAN Reader* (Singapore: Institute of Southeast Asian Studies, 2015), pp. 17–22.

Severino, Rodolfo C., *Southeast Asia in Search of an ASEAN Community: Insights from the Former ASEAN Secretary-General* (Singapore: Institute of Southeast Asian Studies, 2006).

Shiraishi, Takashi, 'The Third Wave: Southeast Asia and Middle-Class Formation in the Making of a Region' in Peter J. Katzenstein and Takashi Shiraishi (eds.), *Beyond Japan: The Dynamics of East Asian Regionalism* (Ithaca: Cornell University Press, 2006), pp. 237–71.

Slaughter, Anne-Marie, *A New World Order: Government Networks and the Disaggregated State* (Princeton: Princeton University Press, 2004).

Solidum, Estrella D., *The Politics of ASEAN: An Introduction to Southeast Asian Regionalism* (Singapore: Eastern Universities Press, 2003).

Towards a Southeast Asian Community (Quezon City: University of the Philippines Press, 1974).

Sriram, Chandra Lekha, *Globalizing Justice for Mass Atrocities: A Revolution in Accountability* (London: Routledge, 2005).

Ssenyonjo, Manisuli (ed.), *The African Regional Human Rights System: 30 Years after the African Charter on Human and Peoples' Rights* (Leiden: Martinus Nijhoff, 2012).

Steinberg, David Joel, *In Search of Southeast Asia* (Sydney: Allen and Unwin, 1987).

Stone Sweet, Alec and Margaret McCowan, 'The Freedom of Movement of Goods' in Alec Stone Sweet, *The Judicial Construction of Europe* (Oxford: Oxford University Press, 2004), pp. 109–46.

Stone Sweet, Alec and Wayne Sandholtz (eds.), *Integration, Supranational Governance and the Institutionalization of the European Polity* (Oxford: Oxford University Press, 1998).

Strange, Susan, *The Retreat of the State*, revised edn. (Cambridge: Cambridge University Press, 1996).

Tanzi, Vito, 'Governance, Corruption and Public Finance: An Overview' in Salvatore Schiavo-Campo (ed.), *Governance, Corruption and Public Management* (Manila: Asian Development Bank, 1999).

Tamanaha, Brian Z., *On the Rule of Law: History, Politics, Theory* (Cambridge: Cambridge University Press, 2004).

Tambiah, Stanley J., *World Conqueror, World Renouncer: A Study of Buddhism and Polity in Thailand against a Historical Background* (Cambridge: University of Cambridge Press, 1976).

Tarling, Nicholas, *Nationalism in Southeast Asia: 'If the People are with Us'* (Oxon: Routledge Curzon, 2004).

Teubner, Gunther, '"Global Bukowina": Legal Pluralism in the World Society' in Gunther Teubner (ed.), *Global Law without a State* (Brookfield: Dartmouth, 1997), pp. 3–28.

Thambipillai, Pushpa and J. Savaranamuttu, *ASEAN Negotiations: Two Insights* (Singapore: Institute of Southeast Asian Studies, 1985).

Tinbergen, Jan, *International Economic Integration*, 2nd revised edn. (Amsterdam: Elsevier, 1965).

Trebilcock, Michael J. and Mariana Mota Prado, *What Makes Poor Countries Poor?: Institutional Determinants of Development* (Cheltenham: Edward Elgar, 2011).

Twining, William, *Globalisation and Legal Theory* (London: Butterworths, 2000).

Un, Kheang, 'The Judicial System and Democratisation in Post-Conflict Cambodia' in Joakim Öjendal and Mona Lilja (eds.), *Beyond Democracy in Cambodia: Political Reconstruction in a Post-Conflict Society* (Copenhagen: Nordic Institute of Asian Studies Press, 2009), pp. 70–101.

Warbrick, Colin and Stephen Tierney (eds.), *Towards an 'International Legal Community'?* (London: British Institute of International and Comparative Law, 2006).

Weatherbee, Donald E., 'Governance in Southeast Asia: The Good, The Bad and the Ugly' in Yoichiro Sato (ed.), *Growth and Governance in Asia* (Honolulu: Asia-Pacific Center for Security Studies, 2004), pp. 179–91.

Weiner, Mark S., *The Rule of the Clan: What an Ancient Form of Social Organisation Reveals about the Future of Individual Freedom* (New York: Farrar, Straus and Giroux, 2013).

Wescott, Clay, 'Combating Corruption in Southeast Asia' in John Kidd and Frank-Jürgen Richter (eds.), *Fighting Corruption in Asia: Causes, Effects and Remedies* (Singapore: World Scientific, 2003), pp. 237–69.

Westwood, Sallie, 'Unequal Nations: Race, Citizen and the Politics of Recognition' in Mary Romero and Eric Margolis (eds.), *The Blackwell Companion to Social Inequalities* (Malden: Blackwell Publishing, 2005), pp. 50–74.

Wolters, Oliver W., *History, Culture and Religion in Southeast Asian Perspectives*, revised edn. (Ithaca: Cornell Southeast Asia Program, 1999).

Woon, Walter, *The ASEAN Charter: A Commentary* (Singapore: National University of Singapore Press, 2016).

Wunderlich, Jens-Uwe, *Regionalism, Globalisation and International Order: Europe and Southeast Asia* (Hampshire: Ashgate, 2007).

Yen, Trinh Hai, *International Litigation in Practice: The Interpretation of Investment Treaties* (Leiden: Brill Nijhoff, 2014).

Zürn, Michael, André Nollkaemper and Randall Peerenboom (eds.), *Rule of Law Dynamics: In an Era of International and Transnational Governance* (New York: Cambridge University Press, 2012).

Journal Articles

Abbot, Kenneth and Duncan Snidal, 'Hard and Soft Law in International Governance' (2000) 54(3) *International Organization* 436–41.

Abdul Aziz, Tunku, 'Malaysia Incorporated: Ethics on Trial' (1999) 58(4) *Australian Journal of Public Administration* 19–25.

Acharya, Amitav, 'Culture, Security, Multilateralism: The "ASEAN Way" and Regional Order' (1998) 19(1) *Contemporary Security Policy* 55–84.

Albors-Lloren, Albertina, 'The European Court of Justice: More than a Teleological Court' (1999) 2 *Cambridge Yearbook of European Legal Studies* 373–98.

Alter, Karen, 'The European Union's Legal System and Domestic Policy: Spillover or Backlash?' (2000) 54(3) *International Organization* 489–518.

'Who are the "Masters of the Treaty"?: European Governments and the European Court of Justice' (1998) 52(1) *International Organization* 121–47.

Andersen, Svein and Nick Sitter, 'Differentiated Integration: What Is It and How Much Can the European Union Accommodate?' (2006) 28(4) *Journal of Integration* 313–30.

Arendshorst, John, 'The Dilemma of Non-Interference: Myanmar, Human Rights, and the ASEAN Charter' (2009) 8(1) *Northwestern Journal of International Human Rights* 102–21.

Austria, Myrna S., 'The Philippines and the AEC beyond 2015: Managing Domestic Challenges' (2015) 32(2) *Journal of Southeast Asian Economics* 220–38.

Baimu, Evarest and Kathryn Sturman, 'Amendment to the African Union's Right to Intervene, A Shift from Human Security to Regime Security?' (2003) 12(2) *African Security Review* 37–45.

Beeson, Mark, 'Sovereignty Under Siege: Globalisation and the State in Southeast Asia' (2003) 24(2) *Third World Quarterly* 357–74.

Bentley, G. Carter, 'Indigenous States of Southeast Asia' (1986) 15 *Annual Review of Anthropology* 275–99.

Berman, Paul, 'From International Law to Law and Globalization' (2005) 43 *Columbia Journal of Transnational Law* 485–556.

Black, Julia, 'Critical Reflections on Regulation' (2002) 27 *Australian Journal of Legal Philosophy* 1–35.

'Decentring Regulation: Understanding the Role of Regulation and Self-Regulation in a "Post-Regulatory" World' (2001) 54 (1) *Current Legal Problems* 103–46.

Bowles, Paul, 'Regionalism and Development after (?) the Global Financial Crisis' (2000) 5(3) *New Political Economy* 433–55.

Braithwaite, Valerie and John Braithwaite, 'The Politics of Legalism: Rules versus Standards in Nursing-Home Regulation' (1995) 4 *Social and Legal Studies* 307–41.

Burley, Anne-Marie and Walter Mattli, 'Europe Before the Court: A Political Theory of Legal Integration' (1993) 47 *International Organization* 41–76.

Caballero-Anthony, Mely, 'Mechanisms of Dispute Settlement: The ASEAN Experience' (1998) 20(1) *Contemporary Southeast Asia* 51–64.

Caporaso, James, 'Regional Integration Theory: Understanding Our Past and Anticipating Our Future' (1998) 5(1) *Journal of European Public Policy* 1–16.

Carothers, Thomas, 'The Rule of Law Revival' (1998) 77(2) *Foreign Affairs* 95–106.

Charney, Michael, 'Warfare in Early Modern Southeast Asia: Introduction' (2004) 12(1) *South East Asia Research* 5–12.

Cheesman, Nick, 'What Does the Rule of Law Have to Do With Democratization (in Myanmar)?' (2014) 22(2) *South East Asia Research* 213–32.

Chew, Melanie, 'Human Rights in Singapore: Perceptions and Problems' (1994) 34(11) *Asian Survey* 939–41.

Chuchu, Fatimah binti Hj Awg and Mukul Saxena, 'Socio-Cultural Hierarchy in the Palace Language of Brunei Darussalam' (2009) 9 *Southeast Asia: A Multidisciplinary Journal* 42–51.

Clarke, Gerald, 'The Evolving ASEAN Human Rights System: The ASEAN Human Rights Declaration of 2012' (2012) 11(1) *Northwestern Journal of International Human Rights* 1–27.

Corbey, Dorette, 'Dialectical Functionalism: Stagnation as a Booster of European Integration' (1995) 49(2) *International Organization* 253–84.

Craig, Paul, 'Constitutions, Constitutionalism and the European Union' (2001) 7(2) *European Law Journal* 125–50.

Crombez, Christophe, 'The Democratic Deficit in the European Union: Much Ado about Nothing?' (2003) 4(1) *European Union Politics* 105–17.

Cutler, Claire, 'Globalization, the Rule of Law, and the Modern Law Merchant: Medieval or Late Capitalist Associations?' (2001) 8(4) *Constellations: An International Journal of Critical and Democratic Theory* 480–502.

Davidson, Paul J., 'The ASEAN Way and the Role of Law in ASEAN Economic Cooperation' (2004) 8 *Singapore Yearbook of International Law* 165–76.

Day, Tony, 'Ties that (Un)Bind: Families and States in Premodern Southeast Asia' (1996) 55(2) *The Journal of Asian Studies* 384–409.

Dee, Philippa, 'Does AFAS Have Bite? Comparing Commitments with Actual Practice' (2014) 35 *Journal of Asian Economics* 46–64.

Deinla, Imelda, 'Public Support and Judicial Empowerment of the Philippine Supreme Court' (2014) 36(1) *Contemporary Southeast Asia: A Journal of International and Strategic Affairs* 128–58.

De Neve, Jan-Emmanuel, 'The European Onion? How Differentiated Integration is Reshaping the EU' (2007) 29(4) *European Integration* 503–21.

Dressel, Björn and Marco Bünte, 'Constitutional Politics in Southeast Asia: From Contestation to Constitutionalism?' (2014) 36(1) *Contemporary Southeast Asia: A Journal of International and Strategic Affairs* 1–22.

Dusza, Karl, 'Max Weber's Conception of the State' (1989) 3(1) *International Journal of Politics, Culture, and Society* 71–105.

Emmerson, Donald, 'Security, Community, and Democracy in Southeast Asia: Analyzing ASEAN' (2005) 6(2) *Japanese Journal of Political Science* 165–85.

Eoseewong, Nidhi, 'The Thai Cultural Constitution' (2003) 3 *Kyoto Review of Southeast Asia*.

Fukunaga, Yuka, 'Securing Compliance through the WTO Dispute Settlement System: Implementation of DSB Recommendations' (2006) 9(2) *Journal of International Economic Law* 383–426.

Gainsborough, Martin, 'Elites vs Reform in Laos, Cambodia, and Vietnam' (2012) 23(2) *Journal of Democracy* 34–46.

Gallagher, Kevin, 'Financial Crises and International Investment Agreements: The Case of Sovereign Debt Restructuring' (2012) 3(3) *Global Policy* 362–74.

Ganesan, Narayanan, 'ASEAN's Relations with Major External Powers' (2000) 22(2) *Contemporary Southeast Asia* 258–78.

Garrett, Geoffrey, 'International Cooperation and Institutional Choice: The European Community's Internal Market' (1992) 46 *International Organization* 556–69.

'The Politics of Legal Integration in the European Union' (1995) 49 *International Organization* 171–81.

Golub, Jonathan, 'The Politics of Judicial Discretion: Rethinking the Interaction between National Courts and the European Court of Justice' (1996) 19(2) *West European Politics* 360–85.

Grainger, Andrew, 'Trade Facilitation: A Conceptual Review' (2011) 45(1) *Journal of World Trade* 39–62.

Gunn, Geoffrey, '"Trophy Capitalism", Jefrinomics, and Dynastic Travail in Brunei' (2008) 6(3) *Asia Pacific Journal*, http://apjjf.org/-Geoffrey-Gunn/2696/article.html

Haas, Ernest, 'Turbulent Fields and the Theory of Regional Integration' (1976) 20(2) *International Organization* 173–212.

Haggard, Stephen, 'The Politics of the Asian Financial Crisis' (2000) 11(2) *Journal of Democracy* 130–44.

Hasan, Zubair, 'Fifty Years of Malaysian Economic Development: Policies and Achievements' (2007) 11(2) *Review of Islamic Economics* 101–18.

Heisenberg, Dorothee, 'The Institution of "Consensus" in the European Union: Formal versus Informal Decision-Making in the Council' (2005) 44 *European Journal of Political Research* 65–90.

Henry, Laurence, 'The ASEAN Way and Community Integration: Two Different Models of Regionalism' (2007) 13(6) *European Law Journal* 857–79.

Hiep, Le Hong, 'Performance-based Legitimacy: The Case of the Communist Party of Vietnam and Doi Moi' (2012) 34(2) *Contemporary South East Asia* 145–72.

Hine, Robert C., 'Regionalism and the Integration of the World Economy' (1992) 30(2) *Journal of Common Market Studies* 115–24.

Hiscock, Mary, 'Changing Patterns of Regional Law Making in Southeast Asia' (1995) 39 *Saint Louis University Law Journal* 933–50.

Hsieh, Pasha L., 'ASEAN's Liberalization of Legal Services: The Singapore Case' (2013) 8(2) *Asian Journal of WTO and International Health Law and Policy* 475–97.

Huelshoff, Michael, 'Domestic Politics and Dynamic Issue Linkage: A Reformulation of Integration Theory' (1994) 38(2) *International Studies Quarterly* 255–79.

Hund, Marcus 'ASEAN Plus Three: Towards a New Age of Pan-East Asian Regionalism? A Skeptic's Appraisal' (2003) 16(3) *The Pacific Review* 383–417.

Itzcovich, Giulio, 'The Interpretation of Community Law by the European Court of Justice' (2009) 10(5) *German Law Journal* 537–60.

Jano, Dorian, 'Understanding the "EU Democratic Deficit": A Two Dimension Concept on a Three Level-of-Analysis' (2008) 14(1) *Politikon: The IAPSS Journal of Political Science* 61–74.

Jayasuriya, Kanishka, 'Globalization, Sovereignty, and the Rule of Law: From Political to Economic Constitutionalism?' (2001) 8(4) *Constellations* 442–60.

Jolly, Mette, 'A Demos for the European Union?' (2005) 25(1) *Politics* 12–8.

Juma, Dan, 'Lost (or Found) in Translation? The Anatomy of the New African Court of Justice and Human Rights' (2009) 13 *Max Planck United Nations Yearbook* 267–306.

Kaur, Amarjit, 'International Labour Migration in Southeast Asia' (2007) *15 Intersections: Gender, History and Culture in the Asian Context*, http://intersections.anu.edu.au/issue15/kaur.htm

Kingsford Smith, Dimity, 'What is Regulation? A Reply to Julia Black' (2002) 27 *Australian Journal of Legal Philosophy* 37–46.

Kinley, David, 'Human Rights, Globalization and the Rule of Law: Friends, Foes or Family?' (2002) 7 *University of California, Los Angeles, Journal of International Law and Foreign Affairs* 239–64.

Koh, Harold, 'Why Do Nations Obey International Law?' (1997) 106 *Yale Law Journal* 2599–659.

Lande, Carl, 'Networks and Groups in Southeast Asia: Some Observations on the Group Theory of Politics' (1973) 67(1) *The American Political Science Review* 103–27.

Lenz, Tobias, 'Spurred Emulation: The EU and Regional Integration in Mercosur and SADC' (2012) 35 (1) *West European Politics* 155–73.

Lev, Daniel S., 'Colonial Law and the Genesis of the Indonesian State' (1985) 40 *Indonesia* 57–74.

Lupel, Adam, 'Regionalism and Globalization: Post-Nation or Extended Nation?' (2004) 36(2) *Polity* 153–74.

Maasdorp, Gavin Grant, 'Economic and Political Aspects of Regional Cooperation in Southern Africa' (1986) 54(2) *South African Journal of Economics* 94–105.

Majone, Giandomenico, 'Europe's "Democratic Deficit": The Question of Standards' (1998) 4(1) *European Law Journal* 5–28.

Mann, Michael, 'The Autonomous Power of the State: Its Origins, Mechanisms and Results' (1984) 25(2) *European Journal of Sociology* 185–213.

Mietzner, Marcus, 'Political Conflict Resolution and Democratic Consolidation in Indonesia: The Role of the Constitutional Court' (2010) 10(3) *Journal of East Asia Studies* 397–419.

Moravcsik, Andrew, 'In Defense of the "Democratic Deficit": Reassessing the Legitimacy of the European Union' (2002) 40(4) *Journal of Common Market Studies* 603–34.

'Preferences and Power in the European Community: A Liberal Intergovernmental Approach' (1993) 31(4) *Journal of Common Market Studies* 473–524.

Murithi, Tim, 'The African Union's Transition from Non-Intervention to Non-Indifference: An Ad Hoc Approach to the Responsibility to Protect?' (2009) 1 *Internationale Politik und Gesellschaft* 90–106.

Murungu, Chacha Bhoke, 'Towards a Criminal Chamber in the African Court of Justice and Human Rights' (2011) 9(5) *Journal of International Criminal Justice* 1065–75.

Mutalib, Hussien, 'Illiberal Democracy and the Future of Opposition in Singapore' (2000) 21(2) *Third World Quarterly* 313–38.

Nishikawa, Yukiko, 'The "ASEAN Way" and Asian Regional Security' (2007) 35(1) *Politics and Policy* 42–56.

Norris, Pippa, 'Representation and Democracy Deficit' (1997) 32(2) *European Journal of Political Research* 273–82.

Nyikos, Stacy, 'Strategic Interaction Among Courts within the Preliminary Reference Process – Stage 1: National Court Preemptive Opinions' (2006) 45(4) *European Journal of Political Research* 527–50.

O'Hagan, Emer, 'Too Soft to Handle? A Reflection on Soft Law in Europe and Accession States' (2004) 26(4) *Journal of European Integration* 379–404.

Piscitello, Daniel Pavón and Jan Peter Schmidt, 'In the Footsteps of the ECJ: First Decision of the Permanent MERCOSUR-Tribunal' (2007) 34(3) *Legal Issues of Economic Integration* 283–93.

Pitarakis, Jean-Yves and George Tridimas, 'Joint Dynamics of Legal and Economic Integration in the European Union' (2003) 16 *European Journal of Law and Economics* 357–68.

Pollock, Mark A., 'Theorizing the European Union: International Organization, Domestic Polity, or Experiment in New Governance?' (2005) 8 *Annual Review of Political Science* 357–98.

Pongsudhirak, Thitinan, 'Thailand Since the Coup' (2008) 19(4) *Journal of Democracy* 140–53.

Rau, Kristen, 'Jurisprudential Innovation or Accountability Avoidance? The International Criminal Court and Proposed Expansion of the African Court of Justice and Human Rights' (2012) 97(2) *Minnesota Law Review* 669–708.

Riekman, Sonja, 'The Cocoon of Power: Democratic Implications of Inter-Institutional Agreements' (2007) 13(1) *European Law Journal* 4–19.

Rittberger, Berthold and Frank Schimmelfennig, 'Explaining the Constitutionalization of the European Union' (2006) 13(8) *Journal of European Public Policy* 1148–67.

Rose, Jonathan, 'The Rule of Law in the Western World: An Overview' (2004) 35(4) *Journal of Social Philosophy* 457–70.

Rosenau, James N., 'The Complexities and Contradictions of Globalization' (1997) 96(613) *Current History* 360–4.

Rüland, Jürgen, 'ASEAN and the Asian Crisis: Theoretical Implications and Practical Consequences for Southeast Asian Regionalism' (2000) 13(3) *The Pacific Review* 421–51.

Ruppel, Oliver and Francois Bangamwabo, 'The SADC Tribunal: A Legal Analysis of Its Mandate and Role in Regional Integration' (2008) 8 *Monitoring Regional Integration in Southern Africa Yearbook* 1–43.

Scheuerman, William, 'Economic Globalization and the Rule of Law' (1999) 6(1) *Constellations* 3–25.

Schmidhauser, John, 'Legal Imperialism: Its Enduring Impact on Colonial and Post-Colonial Judicial Systems' (1992) 13(3) *International Political Science Review* 321–34.

Schwarz, Adam and Roland Villinger, 'Integrating Southeast Asia's Economies' (2004) 1 *McKinsey Quarterly* 37–47.

Scott, James, 'Patron-Client Politics and Political Change in Southeast Asia' (1972) 66(1) *The American Political Science Review* 91–113.

Senden, Linda, 'Soft Law, Self-Regulation and Co-regulation in European Law: Where Do They Meet? 2005 9(1) *Electronic Journal of Comparative Law* 1–27, www.ejcl.org/

Sifft, Stephanie, Michael Bruggeman, Katharina Kleinen-von Königsloöw, Bernhard Peters and Andreas Wimmel, 'Segmented Europeanization: Exploring the Legitimacy of the European Union from a Public Discourse Perspective' (2007) 45(1) *Journal of Common Market Studies* 127–55.

Silverstein, Gordon, 'Globalization and the Rule of Law: "A Machine that Runs Itself?"' (2003) 1(3) *International Journal of Constitutional Law* 427–45.

Solingen, Etel, 'Southeast Asia in a New Era: Domestic Coalitions from Crisis to Recovery' (2004) 44(2) *Asian Survey* 189–212.

Spiga, Valentina, 'Non-retroactivity of Criminal Law: A New Chapter in the Hissène Habré Saga' (2011) 9(1) *Journal of International Criminal Justice* 5–23.

Stone Sweet, Alec, 'Judicialization and the Construction of Governance' (1999) 31 *Comparative Political Studies* 147–84.

Stone Sweet, Alec and Thomas Brunell, 'Constructing a Supranational Constitution: Dispute Resolution and Governance in the European Community' (1998a) 92 *American Political Science Review* 63–81.

'The European Court and the National Courts: A Statistical Analysis of Preliminary References, 1961–95' (1998b) 5(1) *Journal of European Public Policy* 66–97.

Storey, Ian James, 'Creeping Assertiveness: China, the Philippines and the South China Sea Dispute' (1991) 21(1) *Contemporary Southeast Asia* 95–118.

Sturman, Kathryn, 'The Rise of Libya as a Regional Player' (2003) 12(2) *African Security Review* 109–12.

Talib, Naimah, 'A Resilient Monarchy: The Sultanate of Brunei and Regime Legitimacy in an Era of Democratic Nation-States' (2002) 4(2) *New Zealand Journal of Asian Studies* 134–47.

Thio, Li-Ann, 'Administrative and Constitutional Law' (2003) *Singapore Academy of Law Annual Review 2003* 1–12.

Thompson, Mark, 'Off the Endangered List: Philippine Democratisation in Comparative Perspective' (1996) 28(2) *Comparative Politics* 179–205.

Vinuesa, Raul Emilio, 'Enforcement of Mercosur Arbitration Awards Within the Domestic Legal Orders of Member States' (2005) 40 *Texas Journal of International Law* 425–42.

Weiler, Joseph H., 'A Quiet Revolution – The European Court of Justice and Its Interlocutors' (1994) 26(4) *Comparative Political Studies* 510–34.

'The Transformation of Europe' (1991) 100(8) *Yale Law Journal* 2403–83.

Weiler, Joseph H. and Ulrich Haltern, 'The Autonomy of the Community Legal Order: Through the Looking Glass' (1996) 37(2) *Harvard International Law Journal* 411–48.

Zerilli, Filippo M., 'The Rule of Soft Law: An Introduction' (2010) 56 *Focaal – Journal of Global and Historical Anthropology* 3–18.

PhDs

Byrne, Hugh, 'The Classic-Functional Approach to Regional Integration: The Association of South-East Asian Nations (ASEAN) – A Case Study' (PhD Dissertation, Sydney: University of New South Wales, 1980).

Woods, Shelby, 'The Greek Sovereign Debt Crisis: Politics and Economics in the Eurozone' (PhD Dissertation, Washington: University of Washington, 2012).

Reports and Publications

African Union, African Development Back and the UN Economic Commission for Africa, *Framework and Guidelines on Land Policy in Africa: A Framework to Strengthen Land Rights, Enhance Productivity and Secure Livelihoods* (Addis Ababa: AUC-ECA-AfDB Consortium, 2010), www.uneca.org/sites/default/files/PublicationFiles/fg_on_land_policy_eng.pdf

Ando, Mitsuyoannua and Ayako Obashi, 'The Pervasiveness of Non-tariff Measures in ASEAN – Evidences from the Inventory Approach' in Mia Mikic with Martin Wermelinger (eds.), *Rising Non-Tariff Protectionism and Crisis Recovery: A Study by the Asia-Pacific Research and Training Network on Trade* (Bangkok: United Nations Publication, 2010).

Asian Development Bank, *ASEAN Corporate Governance Scorecard: Country Reports and Assessments 2013–2014* (Mandaluyong City, Philippines: ASEAN Development Bank, 2014a).

Strengthening Institutional Knowledge and Capacity of Customs Administrations for Trade Facilitation within the Association of Southeast Asian Nations (Technical Assistance Report, ASEAN Development Bank, August 2014b), www.adb.org/sites/default/files/project-document/81936/46192-001-tar.pdf

ASEAN Secretariat, *ASEAN Annual Report 2006–2007: Becoming One ASEAN* (Jakarta: ASEAN Secretariat, 2007).

ASEAN Economic Community Scorecard (Jakarta: ASEAN Secretariat, 2010).

ASEAN Economic Co-operation: Transition & Transformation (Singapore: Institute of Southeast Asian Studies, 1997).

ASEAN Political-Security Community Blueprint (Jakarta: ASEAN Secretariat, 2009a).

ASEAN Socio-Cultural Community Blueprint (Jakarta: ASEAN Secretariat, 2009b).

ASEANStats: Building Knowledge in the ASEAN Community (Jakarta: ASEAN Secretariat, October 2011), http://aseanstats.asean.org/

ASEAN Statistics Leaflet: Selected Key Indicators 2015 (Jakarta: ASEAN Secretariat, 2015a).

A Blueprint for Growth: ASEAN Economic Community 2015: Progress and Key Achievements (Jakarta: ASEAN Secretariat, 2015b).

Report of the Eminent Persons Group on the ASEAN Charter (December 2006), www.asean.org/storage/images/archive/19247.pdf

ASEAN Secretariat and United Nations Conference on Trade and Development, *ASEAN Investment Report 2013–2014: FDI Development and Regional Value Chains* (Jakarta: ASEAN Secretariat, 2014).

ASEAN Secretariat and the World Bank, *ASEAN Services Integration Report: A Joint Report by the ASEAN Secretariat and the World Bank* (Jakarta: ASEAN Secretariat, 2015).

Corporate Europe Observatory, Lobbying the European Union by Committee (Corporate Europe Observatory Briefing Paper, July 2007), http://archive.corporateeurope.org/lobbyingbycommittee.html

Daboya, Hon. Justice Awa Nana, Community Court of Justice, *ECOWAS: Summary of Activities for the Year 2011* (Activities Report, ECOWAS Community Court of Justice, 2011), www.courtecowas.org

Organisation of Africa Unity, *Lagos Plan of Action for the Economic Development of Africa: 1980–2000* (Addis Ababa: Organisation of African Unity, 1980).

Ruggie, John, *United Nations Special Representative of the Secretary-General on Business and Human Rights, Protect, Respect and Remedy: A Framework for Business and Human Rights* (Report to the UN Human Rights Council, 7 April 2008; UN Doc. A./HRC/8/5).

Stensland, Andreas, Walter Lotze and Joel Ng, *Regional Security and Human Rights Interventions: A Global Governance Perspective on the AU and ASEAN* (Oslo: Norwegian Institute of International Affairs, 2012).

Traimas, Chaowana and Jochen Hoerth, 'Thailand: Another New Constitution as a Way Out of the Vicious Cycle?' in Clauspeter Hill and Jörg Menzel (eds.), *Constitutionalism in Southeast Asia* (Singapore: Konrad-Adenauer-Stiftung, 2008), pp. 301–25.

Vassalos, Yiorgos, '*Secrecy and Corporate Dominance: A Study on the Composition and Transparency of European Commission Expert Groups*' (Brussels: Alliance for Lobbying Transparency and Ethics Regulation in the European Union, 2008).

Wong, Marn-Heong and Andre Wirjo, *Findings from 2013 ASEAN-BAC Survey on ASEAN Competitiveness* (Research Report, ASEAN Business Advisory Council, 2013).

World Trade Organisation, *WTO Training Package: What is Trade Facilitation?* (Geneva: World Trade Organisation, 1998).

Discussion, Working and Research Papers

Barani, Luca, 'Hard and Soft Law in the European Union: The Case of Social Policy and the Open Method of Coordination' (Webpapers on Constitutionalism and Governance Beyond the State No. 2, ConWEB, 2006), www.wiso.uni-hamburg.de/fileadmin/sowi/politik/governance/ConWeb_Papers/conweb2-2006.pdf

Beja, Edsel, Jr, Ronald U. Mendoza, Victor S. Venida and David B. Yap, 'Inequality in Democracy: Insights from an Empirical Analysis of Political Dynasties in the 15th Philippine Congress' (Munich Personal RePEc Archive Paper No. 40104, Munich University, 15 July 2012), http://mpra.ub.uni-muenchen.de/40104/1/MPRA_paper_40104.pdf

Chalk, Peter, *On the Path of Change: Political, Economic and Social Challenges for Myanmar* (Special Report, Australian Strategic Policy Institute, December 2013).

Chalmers, Damian, 'The Much Ado about Judicial Politics in the United Kingdom: A Statistical Analysis of Reported Decisions of United Kingdom Courts Invoking EU Law 1973–1998' (Harvard Jean Monnet Working Paper No. 1/00, Harvard Law School, 2000).

Christiansen, Thomas and Beatrice Vaccari, 'The 2006 Reform of Comitology: Problem Solved or Dispute Postponed?' (EPIASCOPE 20006/3, European Institute of Public Administration, 2006), www.eipa.nl/cms/repository/eipascope/Scop06_3_2.pdf

Coglianese, Cary and Jennifer Nash, 'Government Clubs: Theory and Evidence from Voluntary Environmental Programs' (Corporate Responsibility

Initiative Working Paper No. 50, F. Kennedy School of Government, Harvard University, 2008).

Collinson, Gary and Christopher B. Roberts, 'The Role of ASEAN' in Lesek Buszynski and Christopher Roberts (eds.), *The South China Sea and Australia's Regional Security Environment* (Occasional Paper No. 5, National Security College, Canberra, 2013).

Crouch, Melissa, 'The Judiciary in Myanmar: Beyond Reform?' (Research Paper No. 2016–10, University of New South Wales, 2016).

Dee, Philippa and Anne McNaughton, 'Promoting Domestic Reforms through Regionalism' (Working Paper No. 312, Asian Development Bank Institute, October 2011), www.adb.org/sites/default/files/publication/156167/adbi-wp312.pdf

Dosch, Jörn, 'The ASEAN Economic Community: What Stands in the Way?' (AsiaPacific Issues No. 119, East West Center, September 2015), www.eastwestcenter.org/system/tdf/private/api119.pdf?file=1&type=node&id=35319

Draper, Peter, Durrel Halleson and Philip Alves, 'SACU, Regional Integration and the Overlap Issue in Southern Africa: From Spaghetti to Cannelloni?' (Trade Policy Report No. 15, South African Institute of International Affairs, 2007).

Fukunaga, Yoshifumi, 'Assessing the Progress of ASEAN MRAs on Professional Services' (ERIA Discussion Paper No. 2015–12, Economic Research Institute for ASEAN and East Asia Discussion Paper, March 2015), www.eria.org/ERIA-DP-2015-21.pdf

Halberstam, Daniel, 'Constitutionalism and Pluralism in Marbury and Van Gend' (Public Law and Legal Theory Working Paper No. 104, University of Michigan Law School, March 2008), http://ssrn.com/abstract=1103253

Hill, Hal and Jayant Menon, 'ASEAN Commercial Policy: A Rare Case of Outward-Looking Regional Integration' (Working Paper on Regional Economic Integration No. 144, Asian Development Bank, November 2014).

Hix, Simon and Andreas Follesdal, 'Why there is a Democratic Deficit in the EU: A Response to Majone and Moravcsik' (European Governance Paper No. C-05-02, 14 March 2005), www.connex-network.org/eurogov/pdf/egp-connex-C-05-02.pdf

Intal, Ponciano S., Jr, Dionisius A. Norjoko and Yoshifumi Fukunaga, 'ASEAN Economic Community Scorecard' (Summary of ERIA Research Projects 2014–2015, Economic Research Institute for ASEAN and EAST Asia, April 2015), www.eria.org/Research-Summary-2014-15.pdf

International Trade and Integration Division, Economic Commission for Latin America and the Caribbean, 'MERCOSUR Intra-Regional Trade Statistics International Trade in Latin America and the Caribbean' (Trade Statistics Bulletin No. 19, United Nations ECLAC, 2015), www.cepal.org/sites/default/files/statistical_bulletin_n19.pdf

Isono, Ikumo and Yoshifumi Fukunaga, 'Utilisation of Free Trade Agreements by Service Industries in ASEAN' in Lili Yan Ing and Shujiro Urata (eds.),

The Use of FTAs in ASEAN: A Survey-Based Analysis (Research Project Report, Economic Research Institute for ASEAN and East Asia, August 2015).

Kaufmann, Daniel, Aart Kraay and Massimo Maztruzzi, 'Governance Matters VII: Aggregate and Individual Governance Indicators 1996–2007' (Policy Research Working Paper No. 4652, World Bank, 24 June 2008).

'Governance Matters VIII: Aggregate and Individual Governance Indicators 1996–2008' (Policy Research Working Paper No. 4978, The World Bank, June 2009).

Matyszak, Derek, 'The Dissolution of the SADC Tribunal' (Research and Advocacy Unit, 19 August 2011), www.idasa.org/media/uploads/outputs/files/the_suspension_sadc_tribunal_final.pdf

Menon, Jayant and Anna Cassandra Melendez, 'Realizing an ASEAN Economic Community: Progress and Remaining Challenges' (Economics Working Paper Series, Working Paper No. 432, Asian Development Bank May 2015), www.adb.org/sites/default/files/publication/160067/ewp-432.pdf

Milo, Melanie S., 'The ASEAN Economic Community and the Philippines: Implementation, Outcomes, Impacts and Ways Forward' (Research Paper No. 2, Philippine Institute for Development Studies, 2013).

Moravcsik, Andrew, 'Why the European Community Strengthens the State: International Cooperation and Domestic Politics' (Center for European Studies Working Paper No. 52, Harvard University, 1994).

Pena, Celina and Ricardo Rozemberg, 'MERCOSUR: A Different Approach to Institutional Development' (Focal Policy Paper No. 05-06, Canadian Foundation for the Americas, March 2005), www.focal.ca/pdf/mercosur.pdf

Sepos, Angelos, 'Differentiated Integration in the EU: The Position of Small Member States' (Working Paper No. 17, Robert Schuman Centre of Advanced Studies, European University Institute, 2005).

Suzuki, Sanae, 'Chairship System and Decision Making by Consensus in International Agreements: The Case of ASEAN' (Discussion Paper No. 471, Institute of Developing Economies, July 2014), https://ir.ide.go.jp/dspace/bitstream/2344/1376/1/ARRIDE_Discussion_No.471_suzuki.pdf

Trubek, David, Patrick Cottrell and Mark Nance, '"Soft Law," "Hard Law," and European Integration: Toward a Theory of Hybridity' (Research Paper No. 1002, University of Wisconsin Legal Studies, 2004).

Yasuda, Nobuyuki, 'Law, Legal Culture and Regional Integration: Asian Perspectives' (APEC Study Center Discussion Paper Series No. 7, Graduate School of International Development, Nagoya University, 1996).

Conference Papers

Deinla, Imelda, 'Fostering Rule of Law in African Integration' (Paper presented at the 35th AFSAAP Conference 'Africa: Peoples, Places and Spaces', Canberra, 26–8 November 2012).

Harding, Andrew, 'Strengthening ASEAN Integration: Lessons from the European Union's Rule of Law' (Paper presented at the Conference on the Legal Aspects of Regional Integration: The EU and ASEAN Compared, Centre for European Studies, Chulalongkorn University, Bangkok, 19 February 2001).

Mashayekhi, Mina, Lakshmi Puri and Taisuke Ito, 'Multilateralism and Regionalism: The New Interface' (Paper presented at the United Nations Conference on Trade and Development, Geneva, UNCTAD/DITC/TNCD/2004/7, 2005).

Olayiwola, Wumi and Oluyomi Ola-David, 'Economic Integration, Trade Facilitation and Agricultural Export Performance in ECOWAS Member States' (Paper prepared for presentation at the Eighth African Economic Conference on 'Regional Integration in Africa', Johannesberg, October 2013).

Quisumbing, Purificacion and Benjamin Domingo (eds.), EEC and ASEAN: Two Regional Community Experiences (Paper presented at the Proceedings of the ASEAN Seminar on the EEC Experience on Regional Integration, Manila, 5–8 January 1983).

Speeches

Marcelo, Atty Simeon V., 'Investigating Corruption in the Philippines: A Former Tanodbayan's Experience' (Speech delivered at the 12th Regional Seminar of the ADB/OECD Anti-Corruption Initiative for Asia and the Pacific, Dili, Timor-Leste, 24–25 July 2013).

Pitsuwan, Surin, 'ASEAN's Challenge: Some Reflections and Recommendations on Strengthening the ASEAN Secretariat' (Statement for H.E. Marty Natalegawa, Chair, ASEAN Coordinating Council, 12 December 2011).

Severino, Rodolfo C., 'The ASEAN Way and the Rule of Law' (Speech delivered at the International Law Conference on ASEAN Legal Systems and Regional Integration, University of Malaya, Kuala Lumpur, 3 September 2001).

INDEX